DIRTY WORDS

Also by Mark Morton

Cupboard Love: A Dictionary of Culinary Curiosities

DIRTY WORDS

The story of sex talk

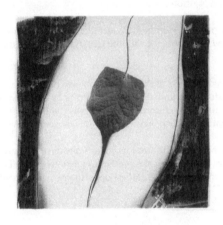

MARK MORTON

Atlantic Books
London

First published in Canada in 2003 by Insomniac Press, Toronto.

First published in Great Britain in 2005 by Atlantic Books, an imprint
of Grove Atlantic Ltd.

Copyright © Mark Morton 2005

1 2 3 4 5 6 7 8 9

A CIP catalogue record for this book is available from the British Library.

ISBN 1 84354 384 2

Cover design: Ghost
Text design: www.carrstudio.co.uk
Printed in Great Britain by Creative Print & Design (Wales) Ltd, Ebbw Vale

Atlantic Books
An imprint of Grove Atlantic Ltd
Ormond House
26–27 Boswell Street
London WC1N 3JZ

For my wife, Melanie Cameron

"Mi hony, mi hert, al hol thou me makest."

CONTENTS

Introduction

TONGUES & LOVERS

$\mathscr{E}$TYMOLOGY IS THE STUDY of where words came from and how they have developed over time. All words have etymologies. For instance, consider the final word in the title of this Introduction: *tongue*. That word is a sex word insofar as it denotes one of the organs used in various sexual activities, ranging from talking dirty to kissing to cunnilingus. But *tongue* also has a long and interesting etymological history. In written English, *tongue* first appeared in the late ninth century in King Alfred's translation of Pope Gregory the Great's treatise on how clergymen should behave themselves (then, as now, they tended not to). Moreover, in spoken English the word *tongue* is undoubtedly even older. It's probably one of the core words in the lexicon used by the original speakers of English: the tribes of Angles, Saxons and Jutes who migrated from northwestern Europe to Britain in the fifth century.

The ancestry of *tongue*, though, can be pushed back even further. Like most other Old English words, it derived from a Germanic source, which is why it resembles the German and Dutch names for the tongue, *Zunge* and *tong*. But even further back, the Germanic source of *tongue* developed from a still older word, one that belonged to a now-vanished language called Indo-European. Latin is one of the many languages that evolved from Indo-European, and thus the word the ancient Romans bestowed on the mouth muscle – *lingua* – is also an etymological cousin of the English word *tongue*. This Latin word is, of course, where we get the word *linguistics* and also, via French, where we get the word *language,* and even, via Italian, where we get the word *linguine,* the name of a dish made of ribbons of pasta that are broad and flat like the tongue.

> The tongue of man is a twisty thing.
>
> *Homer*

When the word *tongue* first appeared in written English, it wasn't spelt as it is now. Instead, it was written as *tunge*. Over time, the *u* in the middle of the word changed to an *o,* so that by the thirteenth century the spelling *tonge* was common. In the sixteenth century, however, it was apparently feared that this spelling might lead people to mistakenly pronounce the *g* as if it were soft, as it is, for example, in the word *sponge*. Accordingly, authors and typesetters began to insert a *u* before the *e* to discourage people from softening the *g* or, as a linguist would put it, from turning the voiced velar nasal into a voiced palato-alveolar affricate.

Assuming that the previous sentence didn't render you entirely comatose, you might be interested to learn that it was quite early in the history of the word *tongue* that it came to denote the language or speech of a person or nation. This sense of the word is still familiar, especially in phrases such as *mother tongue, speaking in tongues,* and *the cat's got your tongue.* The first of those phrases appeared around 1380 in a work by John

Wycliffe. A man may preach the law of God, Wycliffe wrote, not just in Latin but in his *modyr tonge*. The second phrase, *speaking in tongues*, dates back to the sixteenth century, where it arose as the popular name for what is technically known as glossolalia, the sputtering of seemingly incomprehensible words by someone inspired with the Holy Spirit. And as for the idiom *the cat's got your tongue*, it appeared in the mid nineteenth century to describe a person who is made speechless, often in response to hearing some surprising information.

Considering the role of the tongue in erotic activities, it's not surprising that the word itself has been used in explicitly sexual contexts. As early as the 1930s, for example, *tongue* was used as a slang term for cunnilingus, and around the same time *tongue lash* came to denote fellatio. Later, in the 1960s, *tongue bath* and *tongue job* emerged as other slang synonyms for oral sex, and in the 1980s the phrase *tongue sushi* was invented in North America by so-called preppies to allude to especially deep kissing. As for the phrase *tongue-in-cheek*, fear not: that idiom has nothing to do with the buttocks so you can continue to use it in polite company. It arose in the early 1930s, probably inspired by our tendency to give hints as to when we are being ironic through subtle facial movements, such as a raised eyebrow or a slightly protruding cheek.

So much for *tongue*. What about the other word represented in the title of this book, *lover*? Obviously, that word derives from *love*, which – if we seek its ancestral pedigree as we did with *tongue* – can be pushed back to an Old English source, *lufu*. This Old English word developed from a Germanic source, *lubo*, which in turn evolved from an Indo-European word, *leubh*, which meant *to love* or *to desire*. This Indo-European word had several forms, each of which evolved along a unique path, and thus gave rise to different and new words. The word *love*, as mentioned, was one result, and so was the word *leman*, an obsolete or at least archaic word meaning *beloved* or, more idiomatically, *sweetheart*. In 1590, for example, Edmund Spenser used this word in *The Faerie Queene* where the evil Proteus tries to convince the virtuous Florimell "to be his leman and his lady trew." Another Old English word that eventually evolved from the Indo-European *leubh* was *lief*, which originally meant *precious* but later came to function as an adverb meaning *gladly*. This sense of the word was still in use up till the nineteenth century, as evidenced by William Thackeray's 1852 novel *A History of Henry Esmond*, in which the title character says, "I would as lief go there as anywhere." Yet another word that developed from the same Indo-European ancestor was the Latin word *libido*, meaning *desire* or *lust*. This Latin word was adopted by Freud to refer to his conception of the human sex drive, and was introduced to English in a 1909 translation of Freud's *Selected Papers on Hysteria*.

So far so good. It's fairly easy to accept the etymological relationships among *lover*, *love*, *leman*, *lief* and *libido* because of their obvious semantic connections – that is, their meanings all have something to do with love. Things get more complicated, though, when we turn to two other words that are also related to the preceding cluster of words. The first word in question is *believe* which, on the surface, seems to mean something quite distinct from *love*. In fact, there is a semantic connection: we tend to believe in people or things that we love. With this in mind, we can understand how the word *believe* evolved: one of the forms of the Indo-European *leubh* (meaning *love*) gave rise to the Germanic *galaubjan* (meaning *to trust*), which gave rise to the Old English *gelefan* (meaning *to believe*), which became the Modern English *believe*.

The other word in question is *leave*. Here we need to recognize the fact that there are two distinct *leave*s in English, a verb meaning *to depart* and a noun meaning *permission*. Shakespeare puns on these two distinct *leave*s in *King Henry IV Part 1* where the King says to Worcester, "You have good leave to leave us." Nowadays, the *leave* that means *permission* is best known in the phrase *leave of absence*, but even here the distinction is muddied by the fact that a leave of absence (that is, permission to be absent) usually means that you leave (or depart from) your job. In other words, people tend to assume that the two *leave*s are the same word, even though they are etymologically and, strictly speaking, semantically distinct. Of these two *leave*s, it is the one that means *permission* that is related to the previously discussed cluster of love words. Semantically, the path was this: if we love someone, we grant him our trust; and if we trust someone, we are usually willing to give him permission to do something. That, essentially, is how the Indo-European *leubh*, meaning *love*, managed to develop over thousands of years into the English noun *leave*, meaning *permission*.

> I am sure my love's more ponderous than my tongue.
> *William Shakespeare*

Over the centuries, the word *love* has also been assimilated into numerous compound words and phrases. The *Oxford*

English Dictionary lists more than a hundred and fifty such compounds, most of them now obsolete. Among them are *love-blink, love-money, love-day* and *love-apple*. The first of these, *love-blink*, is a Scottish term denoting the come-hither look that besotted young lovers cast toward one another; sexologists have noted that in the early stages of arousal the pupils dilate, thus making the eyes a focal point of erotic non-verbal communication. If forced by circumstances to part from one another, those blinking lovers might partake of the tradition of *love-money*, a nineteenth-century custom whereby a coin is broken in two, with each heavy-hearted lover taking half. That custom appears to be a romanticized version of what medieval lawyers once did with contracts: they cut them in two, along an arbitrary and jagged line, and gave each party half the document; years later, it could be verified that the two halves belonged to the same document by holding one edge against the other. (Such contracts were called *indentured* because the jagged edges of the paper resembled teeth, or in Latin, *dentes*.) Another medieval custom was that of the *love-day*: the two parties of a dispute would have a day set for them, on which they agreed to meet and amicably resolve their conflict. The term was sometimes used metaphorically, as with John Gower in his 1390 dream vision, *Confessio Amantis*: "Helle is full of such descord / That ther may be no loveday." Finally, *love-apple* might already be familiar as a whimsical euphemism: the plural of that term has been used in the twentieth century to denote a woman's breasts and, less commonly, a man's testicles. *Love-apple* is, however, actually much older: it appeared in 1578 as a name for the tomato, and in fact it predates the word *tomato*, which did not appear in

English until 1604. *Love-apple* arose as a direct translation of the French *pomme d'amour*, but the French term itself might have been the result of a mistranslation. The Italians sometimes referred to the tomato as *pomo dei Moro*, meaning *apple of the Moors*, because the fruit was thought to have been imported via Morocco. When the Italian phrase was assimilated into French, it was misconstrued as the similar-sounding *pomme d'amour*.

A similar linguistic mix-up may have resulted in the *love* that is used in tennis. Tennis is, in origin, a French game, and it's possible that French players shouted *l'oeuf*, meaning *the egg*, to express a score of zero; a similar usage can be heard in English when a teacher returns an exam with a *goose egg*, so-called because the oval shape of the egg resembles a zero. When the French term was introduced to England, *l'oeuf* might have been corrupted into *love*. Alternatively, the *love* found in tennis scores might have developed from an earlier sporting idiom, namely, *to play for love*, meaning to play for the love of the game rather than for a wager – or in other words, to play with nothing at stake.

〰

Lover and *Tongue* demonstrate one of the central assumptions involved in any etymological discussion: words have histories, which means their spelling, their pronunciation, and their meaning tend to change over centuries. Of course, we need to qualify this statement somewhat. For one thing, not all words shift in meaning; the word *egg*, for example, means the same thing now as it did a thousand years ago. For another thing, the very notion of spelling becomes problematic once we travel back in history a few hundred years, before the emergence of dictionaries, which went a long way towards standardizing English orthography. In the sixteenth century, for example, almost any word could be spelt a number of ways, and even the name of the most famous writer in English was variously rendered as *Shakespeare, Shagspere, Shaxper*, and so on. Things were even more of a mess in Chaucer's time: that fourteenth-century poet expressed his concern over English spelling in an address to his own poem, *Troilus and Criseyde*:

And for ther is so greet diversitee
In English and in wryting of our tonge,
So preye I god that noon miswryte thee.

If we travel even further back in time, spelling becomes totally moot: there are no written records of English before the eighth century, and none at all for Indo-European.

One final qualification might be this: all words have histories, but sometimes etymologists don't know, or don't know yet, or don't know for certain, what that history is. No one knows, for instance, the origin of the word *prat*, a sixteenth-century synonym for *ass*. Sometimes, too, a word's origin might be highly conjectural – in other words, a guess. Does *nooky*, a twentieth-century slang word for sexual intercourse, derive from *nook*, a word denoting a small out-of-the-way place? It's possible, since nooky often occurs in nooks and crannies, but not certain.

Even with these qualifications, it remains practically true that every word in English has a history, one that might be imagined as extending backward on a horizontal axis, all the way from

Late Modern English to, potentially, some far-off Indo-European ancestor. As well, most words might also be imagined as having a place on a vertical axis, one that represents a single spot of time, but which locates that word amongst other words that mean something similar, or at least belong to the same semantic field. At this moment in time, for example, the words *cock*, *prick*, *pecker*, and *dong*, along with many others, all denote the penis.

The difficulty that arises, then, is how to write about a subject whose members, so to speak, can be organized along two competing axes. Should the hundreds of words in this book be arranged along the horizontal axis (chronologically), or along the vertical axis (thematically or, more properly, semantically)? What I have attempted to do is both. I've grouped the sex words into semantic categories – for example, words denoting the penis or words denoting prostitution – but within each category I have attempted to proceed roughly chronologically.

> Words make love with one another.
> *André Breton*

Considering that chronology is one of the organizing principles of this book, it might be useful to provide a bit more detail about the linguistic timeline that I've so far only implied, and to clarify some of the terms that will often appear.

Of the half million or so words in English, most of them can be traced back to a language that existed about 8,000 years ago in an area north of the Black Sea. Scholars refer to this ancient language as Proto-Indo-European, or just Indo-European for short. I've mentioned above that no written records of Indo-European survive. This means that everything we know about that prehistoric language has been reconstructed by comparative philologists, a huge task that was first embarked upon in the nineteenth century. By examining words from various modern or at least extant languages, philologists were able to work backwards and reconstruct the Indo-European ancestors of those words.

Thanks to comparative philology, we now know that the Indo-European language gave rise to several language branches, including Celtic, Indo-Iranian, Slavic, Baltic, Greek, Italic and Germanic. In turn, as the Indo-European people spread across Europe and parts of Asia, each of these branches developed into numerous languages, many of which, but not all, still exist. From the Celtic branch arose Irish, Gaelic, Welsh and Breton; from the Indo-Iranian branch arose Sanskrit, Urdu, Hindi and Persian; from the Slavic branch arose Russian, Polish and Czech; from the Baltic branch arose Lithuanian and Latvian; from the Hellenic branch arose Greek; from the Italic branch arose the language of ancient Rome – Latin – which in turn gave rise to the Romance languages, namely French, Italian, Portuguese, Romanian and Spanish; and from the Germanic branch arose an East Germanic "twig" that gave rise to Gothic, a North Germanic "twig" that gave rise to Swedish, Danish, Norwegian and Icelandic, and a West Germanic "twig" that gave rise to German, Flemish, Frisian, Dutch and – in the middle of the fifth century – English.

> In German a young lady has no sex, while a turnip has.
>
> *Mark Twain*

The middle of the fifth century is when English emerged because it was then that several Germanic tribes left the northeastern corner of the European mainland, crossed the

North Sea, and settled in what is now called England. The language of these Germanic tribes became Old English, which changed enormously over the following centuries, becoming Middle English around 1100, then Early Modern English around 1500, and finally Late Modern English around 1800, thanks in large part to its exposure to other languages from which it borrowed vocabulary. For instance, in the seventh century, English adopted a few Latin words from the Christian missionaries who had arrived from Rome.

> He who does not love his own language is worse than a stinking fish.
> *Jose Rizal*

From the eighth century to the tenth century, English adopted numerous Scandinavian words from the Vikings who invaded the northern shores of Britain. From the eleventh century to the sixteenth century, English was injected with thousands of French words due to the conquest of England by the Normans. During the sixteenth and seventeenth centuries, English borrowed hundreds of words from Latin and Greek thanks to the revival of classical learning that occurred during the Renaissance. And from the sixteenth century onward, English took hundreds of words from dozens of languages spoken in the diverse lands the English people began to explore and colonize, that is, as they began to do unto others what the Vikings and Normans had done unto them.

A point worth stressing is that some people, such as my first-year English students, mistakenly call the language of Shakespeare Old English. It's not. In fact, Shakespeare wrote in Early Modern English, which is also the language of the King James Bible. The evolution of English can be readily seen by comparing four versions of a passage from Genesis, each from a different stage of the language:

Late Modern English

Now the serpent was the most clever of all the wild beasts that the Lord God had made. And so God has said that you are not to eat from any tree of the garden? he said to the woman.

Early Modern English

Now the serpent was more subtill then any beast of the field, which the Lord God had made, and he said vnto the woman, Yea, Hath God said, Ye shall not eat of euery tree of the garden?

Middle English

But and the serpent was feller than alle lyuynge beestis of erthe, whiche the Lord God hadde maad. Which serpent seide to the woman, Why comaundide God to you, that ye schulden not ete of ech tre of paradis?

Old English

Eac swelce seo nædre wæs geappre ∂onne ealle ∂a o∂re nietenu ∂e God geworhte ofer eor∂an; and seo nædre cwæ∂ to ∂am wife: Hwy forbead God eow ∂æt ge ne æten of ælcum treowe binnan Paradisum?

Clearly, Old English doesn't look much like Modern English – you might even say they're different languages. Then again, you probably don't resemble your grandmother, and yet think of how much, at the genetic level, you owe her: if she hadn't existed, you wouldn't be here. The same is true of Modern English with regard to the debt it owes its historical predecessors. Moreover, just as we can discover a lot about ourselves by learning about our familial ancestors, we develop a better understanding and appreciation of the words we now speak by exploring the ones that came before them.

Some books, like murder mysteries, are meant to be read in one go, over a single afternoon while it's raining outside and you can sit curled up on your couch. This book is a bit different. If you read too much of it at one stretch, you'll probably get a headache, much as you would if you did twenty crossword puzzles in a row. To my mind, the best way to enjoy the extensive etymological lore in *The Lover's Tongue* is to read one chapter, put it down, and come back to another chapter a day or two later. You can, if you want, do the chapters in the order that I've arranged them, but I've also tried to make each chapter self-sufficient. So if, at this moment, you feel like reading about, say, breast words, you can forge ahead and plunge into that chapter right now. And, if you think I've left an important word out, please contact me at here.and.now@shaw. ca, and I might be able to incorporate it into future editions of this book.

> For God's sake hold your tongue, and let me love.
> *John Donne*

Finally, a note about squiggly marks. In scholarly works, Indo-European words often have diacritics, like umlauts and circumflexes, placed over certain letters in order to indicate the precise quality of each sound or phoneme, for instance, whether a given consonant is a plain velar or a palatal velar. As well, Indo-European words are usually preceded by an asterisk to emphasize that they are forms whose existence has been conjectured, not recorded. Thus, the Indo-European source of the word *tongue* would, in a scholarly book, be rendered as *dnghu-. Since this book is intended for non-specialist readers, I've omitted both the asterisk and the diacritics from Indo-European words as well as from other reconstructed words such as the Proto-Germanic ones. For simplicity's sake, I've also rendered Greek and Latin words without diacritics. When I've quoted passages of English from earlier centuries, I've usually retained the archaic spellings in order to preserve the flavour of those texts, but on rare occasions I've silently modernized the spelling of a word to avoid ambiguity.

Chapter One

SHAME ON ME

Smut Words

*I*F YOU'VE READ THIS far, and have made it past *cunnilingus* in the first paragraph, and my bawdy pun on *tongue-in-cheek* in the fourth paragraph, and the flurry of penis words in the twelfth paragraph, then you're unlikely to be offended by the contents of the rest of this book. Bear in mind, though, that the opening sections are fairly tame in that they mostly discuss words pertaining to the emotional, interpersonal or even aesthetic aspects of sex: words relating to physical attractiveness and terms of endearment, for instance. To use the obvious metaphor, these early sections are like etymological foreplay. Later sections become raunchier as they explore the ins and outs of hardcore nouns and verbs: things and actions, organs and motions. I haven't shied away from any word or deed, always bearing in mind a passage from the ancient Roman playwright Terence: "Homo sum; homini nihil a me alienum puto," meaning "I am a man; I consider nothing human foreign to me." In other words, all things – even merkins, codpieces and felching – are worthy of study.

There are those who will not share this liberal perspective. To such folks, this book will seem unseemly; they will call it indecent, indecorous, indelicate, immoral, improper and impure. Those words have long been used to excoriate things, especially literature, that take as their subject the human body, in all its sexual or execratory splendour. What is interesting about that cluster of censorious words is that they all begin with a negating prefix – *un*, *in* or *im*, all of which mean *not*. Those words, in short, all suggest an implicit standard or norm from which unseemly things deviate. This fact might not seem untoward unless we recognize it as a tactic that has been used for centuries to marginalize certain topics and certain groups of people. For example, in the eighth century the word *man* meant *human*, but by the tenth century its sense had narrowed to *male human*. In contrast, the word *woman* was formed around the same time by combining the older word *wif*, which meant *woman*, with *man*, to create *wifman*, which eventually became *woman*. In other words, etymologically a man is a human, but a woman is a "woman human." The implication is that men embody a human standard, and that women are a deviation from that standard. You see the same kind of thinking even today in the small prairie town where I grew up: there, many people still distinguish the "doctors" from the "lady doctors." In that same town, I was also taught in sex-ed class that the difference between men and women is that men have a penis and women do not. I might just as well have been taught that women have a vagina and that men do not, but

> If thought corrupts language, language can also corrupt thought.
>
> *George Orwell*

a close relative of *gusto*. If something is *tasty*, then we undertake it eagerly, with gusto, or – to use another gastronomic term – with relish. Sexually explicit literature is also often called *raunchy*, a word that emerged in 1939, perhaps from the Italian *rancio*, meaning *rancid*, as in food that has gone bad. We might speculate, too, that the same rancid notion might underlie the use of the *blue* and *off-colour* to describe raunchy writing. When food goes bad, it often turns an off-colour, developing a bluish patina or mould. This risqué sense of both *blue* and *off-colour* dates back to the mid nineteenth century. *Crude* is another food-related adjective in that it derives from the Latin *crudus*, meaning *raw* or *unripe*. This origin has been better preserved in the French word *crudités*, the name of an hors d'oeuvre of raw vegetables.

Other words with gastronomic origins have also been used to describe sexually explicit writing, but with a more neutral or even positive connotation. I would, for example, consider it a compliment if someone called this book *racy*, which would suggest a certain liveliness of spirit. That, in fact, was the first meaning of *racy*, although it was applied originally to wines. In the seventeenth century, a racy wine was an especially sprightly vintage. A similar shift in meaning occurred with *spicy*, *saucy* and *salty*. When those adjectives arose they referred only to the flavour of food but eventually came to be used to describe literature that is risqué or titillating. (Incidentally, the word *saucy* and *salty* are cousins: *saucy* – along with *saucer*, *sausage*, *salad* and *salsa* – all derive from the Latin word for salt, *sal*.) To the foregoing list of food-related words, we might also add two words that often appear on the back of novels by Jackie Collins:

sizzling and *steamy*, both of which imply the culinary arts, and both of which seem to have developed their risqué sense in the 1970s.

The tendency to describe sexually suggestive or sexually explicit writing in terms of food seems instinctive. Eating and copulating are fundamental to being an earthly creature: the former is necessary for our survival as individuals, and the latter for our survival as a species. Hence, it's perhaps inevitable that we end up describing sexual matters in terms of food. (This will become even more apparent in the chapter devoted to synonyms for the female breasts.) Conversely, our response to food often seems highly sexualized: compare the ecstatic "oohs" and "aahs" and half-closed eyes evoked by a morsel of chocolate with the vocalizations and facial expressions produced during sex. Both experiences induce a kind of rapture. There might seem to be a parallel, too, between the stages of sex (foreplay, copulation, afterplay) and those of a meal (appetizer, main course, dessert). With both activities, there is even a tendency to omit the first and last stages when pressed for time; the result in the one case is fast-food – in the other, a *quickie*, a usage that was current as early as the 1940s.

Another cluster of words used to describe sexually explicit literature all concern movements of the human body. *Salacious*, for instance, derives from the Latin *salire*, meaning *to jump*, implying that such an action – jumping the bones – might result from reading a salacious book like this one. *Salacious* entered the English language in the mid seventeenth century, and is related to many other words that also derive from the Latin *salire*, including *exult* (which literally means *to jump out*) and *salmon* (that fish is noted for its jumping abilities, especially during spawning season); the last half of *somersault* also derives from the same source. *Titillating* is another word used to describe sexually suggestive works. It derives not from *tit* (an item often found in titillating books) nor from *titter* (the response often provoked by such books); instead, its source is the Latin *titillare*, meaning *to tickle*. Around the same time that the word *titillate* entered English in the early seventeenth century, so did the almost synonymous *prurient*, again from a Latin source: *prurire*, meaning *to itch*. The word *ribald* is similar in that it likely derives from a Germanic source meaning *to rub*. Far more recent than any of these, but also predicated on a bodily movement, is the idiom *nudge-nudge, wink-wink*, which is used to imply the presence of a supposedly covert sexuality. Eric Idle popularized the expression in the late 1960s during a skit on the BBC's *Monty Python's Flying Circus*.

> Do not let your mouth lead you into sin.
> *Ecclesiastes 5:6*

A further group of words employed to describe sexually explicit literature or language comprises terms pertaining to dirt and soil. The most obvious, but also the most recent, is the idiom *dirty word*, which did not arise until the mid nineteenth century. *Smut* also has roots in the soil: that word derives from the German *Schmutz*, meaning *dirt*. When it first appeared in English in 1665, *smut* denoted a fungous disease which turns the seeds of a plant to soot-like powder. Before long, however, *smut* was being applied to bawdy literature, as in this 1698 passage from *A Short View of the Profaneness and Immorality of the English Stage* by Jeremy Collier: "The modern poets seem to use smut as the old ones did machines, to relieve a fainting invention." As for the almost synonymous *filth*, it has been used to denote obscene language and literature since the early eighteenth century, although as early as the tenth century the word was used to denote physical corruption. *Filth* derives from the same Germanic source as *foul*, a word that has been used to disparage obscene materials since the tenth century. The more specific compound *foul-mouthed* is first recorded in Shakespeare, and *sordid* and *obscene* also appeared in his lifetime. Both of these words developed from sources that denoted filthiness: *sordid* from the Latin *sordere*, meaning *to be dirty*, also found in the medical term *sordes*, a name for the feculent crust that accumulates on your teeth when you have typhoid fever. *Obscene* is likely a compound formed from the Latin prefix *obs*, meaning *onto*, and the Vulgar Latin *cenum*, meaning *filth*. To be obscene therefore means *to pile filth onto*. (Incidentally, Vulgar Latin refers to the form of Latin spoken by the common people of the Roman Empire, the plebeians.) Sexually explicit literature is also sometimes disparaged as *nasty*. Nowadays that word is used only in moral or social contexts, but when it appeared in English in the late fourteenth century it referred to things that were physically unclean. Earlier on, the word *nasty* probably developed from the French word *nastre*, which in turn was a shortened form of the earlier *villenastre*. In turn, *villenastre* was a compound formed from the French *vilein*, meaning *farmhand*, and the suffix *astre*. And even further back, the French *vilein* evolved from the Latin *villa*, meaning country house. Both *villain* and *village* also derive from this source, making them cousins of *nasty* despite the fact they do not at all resemble that word.

The list of words that might describe this book can be extended to include the obsolete, the archaic, and the arcane. For instance, I admit that this book is *anacreontic, paphian,* and sometimes even *fescennine*; my critics might uncharitably add that it is *lenocinant* and *lupanarian*, and that I am engaging in *coprophemia, aischrolatreia* and *lalochezia*. The first in that string of words, *anacreontic*, was formed in the early eighteenth century from *Anacreon*, the name of a Greek poet who lived more than twenty-five hundred years ago. Anacreon wrote poems in praise of love, and thus *anacreontic* describes writing that is erotic in nature. Thomas Moore translated the odes of Anacreon in 1800, including this passage from Ode 49:

Sing, sing of love; let music's sound
In melting cadence float around,
While, my young Venus, thou and I
Responsive to its murmurs sigh.
Then waking from our blissful trance,
Again we'll sport, again we'll dance.

This book is also *paphian*, meaning pertaining to sexual indulgence. The word was formed in the early seventeenth century from *Paphos*, an ancient city on the island of Cypress, sacred to Aphrodite, the goddess of love. (Coincidentally, *Paphos* derives from a Greek word meaning *hot*.) The word *fescennine* was likewise inspired by a city: Fescennia, located in the long-vanished nation of Etruria, which is now roughly the Tuscany region of central Italy. In ancient times, a kind of rough and scurrilous poetry came to be associated with this city, and thus the adjective *fescennine*, meaning *obscene*, was formed. A modern equivalent of *fescennine* emerged in 1945, also named after a region renowned for its bawdy jokes and obscene language: namely, the locker room as in *locker-room humour*.

As for the words that might be uncharitably applied to this book, one of them is *lenocinant*, meaning enticing to evil. That seventeenth-century word derives from the Latin *leno*, meaning *pimp*, a man who procures a prostitute for another man. Another word that derives from the same source is *lenociny*, which denotes an enticing medicine: cherry-flavoured cough suppressant is a lenociny, and so are coloured and sweetened children's pain relievers. Further, just as *lenocinant* derives from a source meaning *pimp*, the word *lupanarian*, meaning *lascivious*, derives from a source meaning *prostitute*. That source was the Latin *lupa*, the feminine form of *lupus*, meaning *wolf*. The origin suggests that the ancient Romans considered prostitutes as predators, as she-wolves that preyed upon the otherwise upstanding citizens of Rome. The same attitude is implicit in the modern term *hooker*, implying that prostitutes "snag" their customers, by hook or by crook. The Latin *lupus* is also the generic name for several diseases characterized by skin lesions. Although it's often claimed that lupus was so-named because the facial lesions of its victims resemble the markings on a wolf's head, in fact the disease more likely acquired its name because it seemed to eat up the skin of its victims. In 1590, for example, Philip Barrough wrote in his

> There is only one way to degrade mankind permanently and that is to destroy language.
>
> *Northrop Frye*

A Method of Physick that "Lupus is a malignant ulcer quickly consuming the neather parts; and it is very hungry like unto a woolfe." Similary, the word *cancer*, which is Latin for *crab*, originally denoted a kind of progressive ulcer, and its medical name might have been inspired by the creeping nature of that crustacean.

As for the charge that this book is nothing more than a study in *coprophemia* (shit-speech), *aischrolatreia* (the worship of filth) and *lalochezia* (relieving tension by talking dirty), I deny it, but you – dear reader – can decide for yourself after perusing the remaining two hundred pages of *Dirty Words*.

Chapter Two

BARE BODKINS
Words for Nakedness

*F*ROM THE PERSPECTIVE OF a nineteenth-century logician, nakedness is neither a necessary nor sufficient cause for sex. In other words, it's not necessary to be naked in order to have sex, nor is nakedness all by itself sufficient to result in sex. Nonetheless, modern science has established that those two things – nakedness and sex – frequently occur in tandem. Even in tenth-century England, where a prevalence of cold drafts made bathing something of a rarity, Anglo-Saxon men and wif-men usually doffed their duds before engaging in a bit of the old *forlegenes*. When they did so, they could describe themselves as *unscrydd*, *unbehelod*, *nacod* or *baer*. The first of these words, *unscrydd*, meant *unclothed*, formed from the negating prefix *un* and the verb *scrydan*, meaning *to clothe*. This Old English verb developed from the Indo-European *skreu*, which meant *to cut*: the connection was simply that clothes are cut from fabric, an origin that is paralleled in the word *tailor*, which derives from a Latin source that also means *to cut*. A host of other English words also developed from the Indo-European *skreu*, including *shroud* (which is also cut from cloth), *scroll* (which is cut from parchment), and *shred* (which is a form of cutting). More surprisingly, the mouse-like creature called the *shrew* gets its name from the same Indo-European source: that tiny mammal has a long, sharp snout resembling a cutting instrument. Shrews were once thought to be venomous, and thus *shrew* became a pejorative name for any malignant person, especially women, as in Shakespeare's *The Taming of the Shrew*. From this malignant sense of *shrew*, the word *shrewd* was derived, which originally meant *malicious*, and then weakened to just *cunning*. Still more strangely, the word *scrutiny* derives from the same Indo-European source: that source became the Latin *scruta*, meaning *scraps*, bits and pieces that are cut away and then discarded. This Latin word inspired the metaphor of looking for something so carefully that even the scrap pile, even the rubbish, is sifted and examined – in other words, it is put under *scrutiny*.

> One way of looking at speech is to say it is a constant stratagem to cover nakedness.
>
> *Harold Pinter*

Another word used a thousand years ago to denote nakedness was *unbehelod*; that word appeared, for example, in an Old English translation of the Book of Genesis, which relates how Noah drank too much wine and fell asleep naked – or *unbehelod* – in his tent. Although the last part of this word might resemble *behold*, it has no connection to that verb. Instead, *unbehelod* derived from the Old English *behelian*, meaning *to conceal*.

Even further back, though, *behelian* developed from the Old English verb *helan*, which also meant *to conceal*, to which was added the prefix *be*. This prefix was essentially an intensifier, as it is, for example, in *begrudge* or *befall*. In turn, the Old English *helan* developed from the Indo-European source *kel*, which meant *to cover* or *to conceal*. The transformation of the initial *k* of *kel* into the *h* of *helan* also took place in many other words that developed from *kel*, including *holster* and *helmet*, items that are designed to conceal or cover the things that are thrust inside them. Likewise, the shifting of *k* to *h* occurred with other derivatives of *kel*, such as *hole* and *hollow*, denoting spaces that conceal whatever crawls into them. Even the word *hell* derives from the same source, hell being – etymologically – a hole where the spirits of the dead are concealed. The initial *k* sound of *kel* was retained, however, in some of its other descendents, such as *occult* (the occult arts are the hidden or concealed arts) and *apocalypse* (the *apo* part of that word is a Greek prefix meaning *off*, and thus the entire word essentially denotes a cosmic uncovering). Strangest of all, perhaps, is that the word *colour* developed from the same source: colour, to the primitive imagination, was something that "covered" an object, and which, in the natural world, often served to camouflage or conceal it.

While *unscrydd* and *unbehelod* eventually vanished, *nacod* and *baer* survived from Old English into Modern English, albeit with altered spellings: *nacod* became *naked*, and *baer* became *bare*. Originally, the two words were almost exact synonyms, but over the centuries each has carved out a slightly different usage: nowadays, *bare* tends to be applied to things, like a bare cupboard, whereas *naked* is usually applied to people. There are, however, idioms that belie this tendency, such as *the naked truth* and even *bare naked*. In fact, the latter of those two idioms suggests another tendency with the word *naked*, namely, that it has often been combined with an adjective to form an "augmented" nakedness. Old English, for instance, had *eallnacod* and *lim nacod*, the one meaning *all-naked* and the other *limb-naked* but both having the force of *utterly naked*. The early fifteenth century saw the appearance of *mother naked* – that is, as naked as the day you emerged from your mother – while the early sixteenth century had both *belly naked* and *stark naked*. The latter of these two idioms was originally *start naked*, the word *start* being a now-obsolete word that meant *tail*. To be *start naked* was therefore to be so naked that your tail – that is, your ass – was exposed. The shift from *start* to *stark* occurred as the noun *start* began to decline in use: people mistakenly replaced it with the more familiar-sounding, but totally unrelated, *stark*. A similar shift in pronunciation likely occurred with *buck naked*, which appeared in the early nineteenth century. The *buck* of that phrase might originally have been *butt*, as in *butt naked*, which shifted to the more polite-sounding *buck*. (This shift in pronunciation is known as taboo deformation, and is not uncommon: it occurred in the eighteenth century with the profane *damn*, which prompted the invention of the softer *dang*, and again in the nineteenth century with *God damn it*, which inspired the creation of *doggone it*.) In the 1950s, *bollock naked* arose, similar to *stark naked* in that it implies a state of undress so extreme that one's private parts – in this case the bollocks, or testicles – are dangling in plain view.

> Language is the dress of thought.
>
> *Samuel Johnson*

An alternative explanation for one of the foregoing idioms, *buck naked*, is that it implies a clotheslessness like that of an animal, specifically a male deer. This might seem an unlikely origin until we recall the idiom *as naked as a jaybird*, which was first recorded in English in 1943. An older but equivalent idiom is *naked as a robin*, which dates back to the mid nineteenth century. *Naked as my nail* was current in the mid sixteenth century, the fingernail being one of the few places on the human body that is utterly hairless. Still older are *naked as a worm* and *naked as a needle*, both of which were common in Middle English. This long-standing tendency to amplify the notion of nakedness through the addition of quasi-redundant adjectives such as *buck* and *stark*, or through the use of similes invoking needles, worms or robins, reflects the peculiar psycho-social valence of nakedness: nakedness is rarely a bare fact; it usually invokes or assumes an emotional or moral response. Thus, a woman glimpsed through a window is usually not reported to be *naked* but *stark naked*, even though there is no denotative difference between those two descriptions; the difference, rather, lies in the air of moral outrage, or salacious glee, that adjectives like *stark* or *bare* or *buck* evoke. Likewise, a four-year-old boy running across a beach will not prompt onlookers to exclaim "That child is naked!" but rather "That child is naked as a jaybird!" The implication here is that the youngster's nakedness has not transgressed, but transcended, the usual social taboos. In other words, the jaybird simile implies that the nudity is not sinful but natural, like the unclad state of the rest of God's creatures. As a sidenote, it's interesting to observe that when creatures are anthropomorphized, as they are in Disney cartoons, they tend to acquire clothing. Goofy wears both trousers and shirt, and Mickey Mouse wears shorts. Somewhat perversely, Donald Duck wears a vest but no pants.

Through the centuries, English has also acquired new words pertaining to nakedness. The thirteenth century, for example, saw the emergence of *strip*, a word which not only meant *to make naked* but also *to plunder*. The concurrence of these two senses is an early example of a long-standing tendency to associate sex with violence. The derivative *stripper* emerged around 1930 to denote a woman who is paid to remove her clothing in front of a male audience. Even here, with this modern formation, there is perhaps a vestigial sense of *plunder*, at least to the extent that the male gaze can be construed as a kind of visual assault. On the other hand, the word *striptease*, which also appeared in the 1930s, might imply a reversal of the power dynamic, since the person doing the teasing – and therefore the person ostensibly in control – is the female stripper. The word *peel* underwent an evolution somewhat parallel to that of *strip*. When it emerged in the fourteenth century, it meant *to plunder* or *to pillage* (in fact, *peel* and *pillage* derive from the same source); then in the eighteenth century, *peel* came to mean to remove one's clothes; and around 1950 the word *peeler* arose as a synonym for *stripper*. In contrast, the Old English word *unwry* did not undergo the same evolution as *strip* and *peel*: that word, which appeared in the thirteenth century, also meant *to make naked*, but it vanished from the language by the early fifteenth century. Had it not, lecherous men might now be crowding into "unwry clubs."

In Early Modern English more *naked* words emerged, some of which survived into current English, and some of which did not.

Tirl, for example, appeared in the early sixteenth century, and was used to describe the action of removing someone's clothes. The word is nearly obsolete, but one of its cognates is still familiar: *turf*, a layer of sod that is peeled from the earth. *Devest* appeared at the end of the sixteenth century, literally meaning *to unclothe*; like the word *vest* itself, *devest* evolved from the Latin *vestire*, meaning *to clothe*. Nowadays, the variant form *divest* is familiar, but it tends to be applied to abstractions: "I will divest myself of responsibility." The early seventeenth century saw a flurry of new phrases meaning *naked*, including *in the buff*, *in stag* and *in cuerpo*. The first of these, *in the buff*, is related to the word *buffalo*. The buffalo in question, though, was not the American bison which is popularly and mistakenly referred to as buffalo, but rather a kind of wild ox found throughout southern Europe. *Buff* arose as a shortened name for this creature, and then later came to denote a kind of leather made from the buffalo hide. Still later on, the fuzzy texture and whitish-yellow colour of this leather inspired Western Europeans to perceive its resemblance to their own pale skin, and thus *buff* became a colloquial term for bare skin. The *buff* that means *fan* or *enthusiast* is the same word. In the early twentieth century, volunteer firefighters in New York wore buff-leather coats to protect themselves from falling embers. These firefighters came to be known as *buffs*, but the term was later applied to the civilian onlookers who crowded near blazing buildings, eager to see another conflagration. The enthusiasm of these fire buffs eventually prompted the extension of the word to other enthusiasts, such as film buffs.

The idiom *in stag* also has an animal origin: a stag is a male deer in its sexual prime, and thus for a man to be *in stag* suggests not just nudity, but a bold and assertive nakedness. *Stag* has been used in other sexual idioms as well. For instance, four hundred years ago the phrase *to wear the stag's crest* meant that a husband had an unfaithful wife, the allusion being to the horns or antlers that a cuckold was metaphorically said to sprout. In the early twentieth century, *to go stag* meant that a man was attending a social function without a female companion. And today, at least in parts of North America, the friends of a man about to be married will throw him a *stag party*, often held the night before the wedding. Again, the implication may be that the man, like his animal counterpart, has reached his sexual prime, as evidenced by his imminent marriage. On the other hand, it may be relevant that *stag* has also been used since the eighteenth century to denote a domestic animal – a bull, ram or hog – that has been castrated.

The phrase *in cuerpo*, like *in the buff* and *in stag*, entered the English language in the early seventeenth century, but unlike those two phrases it was a direct adoption of a Spanish idiom literally meaning *in body*, and idiomatically meaning *naked*. Further back, the Spanish *cuerpo* developed from the Latin *corpus*, also meaning *body*, and from which other English words such as *corpse* and *corporation* were derived. Tobias Smollett employed this Spanish idiom in a 1753 novel, in which the hero Ferdinand, also known as Count Fathom, delivers a message to a nude Major:

He got up and opened the door *in cuerpo*, to the astonishment of Ferdinand, who had never before seen such an Herculean figure. He made an apology for

receiving the Count in his birthday suit, to which he
said he was reduced by the heat of his constitution.

The passage is also notable because it contains the first recorded
instance of *birthday suit*, which, like *mother naked*, implies
the nakedness of birth. However, a similar phrase had been
employed a few years earlier, in 1749, in John Cleland's *Memoirs
of a Woman of Pleasure*, where Fanny Hill, standing naked in
the midst of orgiastic onlookers, is relieved to learn that her
birthday finery is superior to that of anyone else:

> I now stood before my judges in all the truth of
> nature…. My breasts, which in the state of nudity
> are ever capital points…maintained a firmness and
> steady independence of any stay or support that dared
> and invited the test of the touch. Then I was as tall,
> as slim-shaped as could be consistent with all that
> juicy plumpness of flesh, ever the most grateful to the
> senses of sight and touch, which I owed to the health
> and youth of my constitution. I had not, however, so
> thoroughly renounc'd all innate shame as not to suffer
> great confusion at the state I saw myself in; but the
> whole troop round me, men and women, relieved me
> with every mark of applause and satisfaction, every
> flattering attention to raise and inspire me with even
> sentiments of pride on the figure I made, which, my
> friend gallantly protested, infinitely outshone all other
> birthday finery whatever.

Another synonym for *naked* that arose in the eighteenth century was *abram*. This was a cant term, meaning that it belonged to the slang register of language. The word was in use among members of the London underworld, and probably developed from the phrase *abram-man*, which denoted not a crazed and half-naked beggar, but a person *posing* as a crazed and half-naked beggar: the grift was undertaken to elicit sympathy (and coins) from passers-by. In turn, *abram-man* probably arose from the Abraham Ward of Bethlehem Hospital, an institution which housed insane patients, and which allowed its inmates to go free on certain days of the year in order to panhandle. The name of the hospital itself was also the source of another English word: *Bethlehem* was corrupted to *bedlam*, which became synonymous with the kind of lunatic kerfuffles and mad hurly-burly that occurred in that institution.

English continued to develop new *naked* words as it entered its Late Modern stage. *Adamitism*, for example, appeared in 1831 as a generic name for social or religious sects that advocated public nudity. The name was inspired by Adam, for whom nakedness was so natural that it was only after he and Eve ate from the Tree of Knowledge that he came to the conclusion that he wasn't wearing any pants. In the 1611 King James Bible, this pivotal moment is rendered thus: "And the eyes of them both were opened, and they knew that they were naked; and they sewed fig leaves together, and made themselves aprons." However, in an earlier English translation, the fallen Adam and Eve are said to have "made themselves breeches," a translation that has resulted in that 1560 version sometimes being identified as "The Breeches Bible." Thanks to this biblical story, fig leaves have long been appended to what were originally nude sculptures and paintings. For example, when it was sculpted in the fourth century BC, the Roman statue *Apollo Belvedere* was literally bollocks naked. After the piece was rediscovered in the fifteenth century, however, it had a fig leaf affixed over its godly genitals. In the nineteenth century, commercially-made copies of great artworks also incorporated the fig leaf to placate prudish customers; Queen Victoria is

> The difference between the right word and the almost right word is the difference between lightning and the lightning bug.
> *Mark Twain*

said to have had a copy of Michelangelo's *David* that sported a removable leaf. Ironically, in the late twentieth century, the connotation of the fig leaf became inverted. It is now employed in advertisements for porn theatres and escort services to suggest not modesty but titillation.

Around the same time that Queen Victoria was fiddling with the fig leaf on her *David*, the word *nude* came to denote the undressed human figure. Prior to this, dating back to the mid sixteenth century, *nude* had been in use, but it was a legal term, denoting a promise that was not formally recorded. For instance, if two peasants met in a field and agreed to trade a goat for a bushel of wheat, the agreement would be a nude promise, because no one else had witnessed that verbal contract. Earlier on, *nude* derived via Latin from an Indo-European source, *nogwo*, meaning *naked*. The Indo-European source also developed, via the Germanic language branch, into the English word *naked*, and also, via the Hellenic language branch, into the ancient Greek word for *naked*, which was *gumnos*. From this Greek source, English derived the word *gymnast*, the connection being that ancient Greek athletes used to train in the nude.

But hold on. If we back up for a moment and reconsider the Indo-European *nogwo* and the ancient Greek *gumnos*, we might be struck by how little they resemble each other. In part, the difference is due to metathesis, which means that two sounds in a word trade places: here, the *n* and *g* of *nogwo* switched spots and resulted in *gonwo*, which eventually changed further into the Greek *gumnos*. The metathesis of these two sounds was another instance of the previously-mentioned taboo deformation. In other words, at some point in prehistory, the Indo-European people came to associate nakedness with the sacred or with the profane, and so even their word for nakedness became taboo. To get around the awkwardness of having a word for something, and yet not being allowed to speak it, the pronunciation was altered, just as we saw previously with the change from *butt naked* to *buck naked*. Another unspeakable word from the distant past is the sacred Tetragrammaton, that is, the four letters – YHWH – that composed the name of God for the ancient Hebrews. In the third century BC it became taboo to pronounce that name; later on, in the seventh century, vowels were inserted between these sacred consonants to make *Yehowah*, and still later on, medieval Christian scholars Latinized the name by spelling it *Jehovah*.

Also in Queen Victoria's lifetime, the word *togless* and the phrase *in the altogether* emerged as synonyms for *naked*. The first of these developed from *tog*, an early-nineteenth-century name for any outer garment; in turn, *tog* appears to be a shortening of *togman*, a kind of sixteenth-century cloak; further back, *togman* developed from the Latin *toga*; and the name of that Roman outfit was derived from the Latin verb *tegere*, meaning *to cover*. The phrase *in the altogether* was first recorded in 1894, and seems to have been originally used to describe models who posed nude for artists; the idiom likely evolved from the use of *altogether* to mean *entirely*, as in "She was altogether naked." In the twentieth century, jocular variations of older words appeared, such as *starkers* in the 1920s from the earlier *stark naked*, and *nuddy* in the 1950s from *nude*. *Stitchless* also appeared in the 1950s, followed by *skinny-dip* in the mid 1960s and *streak* in 1974, both of which reflect fads popularized by North American college students. In 1970 the phrase *full frontal nudity* likewise arose in response to a change in American cinema. Hollywood versions of the fig leaf – the casually held bath towel, the crotch-high fern, the carefully positioned cup of coffee – gave way to *the full monty*. Incidentally, that phrase predates the 1997 film entitled *The Full Monty*, but no one is sure where it originates. It might, for example, derive from the casinos of Monte Carlo, where the full Monte would imply hitting the jackpot. Alternatively, it might derive directly from the Spanish *monte*, meaning *mountain*, since men, especially when they are discussing their unclad genitals, are apt to make a mountain out of a molehill.

Chapter Three

THE GRAMMAR OF GLAMOUR

Words to Describe Physical Attractiveness, or Lack Thereof

I SUGGESTED EARLIER THAT nakedness in itself is not sufficient to cause sex; what is also normally needed is for at least one of the individuals to be attracted to the other individual or, as the case may be, to the riding crop, stiletto heels, and strap-on dildo of the other individual. Since 1924, this ability to attract has been called *sex appeal*. More recently, it's also been called *that certain something, the old stuff, this and that, it-ness* and *oomph*. In addition, a person in possession of the aforesaid *oomph* might also be said *to have plenty of snap in her garter*, or *to have what it takes* or *to have a lot of what she's got*. Clearly, from a lexicographer's point of view, the preceding phrases are woefully inadequate. At best they are elliptical (*that certain something*) and at worst they are tautological: asserting that *she has a lot of what she's got* is tantamount to defining a word by saying that it's used to denote the thing it means. Still, the very fact that those words and phrases are so loose and baggy suggests that there is something almost pre-linguistic about sexual attractiveness: the desire it provokes is so visceral that it's as if the language centre of our brain is short-circuited, and we are reduced to the nebulous grunts and "oomphs" from which human language might have arisen a hundred-thousand years ago. We see this, too, in the vocalizations produced by certain men when an attractive woman walks by: rather than use words like modern humans, they emit a whistle, one that is tellingly called a *wolf whistle*. I also recall witnessing, in my youth, a young man convey his appreciation of a woman's attractiveness by removing his shoe and thumping it against his head, while simultaneously making whooping sounds.

The visceral, almost physical, effect of that certain something is evident in many of the words used to describe sexually attractive individuals. For example, when we call someone *striking* or *stunning*, those adjectives imply an attractiveness that impacts the beholder like a blow to the head. Likewise, the French phrase *coup de foudre*, literally meaning *stroke of lightning*, is sometimes used to describe the metaphorical whack that is experienced with love at first sight. (The English word *astonish* parallels the French idiom: it means *thunderstruck*, deriving from the Latin *tonare*, meaning *to thunder*.)

> The magic of the tongue is the most dangerous of all spells.
>
> *Edward Bulwer-Lytton*

The powerful, even dangerous, impact of a sexually attractive person is suggested by *stunning* and *striking*, but it's also implicit in other synonyms. Such a person can be *arresting, captivating* or *taking*, all of which imply the power to seize hold of the beholder and enthrall him, that is, to make him a thrall, or slave. Even the word *fetching*, which now sounds so quaint, originally had this conquering sense: it derives from the Old English *fet*, meaning *to seize*, and thus is semantically parallel to the word *rape*: the name of that sex crime derives from the Latin *rapere*, meaning *to seize by force*. The fact that the word *rapture* – a kind of ecstasy that seizes hold of you – comes from the same Latin source as *rape* is a further example of how words denoting sexual attractiveness or sexual pleasure are often kissing-cousins to words denoting danger or violence. Danger is even implicit in words such as *alluring* and *attractive*. The former word is related to *lure*, which in the Middle Ages was an apparatus used to trick falcons into approaching so that they could be captured. The latter word, *attractive*, evolved from the Latin *trahere*, meaning *to drag*: attractive people have the power, it would seem, to drag us willy-nilly toward them, like the sirens of classical mythology who lured sailors toward dangerous rocks, or (less poetically) like a John Deere garden tractor, a machine whose name also derives from the Latin *trahere*.

The fear (or fantasy) that our will can be overpowered by a sexually attractive person is also apparent with the words *bewitching* and *enchanting*. Both of those words denote attractiveness or sex appeal, and both derive from the field of necromancy, or black magic. The Latin source of *enchanting* was *canere*, meaning *to sing*, which also gave rise to the word *incantation*, a magic chant or spell. (*Canere* looks as if it might also be the source of *canary*, but it's not: that song bird actually takes its name from the Canary Islands, which the ancient Romans used to call *Canaria Insula*, meaning *Island of Dogs*.) The word *charming* is another word that suggests the seemingly magical influence of a sexually attractive individual; it derives from *charm*, as in *magic charm*, which in turn developed from the Latin *carmen*, meaning *song*.

Even the word *glamorous* has magical associations: the noun from which it was formed, *glamour*, was originally used in Scotland to denote a spell or enchantment. In 1721, for example, the Scottish poet Allan Ramsay wrote a glossary of difficult words in which he explained *glamour* as follows: "When devils, wizards or jugglers deceive the sight, they are said to cast glamour o'er the eyes of the spectator." What is more interesting about *glamour* is that it arose as a corrupt pronunciation of the word *grammar*, the name of the system of rules that control how words are put together to make sentences. To the popular imagination, there has often been a connection between the ability to control language and the ability to cast magic spells. In fact, even the word *spell* implies this connection: knowing how to put letters together to make words means knowing how to spell, or how to cast a spell. Likewise, it's easy to see how, in the early eighteenth century, a scholar or a priest with an arcane knowledge of grammar – especially of Latin grammar – might seem like a magician to an uneducated peasant on the moors of Scotland. Thus, *grammar* – or *glamour*, as it was pronounced there – came to be associated with hocus-pocus. Indeed, even that latter term reflects the association of language and magic:

hocus-pocus, which appeared in the early seventeenth century, might very well be a corruption of a Latin phrase chanted during mass, *hoc est corpus,* meaning *this is the body.* In turn, in the mid nineteenth century, *hocus-pocus* was corrupted to *hokey-pokey* and probably even *hanky panky,* both of which signified deception. In the 1930s, the meaning of *hanky panky* shifted again from *deception* to its present-day sense of *furtive sexual groping.* (Some etymologists derive *hanky panky* from the Romany *hakk'ni panki,* the name of a sleight-of-hand trick where a bag of coins is replaced with a bag of stones; it's possible, however, that the Romany term derived from *hanky panky,* rather than the other way around.)

Even the word *pretty,* which is now one of the meekest compliments for an attractive individual, originally possessed a sinister meaning. A thousand years ago, that word meant *crafty* or *deceitful,* and it evolved from an earlier Old English word, *prat,* that denoted a trick or a deception. Bit by bit, however, the sense of *pretty* shifted, so that over the course of centuries it slid from meaning *deceitful* to meaning *cunning,* and from *cunning* to *clever,* and from *clever* to *pleasing,* and from *pleasing* to *attractive.* This transformation did not occur at a smooth pace, but rather in fits and starts. In fact, one of the most remarkable things about the word *pretty* is that it seems to have dropped out of written English for about four hundred years, from the eleventh century to the fifteenth century. During those four centuries, the word must have been current in spoken English, but for mysterious reasons was eschewed by writers.

One other curious fact about *pretty* is that it is often employed in conjunction with the word *little,* and that the sequence of those two conjoined adjectives was once far more fluid than it now is. In other words, nowadays it is far more usual to say something like "my pretty little dog" rather than "my little pretty dog." In fact, a search of the Internet for the phrase *pretty little* results in 181,000 hits, whereas a search for *little pretty* comes up with only 8,000 hits. Up until the late eighteenth century, however, *little pretty* seems to have been as acceptable as *pretty little*. In 1665, for example, Samuel Pepys wrote in his diary about "a little pretty daughter of my Lady Wright's" and in 1735 the playwright Richard Sheridan wrote a letter to Jonathan Swift about having "written a little pretty birthday poem." The more recent tendency to consistently place *pretty* before *little* is reflected in other adjective pairs, too. For example, a quick search of the Internet, which provides a rough snapshot of contemporary English usage, reveals that *hot sexy men* is about eight times more frequent than *sexy hot men*, and *big strong man* appears seventy times more often than *strong big man*. Linguists have attempted to explain our instinctive tendency to favour some adjective sequences over others by suggesting that we place the most essential modifier closest to the noun. This explanation works with a phrase such as *delicious red wine*, which sounds much more natural than *red delicious wine*; in this case, the fact that the wine is red is more essential than the fact that it is also delicious, and so the adjective *red* is placed closest to the word *wine*. But it's more difficult to see why the fact that a certain man is sexy is more essential than the fact that he is also hot; if anything, *sexy* and *hot* are synonymous, at least in this context. Perhaps the most that can be said is that some aspects of language remain mysterious.

If *pretty* didn't mean *pretty* a thousand years ago, then what did? Actually, at that time the English language possessed several words to describe sexually attractive individuals, the most prevalent of which were *fair* and *comely*. Of these two, *fair* is the oldest: its earliest recorded appearance is in a manuscript written around the year 888. Further back, *fair* evolved from an Indo-European source that meant *to make pretty*. The word *fawn* – not the noun that means *young deer*, but the verb that means *to show delight* as in "She fawned all over him" – derives from the same Indo-European source. Further, the adjective *fair*, meaning *to be free from bias* as in *fair play*, is actually the same word as the *fair* that means *attractive*: when people are fair to each other, it is beautiful; when they aren't, things get ugly. (The other *fair*, the one that denotes a community celebration as in *North Dakota State Fair*, derives from a totally different Indo-European source, one that denoted religious festivals.) In the nineteenth century, the adjective *fair* lost some of its force as it ceased to mean *very attractive* and came instead to denote someone or something which is just slightly better than average, as in *fair weather* or *fairly good*. In this regard, *fair* evolved, over the centuries, in the opposite direction as *pretty*: the former developed a less positive sense, and the latter developed a less negative sense. The other sub sense of *fair*, the one meaning *light-complexioned*, arose in the sixteenth century, back when *fair* still retained its full sense of *beautiful*. This sense of *fair* arose as the people of England

> A definition is the enclosing of a wilderness of idea within a wall of words.
> *Samuel Butler*

came to associate their ideal of beauty with the colour of their own skin: to put it bluntly, a fair (or beautiful) woman was a white (or light-complexioned) woman. Shakespeare played on the shifting senses of *fair* in *Othello*, where the conciliatory Duke offers some advice to the bigoted father of Desdemona: "If vertue no delighted beautie lacke, / Your son-in-law is farre more faire than blacke."

The word *comely* has been in the English language almost as long as *fair* – more than a thousand years. Although *comely* looks as if it might be related to the verb *come*, it isn't; rather, *comely* derives from the Old English *cyme*, which meant *exquisite*. (In contrast, the adjective *becoming*, which can sometimes mean *attractive* as in "That dress is very becoming," does in fact derive from the verb *come*.) Nowadays, *comely* has almost become archaic: that is, it's not yet obsolete, but it's rarely used outside of self-consciously old-fashioned contexts. The same is true of words such as *tempest* and *wench*: people are still familiar with those words thanks to idioms like *a tempest in a teapot* and thanks to the fact that plays like *The Taming of the Shrew* are still taught in high schools, but no one is likely to incorporate them into casual conversation. You will probably never hear your teenager say, "Some comely wenches got totally drenched in the tempest on their way to the mall."

From the beginning of the eleventh century to the end of the fifteenth century, no new words denoting physical attractiveness emerged in English. Then, in the sixteenth century, several appeared, all of which are still current. *Gorgeous* was the first, and it appears to have developed from the French *gorgias*, which meant *elegantly dressed*. Further back, this French adjective might have evolved from the French noun *gorge*, meaning *throat*, which also became the English verb *gorge*, meaning *to eat greedily*, that is, to stuff food down your throat. The connection between the throat and being elegantly dressed is that the throat is often the site of sartorial accessories such as necklaces and ties. Further back, *gorge* evolved from a Latin source from which we also derived *regurgitation*, which makes that vomit-related word a cousin of *gorgeous*. Shortly after *gorgeous* emerged, the adjective *beautiful* appeared in 1526, although the noun *beauty* had been current since the thirteenth century. Both words developed from the Latin *bellus*, meaning *beautiful*, from which English also derived *embellish*, literally meaning *to make beautiful*; that Latin root is also present in *belladonna*, an Italian name for a poisonous plant sometimes known as deadly nightshade. The plant might have acquired the name *belladonna*, which means *beautiful lady*, from the fact that sixteenth-century women used to put drops of its juice into their eyes in order to dilate their pupils, that is, in order to artificially produce the erotic love-blink mentioned in the Introduction.

Near the end of the sixteenth century, the word *handsome* came to mean *attractive*. The word *handsome* had, in fact, existed in English since the fifteenth century, but at the time it did not refer to a person's appearance but rather to the ease with which a material could be manipulated; clay, for example, is more handsome than stone. Naturally, artisans tended to favour handsome materials – they found them more "attractive." Eventually this sense of *handsome* came to dominate and was applied to humans, especially men. It was not for another hundred years that another synonym for *attractive* appeared in English:

namely, the compound *well-looking*, which is first recorded at the beginning of the eighteenth century. This compound may sound strange now, but at that time it was commonly used as it is, for example, in William Thackeray's novel *Vanity Fair* where a philandering husband comments to his wife that "the sisters were rather well-looking young women." By the end of the eighteenth century, the synonymous *good-looking* had appeared, and the two rival compounds duked it out till the end of the nineteenth century, at which point *well-looking* vanished and *good-looking* prevailed.

In the early nineteenth century, *cute* acquired its current sense of *pertly pretty*, a development from its earlier sense of *keen-witted*. The original form of the word was *acute*, which developed from the Latin *acuere*, meaning *to sharpen*. Some words, such as *toothsome*, have acquired their sense of *sexually attractive* only over the last few years. That word was originally gastronomic: it referred to food that was delicious, or pleasing to the tooth. Its recent shift in sense hints at a long-standing tendency to extend food adjectives, such as *scrumptious*, to sexually attractive people, ones to whom we might say, "I could just eat you up!"

English is also blessed with many words for denigrating individuals deemed sexually unattractive. *Ugly* is one of the oldest: it emerged in the thirteenth century from a Scandinavian source, which might imply that the Viking invaders did not find northern England (or perhaps its inhabitants) to be especially appealing. The word *homely* was first applied to human features in the late sixteenth century; prior to that, *homely* had a neutral sense, simply meaning *having to do with the home*. The word acquired a pejorative sense because of the tendency to equate home life with plain, dull things, while places outside the home came to be associated with refinement. For example, the word *courtesy* developed from *court*, thanks to the medieval delusion that the members of the royal court – the Lords and Ladies who surrounded the British monarch – treated each other with dignity and respect. Nowadays, new synonyms for *ugly* and *homely* continue to be coined, if only because adolescents need a semantically rich field of words with which to insult one another. *Gross*, for example, came to mean *repulsive* around 1960; much earlier, in the fifteenth century, that word simply meant *large*. A closely related word is *groceries*, which originally denoted large items of foodstuffs; small and specific items, such as spices, were sold in stores that used to be called *spiceries*, a word that derives from the same source as *species* and *specific*. Around the same time that *gross* developed its *repulsive* sense, the early 1960s, the word *grody* was invented. It was derived from *grotesque*, which in turn developed from *grotto*, a dank and creepy cavern.

Chapter Four

ARDOR VENERIS

Words of Love and Desire

*S*OMETIMES PEOPLE FIND EACH other so attractive that they *fall in love at first sight*, an idiom that dates back to at least the late sixteenth century. It's found, for example, in Christopher Marlowe's poem *Hero and Leander*, where the speaker asks, "Who ever loved, that loved not at first sight?" A similar expression is used even earlier in Chaucer's fourteenth-century poem *Troilus and Criseyde*, where Criseyde "lightly loved Troilus / Right for the firste syghte." When love happens so suddenly, we often say that we've been *smitten*, a usage that dates back to the mid seventeenth century. The word *smitten* is the past participle of the verb *smite*, meaning *to strike*. This verb remains familiar because of its frequent use in the King James version of the Old Testament, where its various forms – *smite, smote, smiting, smitten* – appear 391 times. (Things get less wrathful in the New Testament, where it occurs a paltry thirty times.) In origin, the word *smite* – and thus *smitten* – derives from an Indo-European source that meant *to smear*. Etymologists speculate that the word shifted from meaning *smear* to meaning *strike* because of an ancient method for building the walls of a hut: twigs were woven together and then daubed with mud, an action that would require both smearing and striking. Another idiom that implies the notion of being struck is *head over heels*, which has been used as a synonym for *in love* since the early nineteenth century. However, when the idiom appeared in the mid eighteenth century, it denoted a literal tumbling backwards, such as when you're socked in the noggin. The problem with the idiom *head over heels*, though, is that it doesn't make sense: if your head is over your heels, then you're standing up, not falling down. The idiom would make more sense if it were *heels over head*, and in fact that is the form it had for hundreds of years, dating back to the fourteenth century, until people began to mistakenly reverse the order of the words.

Many terms denoting love embody fire metaphors. Allusions to the *flames of love* date back to the fourteenth century, and *flame* has been used since the mid seventeenth century to denote a sweetheart. Nowadays, this romantic sense of *flame* has come to be especially associated with long-defunct relationships, as in the familiar expression *an old flame*; it's unlikely that you will ever hear someone refer to a *young flame* or a *recent flame*. The word *burn*, too, has long been associated with the passions, love in particular. In his 1568 collection of poetry, for example, Alexander Montgomerie refers to "that fervent fyre of burning love," and in Shakespeare's *The Two Gentlemen of Verona*, Lucetta says,

I doe not seeke to quench your Loves hot fire,
But qualifie the fires extreame rage,
Lest it should burne above the bounds of reason.

The fire metaphors continue in idioms such as *to carry a torch*, meaning *to persist in an unrequited love*, which dates back to the 1920s. That idiom also inspired the term *torch song*, denoting a ballad about a dead love affair. The fire metaphor is even at the heart of the adjective *ardent*, often used in phrases such as "an ardent love affair." That word derives from the Latin *ardere*, meaning *to burn*, which is also found in *aguardiente*, meaning *burning water*, the name of a Spanish rum. The word *hot*, too, has been featured in amorous

> Love is a fire. But whether it is going to warm your heart or burn down your house, you can never tell.
> *Joan Crawford*

idioms since at least the early fourteenth century. Shakespeare, for example, uses the word *hot* as a synonym for *lusty*. In *Henry IV Part 1*, Hal refers to a "hot wench in flame-coloured taffeta," and in *Othello* Iago implies that Desdemona and her supposed lover are "hot as monkeys." In mating season, female animals are said to be *in heat*, an idiom that emerged in the late eighteenth century, echoed by more recent slang phrases including *hot nuts*, *hot pants* and *hot and bothered*, all of which signify sexual arousal. Even *turned on*, which gained currency in the 1960s, implies heat by invoking a metaphor of an appliance – a stove or oven – being turned from off to on.

The tendency to construe love in terms of fire and heat probably results from the fact that love – and, even more, sexual desire – literally warms you: your body temperature rises the moment you begin to flirt. In ancient times, this warmth was attributed to the belief that love "heated the blood," though it might actually have more to do with an increased heart-rate. The association of love with the heart is long-standing. In documents written in English, it can be traced back to the twelfth century, and phrases such as "He gave her his heart" appear as early as the fourteenth century. The heart, however, was not the only organ associated with love and desire. From the fourteenth to the seventeenth century, the liver was also thought by some to be the seat of noble emotions such as love and courage. Even today, the phrase *lily-livered*, denoting a liver lacking in blood, is used to mean *cowardly*. In origin, the word *heart* derives from the synonymous Indo-European *kerd*, which also evolved into the Latin *cor* (from whence we get *courage* and *cordial*) and the Greek *kardia* (from whence we get *cardiac*).

The traditional icon of the heart – a symmetrical figure, with two plump lobes at the top and a pointed bottom – can be traced back to at least the fifteenth century, where it appeared on playing cards. The curious thing about that icon is that it doesn't resemble a real human heart; in fact, some anthropologists have speculated that the heart icon actually emerged as a stylized representation of female human buttocks. That icon is sometimes referred to as a *valentine heart*, since it is *de rigeur* on cards exchanged on Valentine's Day. Incidentally, the practice of giving valentine's cards dates back to the early nineteenth century, but even older is the belief that St. Valentine's Day is when birds choose their mates, as is the case in Chaucer's *Parlement of Foules*.

While many words construe love in terms of fire and heat, others equate the experience with being drunk. For example, in the sixteenth century, the word *besotted* came to describe someone who was head over heels in love, but the word *sot* itself meant *drunkard*. Thomas Nashe, for example, writing in 1592, noted that "the Danes are bursten-bellied sots, that are to be confuted with nothing but tankards or quart pots." Likewise, the word *potty*, which became a synonym for *in love* in the 1920s, derives from the *pot* that denotes a drinking tankard. Shakespeare's portly Falstaff, for example, is often calling for a pot of ale. (The other *pot*, the one which is smoked, also causes intoxication, but it derives from the Mexican-Spanish word *potiguaya*.) Likewise, the word *dippy*, which has described infatuated lovers since the early twentieth century, was probably inspired by the notion of a person taking too many "dips" from the punch bowl.

Other words construe love not as drunkenness, but as madness. The word *dote*, for example, has been used since the mid fifteenth century as a synonym for *love*, and yet earlier on, dating back to the thirteenth century, it meant *to be deranged*. This sense of the word is still evident in the derivative *dotage*: when elderly folks begin to suffer from dementia, they are said to be *in their dotage*. More recent is the idiom *to be crazy about* someone. That phrase seems to have become current in the 1890s, thanks to the song "Daisy Bell," which features the lyrics "Daisy, Daisy, Give me your answer, do! I'm half crazy, All for the love of you!" The word *crazy* has been used to mean *insane* since the early seventeenth century, but its original sense, going back to the late sixteenth century, was *full of cracks*; the walls of an old ship or building, for example, might be described as crazy. The word *infatuated*, too, has denoted a kind of irrational love since it appeared in the mid seventeenth century. That sense is reflected in the word's etymology, which goes back to the Latin *fatuus*, meaning *foolish*.

Usually an infatuation is fleeting. At first you might feel a tightness in your chest, but that physical symptom usually goes away in a few weeks. If it does, what you experienced was probably a *crush*, so called because of the feeling of thoracic constriction. (If it doesn't go away, and you are over fifty, it's probably angina.) Sometimes this kind of infatuated love is referred to as *limerence*, a term coined in 1976 by psychologist Dorothy Tennov. Unlike most scientists, Tennov did not derive her new word from Greek or Latin roots; she has stated, in fact, that she wanted to create a word that had no etymological connection to other love words, in order to distinguish this phase of the love experience from all others. Accordingly, Tennov created *limerence* based on the subjective feelings that its letters and syllables evoked, though she has said that if she were to create the word over again, she would employ a different first letter.

On the Internet, *limerence* is often misspelt *limerance*, perhaps because of the influence of *romance*. That word is surprising because it didn't come to denote a love affair until the early nineteenth century, and yet it has existed in English since the fourteenth century. When it first appeared, *romance* denoted the language we now call *French*, the connection being that French evolved from Latin, which was the language of Rome. Because that language – French or "Romance" – was the vernacular tongue of France, it became the language used for popular stories of adventure and heroism; Latin, in contrast, was reserved for tedious discussions about the nature of angels. Eventually such heroic tales came to be known as *romances*. Naturally, these literary romances often featured a love intrigue, and thus by the seventeenth century the word *romance* came to denote a narrative centring on two lovers, such as those now published by Harlequin. Finally, in the early nineteenth century, the word expanded from fiction to the real world, as it came to signify an amorous affair, as well as the sensibility associated with such affairs, as in "Stanley, he don't go for no romance."

Romance and romantic love are often presented as an ideal, but of course there are other kinds of love as well, such as *cupboard love* and *narcissistic love*. The first of these, *cupboard love*, appeared in the mid eighteenth century to denote feigned love, that is, love that is pretended in hopes of getting a meal or snack. A parallel term, also from the eighteenth century, is *cream-pot love*, named after the pot of cream that young men hoped to get from dairy maids by faking woo. *Narcissistic love*, also known as *self-love*, acquired its name in the early nineteenth century from Narcissus, the beautiful young man in Greek mythology who fell in love with his own watery reflection, and pined away until he was pitied by the gods and transformed into a flower.

> Language was born in the courting days of mankind; the first utterances of speech I fancy to myself like something between the nightly love lyrics of puss upon the tiles and the melodious love songs of the nightingale.
>
> *Otto Jespersen*

Since the mid 1980s, the phrase *in lust with* has been popularized as a counterpart to the much older *in love with*. Together, the two phrases embody a notion that extends back centuries: namely, that love and lust are distinct, even antithetical. Yet really, love and lust are simply two forms of desire, one seeking an emotional bond and the other a physical bond; ideally, the two can overlap and work well together like George and Gracie, or Chang and Eng; but when they don't, they transform into Jekyll and Hyde, each one plotting the destruction of the other.

The word *lust* has been a remarkably stable word. In English it has meant *sexual desire* for over a thousand years, and even its spelling hasn't really changed: in Middle English, it was sometimes spelt with an *e* at the end, but the usual Old English form was *lust*. Even further back, the Indo-European source, *las*, meant much what the word now means: *wanton*, though it also had the sense of *eagerness*. This latter sense, *eagerness*, is apparent in one of the other words that derived from the Indo-European *las*: namely, *wanderlust*, literally meaning *eager to wander*. On the other hand, the *wanton* sense of *las* has been retained in one of its other descendents, *lascivious*.

Over the centuries, dozens of words have been used as synonyms for *lust*, including four from the sixteenth century, all of which, curiously, begin with the letter *r*: *rank*, *riggish*, *ruttish* and *rammish*. The first of these, *rank*, derives from the Danish *rank*, meaning *erect*. That word was adopted by English in the eleventh century, to mean both *proud* and *fully-grown*. By the fourteenth century these two senses had merged, and *rank* came to signify things that grew too luxuriantly – a garden overtaken by rhubarb, for example, might be described as rank. Such too-luxuriant growth is sometimes the result or cause of decay, and this fact led to *rank* acquiring its current sense of *bad smell*. This smell sense might also have contributed to the sexual desire sense of the word, since female animals signal when they are in heat by emitting a "rank" odour. However, the sexual sense of *rank* probably also developed from the notion of luxuriant growth, which would have suggested fertility, and therefore sexual desire.

The word *riggish* also denoted lust, specifically that of women. This gendered use of the word results from the fact that it developed from *rig*, which in the mid sixteenth century was used as a name for a wanton woman. Earlier on, this sense of *rig* might have developed from the *rig* that denoted an imperfectly castrated horse, a beast that would continue, unlike a gelding, to manifest sexual desire. Even further back, the name of this quasi-gelded horse was *ridgel*, so called because the animal's testicles were thought to remain near the *ridge* of its back, which is why they escaped being snipped off.

Ruttish also has its origin in the barnyard: it derives from the noun *rut*, which in the early fifteenth century came to denote the sudden lustiness that afflicts male animals every spring. The scientific name for this annual sexual desire is *estrus*, which derives from the Greek name for the gad-fly, the notion being that those biting insects can drive a beast into a frenzy. Although *ruttish* originally applied to male animals, the term switched genders when it was extended to humans. For example, writing in 1577, Richard Stanyhurst noted the proverb, "Rutting wives make often rammish husbands." This proverb also provides an instance of the word *rammish*, which came to mean *lustful* because of the long-standing belief that rams and goats are horny creatures. Indeed, *goatish* itself was also used, from the sixteenth century, to denote sexual desire. Goats might also have inspired the use of the word *horny*, a synonym for *lustful* that emerged in the 1880s. More likely, however, the horn in question was that of a cow or bull, since *horny* seems to have developed from the slang use of *horn* to mean *erect penis*, and – in terms of shape – a bull's conical horn resembles a man's erection much more than the curlicue horn of a ram or goat.

Chapter Five

MY SWETE
HURLE BAWSY

Terms of Endearment

*A*T ONE END WE have *darling* and at the other end *snookums*. Both words are terms of endearment, also known as *hypocorisms*, but they are separated by more than eleven centuries of love, loss, heartache and sex. Indeed, terms of endearment are, most of the time, verbal precursors of sex: if two people are in bed, with arms and legs entwined, with one or more organs poking into one or more orifices, chances are that they have, at some point in the near or distant past, exchanged utterances such as "Oh, sweetheart," or "Oh, lambkin," or "Oh, creepmouse." In fact, one way of distinguishing hypocorisms is to understand that they are vocatives, which means that they are, or plausibly could be, preceded by the exclamation "Oh." This is important because there is another cluster of words that share many of the characteristics of terms of endearment, but which are used for an entirely different purpose: specifically, they are used to objectify a person by defining him or her only in terms of sexuality, and thus we might call them terms of objectification. *Bitch*, for example, is a term of objectification in that it equates a woman with a female dog, with the implication being that her sexual behaviour is animal-like; *lambkin*, on the other hand, is also a term drawn from the barnyard, but it is a term of endearment intended to suggest tenderness and intimacy. "Oh, lambkin" has been uttered countless times since the sixteenth century; "Oh, bitch" has probably never been murmured, or if it has, then it was with a very different kind of "Oh."

Many terms of endearment used by lovers have origins that defy etymological investigation, sometimes because they are invented in imitation of the nonsense vocalizations that parents often produce when coddling their infants. Still, even though such vocalizations may be nonsense, they are not totally arbitrary. They tend to make use of internal rhyme, and certain syllables recur among the different formations: *ums*, for instance, is found in *diddums* (employed to soothe fussy babies since the nineteenth century), in *pussums* (applied to beloved cats since 1924), and also in *pookums*, a traditional name for a teddy bear.

> More than kisses,
> letters mingle souls.
> *John Donne*

That same syllable is also found in *snookums*, which originated around 1919 as a term of endearment applied by a parent to a child but soon adopted by spoony couples across North America. The *snook* part of that word is likely a nonsense formation, since it seems to have little connection to any of the earlier *snook*s in English: an obsolete *snook* that denoted a promontory of land; a zoological *snook* denoting the sergeant fish; and a pejorative *snook* that denotes a derisive gesture.

Slawsy-gawsy was another term of endearment, now thankfully obsolete, which seems to have arisen as a nonsense formation. It was used, along with numerous other terms of endearment, in a sixteenth-century bawdy poem called "In Secreit Place This Hyndir Nycht" by Scottish poet William Dunbar. The woman in the poem addresses her lover thus:

> My belly huddrun, my swete hurle bawsy,
> My huny gukkis, my slawsy gawsy,

which means something like

> My big lummox, my sweet unweened calf,
> My honey cakes, my slawsy gawsy.

To this, her beloved replies,

> My kyd, my capirculyoun,
> My bony baib with the ruch brylyoun,
> My tendir gyrle, my wallie gowdye,
> My tyrlie myrlie, my crowdie mowdie,

which obviously needs no translation.

As strange as the phrases in Dunbar's poem might seem, they are nonetheless representative of most terms of endearment for the past thousand years. For instance, in *slawsy gawsy* and *tyrlie myrlie* we see the use of rhyme which also characterizes still-current forms such as *lovey-dovey*, which appeared in 1819, and *honey bunny*, an early version of which can be traced back to a collection of poems called *Pills to Purge Melancholy*, published in 1719 by Thomas D'Urfey, in which a smitten lover exclaims the immortal line, "My Juggy, my Puggy, My Honey, my Bunny." Like the aforementioned Dunbar, D'Urfey also wrote bawdy verse, including this passage from a poem entitled *My Mistress' Cunny*:

My mistress is a hive of bees
In yonder flowery Garden:
To her they come with loaden thighs,
To ease them of their burden.
As under the bee-hive lieth the wax,
And under the wax is honey,
So under her waist her belly is placed –
And under that, her cunny.

Other rhyming terms of endearment include the now-obsolete *golpol* and *kicky-wicky*. The first of these appeared in the sixteenth century as a shortened version of *gold-poll*, with *poll* being an old word for *head*. (In fact, when you take a poll you are, etymologically, counting heads.) The modern equivalent of *golpol* is *blondie*, although that word is perhaps closer to being a term of objectification, rather than endearment. The second rhyming hypocorism, *kicky-wicky*, also dates back to the sixteenth century and perhaps derives from the French *quelque chose*, meaning *something*. That French phrase is also the source of the English *kickshaw*, a culinary term denoting a fancy French dish, an exotic "something or other" as opposed to a more familiar and substantial English meal.

The strange phrases in Dunbar's bawdy poem also include names of food, another characteristic of many terms of endearment. *Huny gukkis*, as mentioned earlier, refers to honey cake, and in the sixteenth century *crowdie mowdie* was a kind of porridge. Contemporary counterparts to these food-related endearments include *honey*, *sugar*, *sugar-pie*, *sweetie-pie* and *sweetpea*, although many of these, or variations of these, have been in use for centuries. For example, in a fourteenth-century romance called *William and the Werwolf*, the protagonist William tells his beloved Melior, "Mi hony, mi hert, al hol thou me makest," meaning "My honey, my heart, you make me completely whole." In contrast, the word *sugar* became a term of endearment much more recently: it's not recorded with that usage until 1936, although as a name for a substance with the chemical formula $C_{12}H_{22}O_{11}$ it is of course much older, dating back to the thirteenth century. (In origin, *sugar* derives not from an Indo-European source, but from a Semitic one, the Arabic *sukkar*, which is also the source of the German *zucker*. This word is familiar in North America as a surname – ancestors of the Zucker family, or of the Zuckerman family, were likely sugar merchants.) *Sweetheart* dates back to the thirteenth century, *sweetling* to the mid seventeenth century, and *sweetikins* to the late sixteenth century: "She is such a honey sweetikins," wrote Thomas Nashe in 1596. *Powsoddy*, a now obsolete name for a pudding, was also used as a hypocorism in the late sixteenth century, paralleling the affectionate use of the word *pudding* itself in our own century, though lovers usually alter the pronunciation to *puddin*. (In origin, *puddin* had a slightly pejorative sense, as it derived from *puddinghead*, a nineteenth-century name for a dim-witted but amiable person.) In the first three decades of the twentieth century, the name of another food item, the *crumpet*, was also used to address the beloved; in contrast, the names of other forms of cooked dough – such as *pancake* and *cruller* – have met with little success when used as terms of endearment, at least in my experience. *Cabbage*, however, has enjoyed unlikely success as a hypocorism, a usage that dates back to the mid nineteenth century; this usage arose as a direct translation of *chou*, which French lovers had been calling each other for a long time: "Oh, mon petit chou" – "Oh, my little cabbage."

One of the other strange phrases in Dunbar's poem is *my swete hurle bawsy*, meaning *my sweet unweened calf*, which suggests another motif pertaining to terms of endearment, namely, the tendency to identify the beloved with critters and varmints. The speaker in Dunbar's poem, for example, goes on to address his sweetheart as *my kyd*, the name of a young goat, and also *capirculyoun*, a peculiar word that looks as if it might be related to the Latin *caprum*, meaning *goat*, from which we also derive *Capricorn*, the zodiacal goat. Nowadays, we still evoke the animal world in amorous contexts by using phrases such as *puppy love* and *doe eyes*. Some lovers, too, call each other *pet*, and in fact terms of endearment are sometimes called *pet names*. The heyday of beastly hypocorisms, however, was from the fifteenth to the eighteenth centuries, a time when people interacted with animals not just in their McNugget or Quarter-Pounder incarnations, but as fellow creatures, sharing the same plot of farmland, if not the same house. In that four-century period, lovers affectionately called each other dozens of animal names, including *turtle, bawcock, chuck, sparrow, lady-bird, mouse, lambkin, bulkin, miting, coney, marmoset* and *sparling.*

Of all these, *turtle* is the oldest term of endearment, first used in that sense in the mid fifteenth century. The turtle in question, however, is not the shell-covered reptile, but rather the turtle dove, a bird traditionally admired for its devotion to its mate. Moreover, the *turtle* of *turtle dove* is not related to the reptilian *turtle.* In the ninth century, the bird's Old English name was *turtur*, which was adopted directly from Latin. In turn, this Latin name of the bird likely arose in imitation of its cooing. By the eleventh century, the Old English *turtur* had developed a diminutive form, *turtle*, which was used to denote small doves. The diminutive *turtle* eventually became so familiar that it had an influence on the similar-sounding but unrelated *tortue*, meaning *tortoise*, which came to be pronounced and spelt just like the name of the bird. As a result, *turtle* ended up referring both to a bird and a reptile. (Incidentally, that reptile's earlier name, *tortue*, evolved from the Latin *tortus*, meaning *twisted*, in reference to the crooked or "twisted" feet of some turtle species.)

Many of the other terms of endearment in the preceding list are also bird names. This is obvious with *sparrow* and *lady-bird*, but less so with *chuck* and *bawcock*. The word *chuck*, however, is merely a variant of *chick* (unrelated to the *chuck* of *woodchuck*, which is Cree in origin); *bawcock* is simply a corruption of the French *beau coq*, meaning *beautiful cock* or, more idiomatically, *fine rooster*. These two terms were linked by Pistol, in Shakespeare's *Henry V*: "Good bawcock, bate thy rage; use lenitie, sweet chuck!" Of the remaining words in the preceding list, several are animal diminutives: a *lambkin* is a little lamb and a *bullkin* is a little bull (just as a *mannequin* – originally *mannikin* – is a little man; a foreskin, however, is just a little piece of skin). As for *miting*, it's not linguistically a diminutive, but in the fifteenth century it did denote any diminutive creature; the word developed from *mite*, the name of a tiny insect.

John Skelton employed *miting*, along with several other terms of endearment, in his poem "The Tunnyng of Elynour Rummyng," in which the hideous Elynour rejoices in the hypocorisms her husband has bestowed upon her:

> He calleth me his whytyng,
> His mullyng and his mytyng,
> His nobbes and his conny,
> His swetyng and his honny.

The origin and precise meaning of several of the words used by Elynour's husband – such as *nobbes* and *mulling* – have been lost in the five centuries since Skelton wrote his poem. *Conny*, however, remained in use until the nineteenth century as *coney*, a synonym for *rabbit*. Indeed, *coney* was the original and earliest name for that burrowing rodent. (Rabbits are, technically, rodents.) Even today, *coney* survives in *Coney Island*, a New York island where rabbits were bred before it became a well-known amusement park. It's interesting that the earliest spellings of *coney* – dating back to the fifteenth century – employed a *u* in place of what is now an *o*, and that the original pronunciation of the word was such that it rhymed with *honey*. Over the centuries, however, the spelling and pronunciation were consciously altered by prudish scholars, in order to diminish the accidental resemblance of the animal's name to the unrelated *cunny*, meaning *cunt*.

Another rodent whose name has been borrowed as a term of endearment is the mouse. For instance, in a mid-sixteenth-century dramatic interlude called *The Triall of Treasure*, one lover exclaims to another, "My mouse, my nobs, and cony swete, / My hope, and joye, my whole delight." This tender usage is puzzling considering that shrews and rats, relatives of the mouse, were considered baneful creatures. Nonetheless, *mouse* was evidently so popular among couples that spin-off hypocorisms appeared, such as *creep-mouse* and *flitter-mouse*, the latter of which also denoted the bat, a kind of fluttering mouse. John Palsgrave employed the former term in his 1540 play, *The Comedy of Acolastus*, in which he thanks "my lyttell sparowe, or my pretye crepemous" and Ben Jonson employed the latter term in his 1610 play, *The Alchemist*, in which the title character tells Dol Common that she is "My fine flitter-mouse, / My bird o' the night." Amazingly, the word *mouse* is closely related to both *muscle* and *mussel*. The Latin name for that rodent, *mus*, evolved directly into the word *mouse*, while a diminutive of the same Latin word – *musculus*, meaning *little mouse* – evolved into *muscle* and *mussel*. The connection between a mouse and muscle is that certain muscles, like the bicep, seem to run up and down the arm or leg when flexed, rather like a mouse; and the connection between a mouse and a mussel is that the small size and grey colour of that mollusk make it a kind of "mouse of the sea."

More exotic creatures have also lent their names to romantic use. For example, *marmoset*, the name of a small monkey, was used by lovers – usually by the male to address the female – from the sixteenth to the eighteenth century. Even stranger, *sparling*, an old name for a fish now known as the smelt, was employed as a hypocorism in a 1530 poem by an obscure writer named John Redford. One wonders, though, whether Redford might have been driven to use *sparling* simply because he needed a rhyme for the word that ended the previous line – *darling*. Incidentally, the word *darling*, the oldest term of endearment in the English language, derives from the word *dear* and the suffix *ling* (the suffix is also found in words like *earthling*). In Old English, the word *dear* meant *worthy*. In the fifteenth century it began to be used in the salutation of letters, and during the Second World War this convention prompted the term *Dear John letter*, a letter sent to an overseas soldier by a wife confessing her infidelity.

Chapter Six

STUDS, JADES AND BITCHES

Terms of Objectification

$\mathcal{I}$N THE PRECEDING CHAPTER I suggested that in some ways terms of endearment resemble terms of objectification. Both make great use of metaphor: a person is identified with something like an animal or a food, the only difference being the attitude underlying the usage. I mentioned, for instance, that in the early twentieth century the word *crumpet* was used as a term of endearment for both sexes. That usage ended in the 1930s as *crumpet* developed a new sense. Namely, it came to be used as a collective noun for women construed as sex objects. "That's a nice bit of crumpet," one leering man might say to another, pointing not to his breakfast plate, but to a woman across the room. Not surprisingly, as this sense of *crumpet* arose, it drove the other sense into extinction. After 1930, whispering "My crumpet!" into your sweetheart's ear would be tantamount to calling her a *broad* or a *skirt* or a *piece of ass*. The difference in attitude that underlies the distinction between terms of endearment and terms of objectification is perhaps best represented by the words that precede them: if terms of endearment are usually preceded by *oh* or *my*, then terms of objectification are usually preceded by *a* or *you* – thus, "My lambkin" or "Oh, darling" versus "A fox" or "You bitch."

Another characteristic of terms of objectification is that they are divided along gender lines to a much greater degree than terms of endearment. *Darling* and *sweetheart*, for example, are addressed equally toward men and women, and while a hypocorism such as *mouse* might be used more by men in reference to a woman, it would not be terribly unusual for a woman to affectionately address a man with that word. (Nor, for that matter, would it be unusual for that word to be used in same-sex relationships.) In contrast, because terms of objectification place so much more emphasis on the mere sexuality of the person in question, the gender distinctions are much more rigid. While a man can bitch about something, he can't usually be a bitch – and if he is called that, the usage is employed to overtly challenge his masculinity. Some terms of objectification even develop a distinct gendered counterpart: after *cheesecake* emerged in the 1930s to denote women photographed in sexy poses, the term *beefcake* emerged in the 1940s to denote the male equivalent. Similarly, beginning in the nineteenth century, the word *bastard*, which was originally applied to any illegitimate child, male or female, began to be used as an insult specifically aimed at men. This shift in sense likely arose in order to supply *bitch* with an

> In my youth there were words you couldn't say in front of a girl; now you can't say girl.
> *Tom Lehrer*

alliterative counterpart. Indeed, the phrase *the bitch and the bastard* has become a contemporary idiom, as evidenced by the fact that it is the name of both an erotic paperback novel (by Wendy Harris) and a play (by Scott McKay).

However, although some terms of objectification exist in gendered pairs, most do not. In fact, the number of such terms that target women has, over the centuries, far exceeded the number that target men. This disproportion is due in part to the fact that history, at least until recently, was written by men. Most of the documents from which we derive our understanding of the past, and of past languages, were produced by male historians, male playwrights, male novelists, and so on. It might also be true, however, that men are more fertile when it comes to inventing collective nouns that construe women as sex objects, perhaps because they have an overdeveloped impulse to categorize, or perhaps because their higher level of testosterone predisposes them to see everything, or at least an awful lot of things, in terms of how it relates to their penis. In any event, the number of words and idioms that construe men in sexual terms is quite small.

Stud is one notable example: it's been used since the late 1920s as a synonym for *young man*, but always with a connotation that implies vigorous sexuality. This sense evolved from the late-nineteenth-century usage of *stud* to denote a womanizer, a man excelling in the art of seduction. Earlier on, all senses of this word pertained to horses: since the early nineteenth century, a stud was a stallion, a male horse kept, as the *Oxford English Dictionary* delicately puts it, "for the purpose of servicing mares." Before that, in the fourteenth century, *stud* referred to a group of horses kept for breeding, and its earliest usage, in the eleventh century, was to denote the stable where horses were kept for that sexual chore. *Stable*, in fact, derives from the same source as *stud*: both words developed from *sta*, an Indo-European source that meant *to stand*. Moreover, the number of other English words that have developed from the Indo-European *sta* is enormous – more than a hundred. They range from *stage* (a place where one stands in front of others), to *stool* (a piece of furniture which stands on three legs), to *statue* (a carved, standing figure), to *solstice* (the point in the year at which the sun "stands still," before beginning to move back toward the celestial equator). Even the *stan* in country names such as *Afghanistan* derives from this Indo-European source: the Indo-Iranian derivative, *stanam*, meant *nation*, that is, *the place where we stand*.

Although other collective nouns denoting men have existed in English, only a few of them have sexual connotations, such as *buck* and *shaver*. *Buck*, for example, implies the aggressive sexuality of a male deer in its prime, as suggested earlier in reference to the phrase *buck naked*. In England, it was used since the eighteenth century to describe dashing young men, and in North America it was used in the nineteenth century to denote Native Americans and Black slaves: "A buck nigger," advised a gentleman's handbook published in Philadelphia in 1835, "is worth the slack of two or three hundred dollars." Five years later, in an adventure novel called *Greyslaer*, Charles Fenno Hoffman wrote, "There they lay on the grass, six big buck Injuns, likely fellows all." Such usages are congruent with the long-standing racist tendency to regard African-Americans and Native Americans as enjoying more sexual prowess than Caucasians, a tendency that tends to get polarized into either anxiety (as seen, for example, in films ranging from *Birth of a Nation* to *To Kill a Mockingbird*) or fantasy (as seen, for example, in innumerable porn movies that feature a black male with one or more white females, a sub-genre known in the porn industry as *black on white* or *ebony fuck*). The word *shaver* has also been used as a collective noun for men, and it also seems to be founded on an aspect of sexuality: namely, the act of shaving, which becomes necessary only after sexual maturity. When the word originated in the late sixteenth century, it denoted men, specifically men at their lusty prime, as in this passage from a 1602 pamphlet by Samuel Rowlands: "Such jollie shavers have I knowne...to sit up all night...quaffing and swilling at the Taverne." However, within a hundred years the word shifted in meaning, and came to denote adolescent males, boys who were just beginning to shave and who had not yet matured to the point where they could sport a full beard. It's this latter sense of the word that is still current, just barely, today. I recall, for example, my grandfather referring to me as a *young shaver*.

As for another handful of collective nouns – including the obsolete *churl* and *jack*, and the still-current *gaffer*, *bloke*, *guy*, *fellow*, *chap* and *dude* – they are gendered terms insofar as they refer specifically to men, but none of them seems to be especially sexual in origin or connotation. On the other hand, male epithets such as *tomcat* do have sexual implications, but they are not really used as collective nouns. You would not say, "Mike was out with the tomcats last night" in the same way that you might say "Sheila was out with the chicks last night." Instead, words such as *tomcat* or *lecher* seem to be used in more specific contexts to denote a particular kind of sexual behaviour, and so they are discussed in Chapter Eighteen devoted to wanton words.

When we turn to terms of objectification that have targeted women, the story is quite different. There are dozens of such terms, and all of them have either emerged from a male view of female sexuality, or else they have come to imply a male view of female sexuality. To take an obvious example, the word *breeder* has been used since the sixteenth century as a synonym for *woman*. In Shakespeare's *Henry VI Part 3*, for instance, Richard tells his brother Edward to inscribe the image of three daughters in his shield, because "You love the breeder better than the male." (Since the 1970s, however, *breeder* has been used by some members of the gay community to refer disparagingly to any heterosexual person, male or female.) Another obvious example is *cooler*, which was current in the seventeenth and eighteenth centuries, and which likely came to denote women because they cool (by satisfying) a man's sexual heat. In contrast, a word like *bimbo* has a non-sexual origin – it comes from the Italian *bambino*, meaning *baby or child*, as does the name *Bambi* – and yet in the early twentieth century it came to denote women as sexual objects. For some reason, too, the word *bimbo* has become almost inextricably linked to a certain hair colour: an Internet search results in more than 22,000 hits for *blonde bimbo* and a paltry 1,100 for *brunette bimbo*.

As with terms of endearment, many of the words that denote women as sex objects are drawn from the dinner table. One difference, however, is that these terms of objectification are not so much sweet as savoury; or, to put it another way, they tend to regard women as meat. The word *meat* itself has long been used in this way. For example, in Shakespeare's *Henry IV Part 2*, the aptly named Doll Tearsheet rejects the advances of Pistol in favour of Falstaff by saying, "Away, you mouldie rogue, away! I am meat for your master." The specific names of various kinds of meat were similarly employed as terms of objectification, including *mutton, beef* and *fish*, all of which make an appearance in Shakespeare's plays. In *Measure for Measure*, Lucio slyly claims that the Duke "would eat mutton on Fridays," insinuating that he would partake of wanton women even on holy days. In the same play, Pompey Bum says that Mistress Overdone has "eaten up all her beef," meaning that she has worn out her flesh servicing clients. In *Hamlet*, Polonius is called a *fishmonger*, a cant synonym for *pimp*, that is, for someone who procures "fish" for lecherous men. Specific names of fish were also used to objectify women: *ling*, a form of cod, is used this way in *All's Well that Ends Well*, where the clown contrasts country women with courtly women: "Our old ling and our Isbels o' th' country are nothing like your old ling and your Isbels o' th' court." Even *dish*, which sounds so contemporary thanks to the adjective *dishy*, was used in Shakespeare's time to denote wanton women. In *Antony and Cleopatra*, Enobarbus disparagingly refers to the Queen of the Nile as an "Egyptian dish."

Words denoting small bits of food, too, have been used as eroticized synonyms for women, including *morsel* and *piece*. The first of these words, *morsel*, was used in that manner as early as 1412 by Thomas Hoccleve, who wrote of "the beauty of

> No man can tame the tongue. It is a restless evil, full of deadly poison.
> *James 3:8*

this womman, / This tendir yong morsel." Moreover, the origin of the word *morsel* confirms its gastronomic associations: it derives from the Latin *mordere*, meaning *to bite*. The second word denoting a bit of food, *piece*, arose as part of the idiom *piece of flesh*, which appears to have originated as an admiring (though nonetheless objectifying) epithet. In 1593, for example, the unknown author of a popular work known as *Robin Good-Fellowe's News* rapturously penned, "Oh, she is a tall peece of flesh," and in 1759 the English diplomat Charles Hanbury Williams penned this line: "This beautiful piece of Eve's flesh is my niece." By the late eighteenth century, however, *piece* – when used as a metonym for women – had acquired a more derogatory sense, and by 1910 it was being combined with other words to form the idioms *piece of tail* and *piece of ass*, both of which imply that women are consumable tidbits.

Clearly, there is a long-standing tendency to construe women as sexualized food items – or perhaps not *sexualized*, a word which can have positive connotations, but rather *sexified* (or, considering that we're talking about food, *sexi-fried*). In the previous discussion of terms of endearment, the food metaphors didn't really seem creepy; for one thing, they tended to refer to both men and women, and for another, they tended to be items either evoking sweetness or playfully ludicrous in their application, like *cabbage*. With the terms of objectification, the words seem more sinister: the foods in question consistently gesture toward flesh, and the dynamic that is created is one in which men are the eaters and women the eaten. We have descended, in other words, from a seemingly happy world in which either partner can affectionately chirp "I could just eat you up," to a demonic world in which a wicked wolf cries "The better to eat you up!" before jumping out of grandmother's bed and actually devouring the toothsome Little Red Riding Hood. In the happy world of endearments, men and women metaphorically become "one flesh" – "bone of my bone, and flesh of my flesh," as the traditional wedding vows say. In the demonic world of objectification, the image of Jack the Ripper lurks under the surface, frying up the kidney of Catherine Eddowes, making her flesh into his flesh, and bragging about his deed in a letter:

> I send you half the Kidne I took from one women
> prasarved it for you tother piece I fried and ate it was
> very nise. I may send you the bloody knif that took it
> out if you only wate a whil longer.

In one sense, what Jack the Ripper did in Victorian London was simply enact a fantasy that is implicit in the English language, at least implicit in the words that objectify women by equating them to meat. A version of that cannibalistic fantasy is also present in Bram Stoker's novel *Dracula*, in this erotically-charged scene where the vampire is interrupted as he attacks the wife of Jonathan Harker:

> Kneeling on the near edge of the bed facing outwards
> was the white-clad figure of his wife. By her side stood
> a tall, thin man, clad in black. His face was turned
> from us, but the instant we saw we all recognized the
> Count, in every way, even to the scar on his forehead.
> With his left hand he held both Mrs. Harker's hands,

keeping them away with her arms at full tension. His
right hand gripped her by the back of the neck, forcing
her face down on his bosom. Her white night-dress was
smeared with blood, and a thin stream trickled down
the man's bare chest which was shown by his torn-open
dress.

Sex and cannibalism are linked, too, in films such as *Eating
Raoul* and *The Cook, the Thief, His Wife and Her Lover*,
although in those films the sexual dynamics are more complex
insofar as the dinner entrée is not always female.

If consumption is at the heart of the food-based terms of
objectification, one might expect conquest to underlie the cluster
of collective nouns that equate women with animals. The title of
a play such as *The Taming of the Shrew*, for example, suggests
that Kate is a creature that must be tamed, conquered, or – as
cowboys used to do with wild horses – broken. However, most
of the animals whose names have historically been redirected
to women are not creatures that require taming: *bitch, chick,
puss* and *jade* are all names of creatures that have already been
domesticated. The first of these, *bitch*, was used as a collective
noun for women in the early fifteenth century, although its
original sense of *female dog* dates back to the eleventh century.
In the eighteenth century, the pejorative force of the word
was evidently much stronger than it is nowadays: in his 1785
Dictionary of the Vulgar Tongue, which he researched by
frequenting the London pubs of sailors and thieves, Francis
Grose wrote that *bitch* was "the most offensive appellation that
can be given to an English woman, even more provoking than

that of whore." Grose went on to quote what was then a kind of street riposte: "I may be a whore, but can't be a bitch," roughly equivalent to the contemporary "I may be drunk, but you're ugly." The distinction in this retort between *whore* and *bitch* might lie in the notion that even though a whore is a whore, at least she has sex because she chooses to, while a bitch – that is, a female dog – cannot help having sex. Anyone who has seen a dog in heat knows that its desire to copulate is not a choice, but a profoundly physiological impulse. To be in the grip of such biological determinism – that is, to be a bitch – would be worse than being a whore who is exercising her free will.

In the early nineteenth century, *bitch* developed a new sense, namely, *to bungle* or *to ruin*. This sense is still current, as evidenced by my brother-in-law, who recently complained that a car mechanic had bitched his engine. Thanks to the development of this sense, *bitch* began to lose its explicitly sexual connotations through the nineteenth century, so that by the early twentieth century a bitch could simply be someone who complained a lot, a spoiler or party-pooper. Incidentally, it need hardly be said that when a word, like *bitch*, develops a new sense, it doesn't instantly lose its old one: the rival meanings can coexist for centuries. There are even examples of single words that possess nearly opposite meanings, as with the verb *sanction*, which can mean *to authorize* or *to penalize*. Likewise, the verb *cleave* can mean *to split apart* (as in "to cleave an apple") or *to join together* (as in "husband and wife shall cleave together").

Another dog word that was extended to women in the late sixteenth century was *minx*. In *Othello*, for example, Bianca angrily says "this is some minx's token" when she realizes that the handkerchief Cassio gave her once belonged to another woman. Earlier in the same century, however, *minx* had referred not to women, but to lap dogs, as in Nicolas Udall's translation of a work by Erasmus: "There been litle mynxes, or puppees that ladies keepe in their chaumbers for especiall jewelles to playe withall." Strangely, however, this puppy word might in turn have developed from an earlier word – *minikin* – that was originally a term of endearment for women. In other words, a term of endearment applied to women developed into a pet name applied to dogs, which then became a term of objectification applied to women. Even further back, *minikin* was borrowed from Dutch, where *minneken* was formed as a diminutive of *minne*, meaning *love*.

Francis Grose also included *jade* in his *Dictionary of the Vulgar Tongue* as a pejorative appellation for women still current in the eighteenth century. When the word emerged in the late fourteenth century it denoted an old and worn-out horse, but by the mid sixteenth century it was being applied to women, usually with the connotation that the woman in question was ill-tempered. For example, it's employed in a dramatic interlude written around 1560 to describe a "cursed shrew" known as Xantippe:

Such a jade she is and so curst a quean,
She would out-scold the devil's dame I ween.

Nowadays, this *jade* is obsolete, except as it exists in the adjective *jaded*, meaning *dissipated*, which again hearkens back to the original *worn-out horse* sense of the word. In fact, as a noun this pejorative *jade* has been so completely forgotten that it has allowed another *jade*, denoting a green gemstone, to become a fairly common girl's name. In 2001, *Jade* was the seventy-fifth most popular name for U.S.-born female infants, according to the American Social Security Administration. This *jade* derives from the original Spanish name for the mineral, *piedra de ijada*, meaning *stone of colic*, from the belief that the gemstone had the power to cure that intestinal ailment.

Puss was used in the eighteenth century as a derogatory collective noun for women; for example, one of the characters in Henry Fielding's 1732 play *The Modern Husband* says, "I think her an ugly, ungenteel, squinting, flirting, impudent, odious, dirty puss." Earlier on, in the seventeenth century, the word had been a synonym for *cat*, as it still is. Even earlier, however, *puss* had arisen as a proper name for a cat; that is, in the sixteenth century *puss* didn't actually mean *cat*, but rather it was a name sometimes bestowed on cats, much like *Snowball* or *Whiskers* or *Mr. Dinglethorpe* might be nowadays. Over time, however, the proper name *Puss* became the generic name *puss*, just as *Kleenex*, a brand-name, has come to serve as a generic name for all kinds of facial tissues. Even further back, it's possible that the name *Puss* originated from the *pss-pss* sound that humans often make while vainly striving to get a cat's attention. The application of *puss* to women might have been prompted by the old belief that cats were the "familiars" of witches, that is, evil spirits in feline form. As for one of the

> Slang is language which takes off its coat, spits on its hands, and goes to work.
> *Carl Sandburg*

derivatives of *puss* – namely, *pussy* – that word is discussed in Chapter Nine, devoted to women's genitals.

The Bible was the inspiration for another objectifying epithet, *heifer*. That word, which denotes a young and calfless cow, has been a slang term for women since the early nineteenth century. The Canadian satirist Thomas Haliburton used it, for example, in one of his Sam Slick novels in 1853: "I have half a mind to marry that heifer, though wives are bothersome critters when you have too many of them." However, the original source of the "woman as heifer" notion is the story of Samson, found in the Old Testament's Book of Judges. In that biblical story, Samson poses a riddle that the Philistines solve only after they convince his wife to secretly divulge the answer. Enraged, Samson says to the Philistines, "If ye had not plowed with my heifer, ye had not found out my riddle." In other words, if they hadn't exploited his wife, they would still be stumped. This use of *heifer* parallels that of *cow*, an epithet for women that dates back to the late seventeenth century. Here, it was perhaps the milk aspect of the creature – its hard-to-miss udder – that prompted the identification of women with the cow; that dairy aspect is certainly at the heart of several slang words for breasts, such as *jugs* and *creamers*. Considering that *cow* has been used for centuries to denote women, you might think that the word *cowpoke* has sexual implications, but it doesn't. Instead, a cowpoke is simply a cattle handler, one that uses a long pole to poke and prod the little dogies onto a train car.

Another barnyard animal whose name has become a pejorative collective noun for women is the chicken. As early as the fourteenth century, a variant of *chicken* – *chick* – was used to denote children, a usage that might have been inspired in part by the alliteration of *chick* and *child*. Those two words often appeared in tandem, usually in situations that imply that the child is a boy while the chick is a girl. In 1611, for example, Randle Cotgrave wrote "Hee hath nor child nor chicke to care for." In the 1920s, the word *chick* was transferred from children to women, a shift that epitomizes a long-standing tendency to see children, rather than men, as the equals of women. (In my home city of Winnipeg, the municipal pet shelter was established in 1894 as *The Humane Society for the Prevention of Cruelty to Women, Children, and Animals*). The word *chicken* was also used as a collective noun for women, dating back to the mid nineteenth century; this usage probably grew out of an even earlier tendency, in the late eighteenth century, to use *chicken* as a synonym for *prostitute*. Another variant, *chickabiddy*, was also used in the late eighteenth century to denote women, the *biddy* part of that word being a familiar form of the Irish name *Bridget*. More recently, women have rehabilitated the word *chick* by laying claim to it, much as the gay community reclaimed the once pejorative word *queer*. For instance, the term *chicklit* has been invented as a laudatory label for a sub-genre of fiction written by women, with academics presenting lectures sporting punny titles like *From BritLit to ChickLit*. A parallel but less successful rehabilitation of another collective noun occurred in the early 1990s when a movement known as "riot grrrls" emerged from punk rock, with groups like Bikini Kill and Bratmobile. Proponents of this punk-feminist movement changed the spelling of *girl* to *grrrl*, a spelling intended to evoke the anger and menace of a growl.

The new spelling of *girl* never achieved acceptance outside of the Riot Grrrl milieu, due primarily to the fact that most people – even social radicals – are notoriously conservative when it comes to orthography. Attempts to overhaul the English spelling system, which is indeed beautifully ridiculous in its complexity and idiosyncrasies, have always failed. People even resist changes to individual words, as evidenced by the suspicion provoked by *womyn*, a feminist respelling that attempts to take *men* out of *women*. In contrast, people seem more willing to embrace semantic change: when a word shifts in meaning or develops an entirely new meaning, it may initially provoke a few letters to the editor from irate pedants, but before long it slips into standard usage, and the next thing you know, people are using *mouse* to denote not just rodents and loved ones, but the device that sits beside your computer keyboard. This happened to a peculiar degree with the word *girl*: its original usage, which lasted from the thirteenth to the fifteenth century, was to denote any child, whether male or female. By the early sixteenth century, however, *girl* had narrowed in meaning to just *female child*, with the masculine counterpart being signified by *boy* or by the synonymous *knave*, the latter of which eventually came to mean *rascal*.

As mentioned above, the familiar form of *Bridget* – *Biddy* – is represented in *chickabiddy*. The name *Biddy* itself was also used as a collective noun for women in the late eighteenth century, and from time to time one still hears someone say, "She's an old biddy." Personal names have, in fact, often become collective nouns for women regarded as sex objects. This happened with *Jill*, *Tib*, *Moll* and *Judy*. The first of these, *Jill* – sometimes spelt *Gill*

– is a shortened form of *Gillian*, which is the feminine form of the Roman name *Julius*, from whence we also get the name of our seventh month. *Jill* was used pejoratively to denote sexually active women, as evidenced by this passage from Raphael Holinshed's late-sixteenth-century *Chronicles*: "She is a princesse, and the daughter of a noble king, and it evill becommeth thee to call her a gill." The name *Tib*, which is the familiar form of *Isabel*, was used in a similar manner from the early sixteenth century. For instance, in his 1618 tract *The Scourge of Drunkeness*, William Hornby lamented that London had "so many taverns where tinkers and their tibs doe oft repaire," and in 1681 the philologist William Robertson defined *tib* with the Latin phrase *mulier sordida*, that is, *sordid woman*. The name *Moll* is also a short form: it comes from *Molly*, which in turn is a variant of *Mary*, and was in common use as a collective noun for women since the early seventeenth century. *Moll* is still familiar thanks to *film noir* cinema: in movies such as 1935's *G Men* and 1941's *Highway West*, the word *moll* is used in the credits to identify a gangster's unnamed girlfriend. In the early nineteenth century, *Judy* also came to be employed as a pejorative collective noun, a usage that was probably inspired by the Punch and Judy puppet shows that have been popular in England since the mid seventeenth century. In those puppetry performances, Punch physically enacts the linguistic oppression that is effected through terms of objectification: he beats his wife into submission, though it must be admitted that he also beats other characters, including the devil. In Australia, *Sheila* has been used as a collective noun for women since the early nineteenth century; in the U.S., *Betty* came to be used in the same way in the late 1980s.

Dozens of other words have also been used over the centuries to sexually objectify women. They include the following, listed according to when they were first employed as pejorative collective nouns: *wench* (1290), *crone* (1386), *drab* (1515), *mort* (1561), *dell* (1567), *rig* (1575), *dowdy* (1581), *minx* (1592), *baggage* (1596), *hussy* (1650), *dame* (1698), *stammel* (1700), *buer* (1807), *flat cock* (1811), *article* (1811), *bint* (1855), *popsie* (1862), *dona* (1873), *chippy* (1886), *totty* (1890), *tootsy* (1895), *skirt* (1899), *frail* (1899), *frippet* (1908), *gash* (1914), *tab* (1918), *number* (as in *a little blonde number*, 1919), *quiff* (1923), *poule* (1926) and *trim* (1955). Although all these words have intriguing histories, I'll elaborate on only two of them, *wench* and *mort*.

Wench is a curious word because it originated as a neutral term, and later developed into both a term of objectification and a term of endearment. The original sense of the word, around the late thirteenth century, was simply *girl* or *young woman*. However, by the mid fourteenth century *wench* had developed a negative sense as it came to denote sexually active women; this negative connotation was sufficiently faint, though, that it often needed to be reinforced through the use of adjectives, as in *common wench*, *light wench* and *wanton wench*. By the late sixteenth century, the word had undergone what linguists call amelioration as it came to be used as a term of endearment, both from husband to wife and from parent to daughter. In origin, the word *wench* developed from the Old English *wencel*, which – in the ninth century – referred to a toddler. In turn, *wencel* probably evolved from an even older source, *wancol*, which meant *unsteady*. (Our word *toddler* is parallel in that it derives from *toddle*, a verb that means *to walk unsteadily*; in contrast, *infant* comes from the Latin *infans*, meaning *unable to speak*, which is also the source of *infantry*, traditionally the youngest soldiers of the military.)

Much like *wench*, the word *mort* originated with a fairly neutral sense of *girl* or *woman*, but soon developed a lascivious connotation. Although the origin of the word is unknown, it became, in the early eighteenth century, a very popular term among the canting crew, that is, among the thieves and beggars of London who employed a slang-filled language then known as flash lingo. Back then, *to patter flash* meant to speak in the language of the street, or in what was also called *gibberish*, which was a means to baffle eavesdropping authorities, and to test whether or not the person with whom you were sharing your robbery plans was a real *fidlam ben*. As far as the canting crew was concerned, there were numerous kinds of morts, many of them detailed by Francis Grose in 1785 in his *Dictionary of the Vulgar Tongue*. You could be, for instance, a *bleached mort* (a fair-complexioned woman), a *ben mort* (a beautiful woman), an *autem mort* (a married woman), a *strolling mort* (a female pedlar), a *kinchin mort* (a young girl), a *dimber mort* (a pretty woman), a *gentry mort* (a Lady), a *filching mort* (a female pickpocket), a *rum mort* (a superb woman), a *queer mort* (a woman infected with venereal disease), or even a *mort wap-apace* (a woman who waps – that is, copulates – vigorously). About the only thing that a mort wasn't allowed to be, was herself.

Chapter Seven

THE BAWDY BODY

Words for Body Parts Shared by Men and Women

ALTHOUGH SEX THERAPISTS BLITHELY tell their under-endowed male clients that the largest sexual organ in the human body is the brain, this book is not quite so cerebral. Accordingly, I will skip the brain and proceed to what is not only the largest organ in the human body, but is also essential in sex: namely, the skin. The skin, after all, contains millions of nerve endings that respond to tactile stimulation, whether it be a gentle caress, a sensuous massage, or a stern spanking with a ping-pong paddle. Indeed, the beauty of the skin is that while it is smooth, it is not perfectly smooth; if it were, sexual interaction would be a frictionless – and therefore frustrating – experience.

When the word *skin* first emerged in the English language, it referred only to the pelt of an animal; it was not until the early fourteenth century that it was applied to the outer covering of the human body. Prior to this, the usual word for human skin was *hide*, a usage that can still be seen in idioms such as "He tried to save his own hide." The word *skin* developed from a Scandinavian source, as did many other words in English that begin with the *sk* sound, such as *skull, sky* and *skirt*. Old English did, originally, have some native words that were pronounced with the *sk* sound, but these had evolved to the *sh* sound before the Viking invasions took place in the eighth century: for instance, the Old English *scyrte* became *shirt*. In contrast, the Old Norse *skyrta* became the English *skirt*, thus retaining the *sk* sound. Incidentally, both the Old English *scyrte* and the Old Norse *skyrta* developed from the same Germanic source, which means that *skirt* and *shirt* are cousins or, as a linguist would say, doublets, an especially apt term considering that both words refer to garments.

Even further back, the Germanic source of *skin* – *skurtaz* – developed from the Indo-European *sker*, meaning *to cut*. This Indo-European word is also the source of the words *shear, scar* and *scabbard*, all of which plainly have something to do with cutting. It's also the source of *share* in that sharing something demands cutting or dividing it up, and it's even the source of words such as *carnal*, thanks to the loss of the Indo-European word's initial *s*. The immediate Latin source of *carnal* was *caro*, meaning *flesh*, the connection being that flesh is something that is cut from an animal. Carnal knowledge is therefore knowledge of the flesh, just as *chili con carne* is a dish of chilis and flesh, and *carnations* are a flesh-coloured flower, at least as far as pale-skinned Europeans are concerned.

Skin has other connections to sex as well, some ancient and some contemporary. In the fourteenth century, for example, it was used as a verb to mean *to circumcise*. The penis, according to one medieval medical text, "may be cicatrisid or y-skynned" so long as it is "discretly faren," that is, "carefully performed." Six hundred years later, in the 1960s, *skin* was co-opted by the porn industry in the compounds *skin magazine* and *skinflick*. One of the earliest references to a *skinflick* was in the June 13, 1969 issue of *The Daily Colonist*, a newspaper published in Victoria, British Columbia: "We ran family movies for nine years," said a theatre-owner, "and almost went broke. For the last three years, we've been showing skinflicks and doing much better financially."

Although bare skin, and lots of it, is what makes pornography sell, it is the flesh that has traditionally been considered the source of human sexuality, as suggested by the previously mentioned *carnal knowledge*, and by idioms that date back to the Middle Ages, such as *the sins of the flesh*. The adjective *fleshly*, too, has long been used to mean *lustful*, in opposition to things that are spiritual – for verily, as it is written in the Gospel of Matthew, the spirit indeed is willing but the flesh is weak. The word *flesh* has been used in other sexual constructions as well, such as the fourteenth-century phrase *to blend flesh*, meaning *to copulate*, and the sixteenth-century euphemism *strange flesh*, used by William Tindale in his translation of the Bible to allude to the unnatural sex acts that angered God into raining fire and brimstone onto the citizens of Sodom and Gomorrah. *Fleshmonger* was used in the early seventeenth century to denote a pimp, and around the same time *flesh-shambles* emerged as a synonym for *brothel*, a shambles being a messy and temporary marketplace set up for

Callipygian: the condition of having beautiful buttocks.

cutting and selling meat. (A contemporary analogue for *flesh-shambles* is *meat market*, used to describe a bar where finding a casual sex partner is the goal of the patrons.) *Fleshly part* was used in the nineteenth century as a slang term for the vagina, and in the 1970s, *fleshpot* emerged in the U.S. to denote promiscuous women, synonymous with the better-known *sexpot*.

If flesh is the material or substance of which we are made, then our more abstract form or shape is our *body*, a word that clearly has relevance to sexuality; a working title of this book, for example, was *The Bawdy Body*, since so many of the sex words contained herein have ribald reference to the human body. (*The Bawdy Body* was quickly abandoned, as were the working titles *Prick Up Your Ears*, *The Boudoir Bible*, *The English Sexicon* and *Talking Dirty*.) Moreover, just as *flesh* has traditionally been paired with *spirit*, the word *body* has long been linked with *soul*: for example, in religious works the phrase *body and soul* dates back to the fifteenth century, and in the jazz world the song "Body and Soul" dates back to 1930. However, whereas flesh and spirit have tended to be construed as polar opposites, with the former being a clog to the latter, the words *body* and *soul* have tended to enjoy a more amicable relationship: the body is not so much the enemy of the soul as its vessel – the soul is literally embodied. Perhaps for this reason, the sexual applications of *body* have tended to be milder than those of *flesh*. For example, the word *body* might have been the inspiration of *booty*, a word that appeared in American Black English in the 1920s and which was popularized in the 1970s in the phrase *shake your booty*. (It's possible that *booty* instead derived from *butt* or even from *bottom*, but the fact that *booty*, when it first appeared, was sometimes spelt *boody*, strengthens the *body* origin.) Around 1930, another sexually tame application of *body* emerged with the invention of *body urge*, a euphemism for the sex drive. More recently, the compliment "You have a nice body" has become a fairly safe way of introducing an erotic undertone into a casual conversation. That compliment might be received less politely, however, if the speaker were to employ one of the Old English synonyms for *body* such as *flaeschord*, meaning *flesh hoard*. Other obsolete Old English words for *body* included *feorhbold* (literally meaning *life-dwelling*) and *ban-cofa* (literally meaning *bone-chamber*). The latter term is graphic, but not as stomach-churning as the German term Martin Luther used to denote the body: *madensack*, meaning *worm bag*. One other word that once denoted the body is *belly*, which in the thirteenth century signified not just the stomach, but the entire human form. *Belly* also came to refer to the uterus, and so it is discussed further in Chapter Nine, devoted to the female genitalia.

〰

Having dispensed with the body, we can now turn to its parts, starting with one that is shared by both men and women: namely, the *buttocks*. While the medical name for this part of the human anatomy is the *gluteus maximus* (which derives from a Latin source meaning *largest rump*, there being three differently-sized muscles in that area), the earliest English name was the now-obsolete *lenden*, the plural of which was *lendenu*. (The plural form was more common simply because the buttocks have two cheeks.) The Indo-European source of this Old English word was *lendh,* which developed through the Italic language branch into the Latin word *lumbus,* which eventually evolved into the English word *loin.* Other words that derive from the same Indo-European source include *lumbar* and *lumbago,* the latter of which is a pain situated in the loins. While *lenden* became obsolete by the mid sixteenth century, another Old English name for the buttocks, *aers,* survives in a slightly mutated form, *arse.* The Indo-European source of *arse* was *ors,* which also developed into the Greek *oura,* meaning *tail.* The Greek *oura* was combined with another Greek word, *skia,* meaning *shadow,* to form *skiouros,* which not only denoted the *squirrel,* but also developed into the English name of that creature; a squirrel, in other words, is a *shadow-tail,* and its name is a cousin of *arse.* Although the human arse is sometimes loaded with explosive charges, its name has no connection to the similar-sounding *arsenal,* a kind of storehouse for munitions. The coincidental resemblance of the two words has not gone unnoticed by British football fans, who sometimes malign the much-vaunted Arsenal Club as The Arse.

Over the centuries, the degree of vulgarity attached to *arse* has fluctuated greatly. In its early history, it belonged to the standard register of language: that is, it had no taboo connotations, and thus would have been comparable in tone to the modern usage of *buttocks.* In the mid seventeenth century, however, *arse* came to be seen as vulgar slang, so much so that it usually appeared in books with asterisks representing the middle letters – a**e. Since the mid twentieth century *arse* has lost much of its taboo power. In part, this occurred as the American spelling and pronunciation of the word changed to *ass.* This change from *arse* to *ass* probably resulted from the confluence of three factors. First, the pronunciation might have changed gradually and unconsciously, just as the British *curse* became the American *cuss*, or just as the stress on *buttocks* gradually shifted from the last syllable in England to the first syllable in North America. Second, the change in spelling and pronunciation might have resulted from a conscious desire to create a socially acceptable version of the word; we saw this kind of taboo deformation in an earlier section, with regard to *God damn it* becoming *doggone it*. Third, the drift from *arse* to *ass* might have been facilitated by the fact that *ass* – the name of a kind of beast of burden – had already been used for centuries as an insult. For example, in Shakespeare's *Much Ado About Nothing*, Conrade calls Dogberry an ass, prompting the dim-witted Constable to wish that the insult had been written down so that it could be presented in court as evidence of libel: "But, masters, remember that I am an asse; though it be not written down, yet forget not that I am an asse."

Nowadays, to be called an ass evokes an image of two naked buttocks, but in Shakespeare's time, and for many centuries after, the word would not have had that association: it would have merely equated the person with a donkey. Indeed, that beast-of-burden *ass* derives from a source meaning *donkey*, namely, the Latin *asinus*, which is also the source of the word *asinine*, meaning *foolish as a donkey*. Strangely, the Latin *asinus* is also the source of the word *easel*: an easel bears a painter's canvas, just as a donkey bears a rider or supplies. The same kind of thinking prompted the invention of *clothes-horse* to denote a structure on which garments are draped to dry.

The synonyms for *arse* that appeared between 1100 and 1500 nicely represent the three language sources to which most Middle English words can be traced. There are, for example, words of native origin, that is, Old English words that developed new senses in Middle English; there are Scandinavian words that probably were current in spoken English for several centuries before they were recorded in Middle English; and there are French words that were introduced after the Norman Conquest.

Tail and *toute* are both native English words. *Tail* dates back to the ninth century, where it referred not to the appendage that hangs from an animal's hindquarters, but to the hindquarters themselves. (The appendage that we now call a tail was then called a *steort*, which became the noun *start*, which, as we saw previously, became the adjective *stark* as in *stark naked*.) However, even though *tail* existed in Old English, it was not used to denote the human buttocks till the early fourteenth century. The earliest instance of this sense of the word is in a preaching manual called *Handlyng Sinne* by Robert Manning, where he warns that sinners will "go to helle, both top and tayle," in other words both head and arse. By the mid fourteenth century, *tail* was also being used to denote the female genitals, as it was in a satirical poem printed in the early sixteenth century called *Cocke Lorelles Bote*, which mocks the pretended chastity of nuns: "Many whyte nonnes with whyte vayles, / That was full wanton of theyr tayles." This usage eventually developed into the bawdy idiom *a piece of tail*, first recorded in 1846. As for *toute*, this word appeared in the early fourteenth century, but it probably developed from the Old English verb *totian*, which meant *to stick out*, as buttocks tend to do. Although the word *toute* has been obsolete since the mid fifteenth century, it's commonly encountered in English literature survey courses, which often feature Chaucer's *Miller's Tale*. At the climax of that bawdy poem, Nicholas farts in the face of Absolon, just seconds before Absolon employs a hot iron rod to burn Nicholas' arse, or as Chaucer himself wrote, to "brend so his toute."

Crike, *luddock* and *rump* are all arse words that Middle English adopted from Scandinavian sources. The first of these, *crike*, appeared and disappeared in the fourteenth century; it derived from the Old Norse *kriki*, meaning *crack*. The word *crack* has also been used, since the mid twentieth century, to denote the buttocks, or at least the cleft between them, and it – like *crike* – might be distantly related to *creek*, a kind of crack in the land through which water runs. In origin, *crike*, *creek* and *crack* might all derive from a Germanic source that meant *to crack*, and which arose in imitation of the sharp and sudden sound produced when something brittle cracks. If so, then this cluster of words is also

Okole, bahookie and *popo*: words recently adopted as slang synonyms for buttocks, from Hawaiian, Scots and German respectively.

related to *crow*, *crane* and *grackle*, the names of birds whose cry is sharp and "crackling." This *sharp cry* sense of *crack* is also represented in the word *wisecrack*, and in the idioms *to crack a joke* and *to crack a fart*, the latter of which dates back to the mid seventeenth century. The word *luddock*, like the word *crike*, existed only for a single century, the fifteenth, though *lud*, which also denoted the buttocks, was still current as late as the sixteenth century. In origin, *luddock* and *lud* likely derived from a Scandinavian source that meant *thick* or *broad*. Unlike *crike* and *luddock*, the word *rump* is the only arse synonym of Scandinavian origin that did not become extinct. Its Scandinavian ancestor was probably a word meaning *tail*, as evidenced by the fact that Danish, Swedish, Norwegian and Icelandic all have words that sound similar to *rump*, and all of them mean *tail* or *posteriors*. The word acquired a political sense in the mid seventeenth century when it was used to denote a Rump Parliament, that is the remnant or "rump" that was left after Oliver Cromwell expelled those members of parliament who opposed putting King Charles I on trial.

From French, Middle English adopted numerous terms for denoting the buttocks, including *haunch, croupe, fundament, cul, nage* and *bewschers*. The first of these, *haunch*, is unlike most of the others in that its French source, *hanche*, likely developed from a Germanic language, rather than from Latin like most other French words. The Germanic language in question was probably Frankish, spoken in the fifth and sixth centuries in an area that now includes France, but was then known as Gaul. This means that *haunch* travelled from a Germanic language (Frankish) to a Romance language (French) and then back to a Germanic language (English). Likewise, the French ancestor of *croupe*, which has been used to denote the buttocks since the late fifteenth century, also derived originally from a Germanic source, one that meant *lump*. From the same source evolved the word *crop* – not the *crop* that denotes a harvested grain, but the *crop* that refers to the lump near the bottom of a chicken's throat, also known as the craw. In contrast to *haunch* and *croupe*, the French source of *fundament* developed from a Latin word, *fundus*, meaning *bottom*. This Latin word is also the ancestor of *foundation* (the base of a building) and *profound* (as in *deep* or *bottomless*), but is not connected to the *found* that means *discovered*, as in "I found my pants." In the fourteenth century, Middle English also adopted the French word *cul* as a synonym for *arse*. In Modern English, the French word is still known in the phrase *cul de sac*, literally meaning *bottom of the bag* and denoting a blind alley or dead end. Also in the fourteenth century, English adopted the French word *nage*, meaning *buttock*; in turn, this French word evolved from the Latin *natis*, also meaning *buttock*. The word *nage* did not survive the fourteenth century, but one of its derivatives, *natchbone*, which denoted the highest point of a cow's hindquarters, was current up till the nineteenth century. French also contributed the fifteenth-century arse word *bewschers*, which arose as a corrupt form of *beau sire*, a respectful term of address meaning *fair sir*. The application of this salutation to the buttocks was humorously motivated, somewhat analogous to a nineteenth-century name for the arse, the *Sunday face*.

Several other arse words that emerged in Middle English have unknown origins. *Hurdes*, for example, briefly appeared in the mid fifteenth century, but little more is known about it. Likewise, not much is known for certain about *buttock* or *bum*. With regard to the former word, it's not even clear whether *buttock* arose as a diminutive of *butt* (just as *hillock* is a diminutive of *hill*), or whether *butt* arose as a shortened form of *buttock*. (*Buttock* appears in written English in the early fourteenth century, more than a hundred years before *butt*, but it's possible that in spoken English *butt* was the original term.) The issue is muddied further by the fact that there are numerous other *butt*s in the English language, some of which might be related to the *butt* that means *arse*, and some of which clearly are not. The *Oxford English Dictionary* distinguishes fourteen such *butt*s, each of which has at least several sub senses. There is, for example, the *butt* that denotes a kind of flat fish (the vendors of which were known as *butt-women*); there is the *butt* that denotes a large wine cask (the servants who tended these casks was known as *butt-men* or, more commonly, *butlers*); there is the *butt* that denotes a small hill (related to the more common *butte*); there is the *butt* that denotes a thrust from the head of a goat (a head-butt); and, to cite just one more, there is the *butt* of a joke. How these various *butt*s relate to one another, or whether they do at all, continues to puzzle etymologists.

As for *bum*, the Oxford English Dictionary suggests – rather strangely, I think – that it arose through onomatopoeia: in other words, that it was invented in imitation of the sound produced by the thing to which it refers. While such an explanation makes sense for words such as *cuckoo* and *boom*, it seems slightly less feasible for the bum, even though that body part is not always silent. (Then again, the term *bumfiddle* did arise in the late seventeenth century as a synonym for *bum*, probably inspired by the "music" that the buttocks occasionally broadcast.) Some scholars have

> If the tongue had not been framed for articulation, man would still be a beast in the forest.
>
> *Ralph Waldo Emerson*

also suggested that *bum* arose as a shortened form of *bottom*, but that too is unlikely considering that *bottom* was not used to denote the human rear until the late eighteenth century. In the nineteenth century, *bum* came to denote a tramp, though whether this was an extension of the *bum* that means *arse*, or whether it was a shortening of the word *bumbler*, is unclear. However, some other terms obviously have developed from the *bum* that means *arse*, including *bum-roll*, a stuffed cushion that protruded from women's dresses in the mid seventeenth century; *bum-sucker*, which arose in 1877 to denote a sycophant or brown-noser; and *bum-fodder*, which appeared in the mid seventeenth century to denote literature so worthless that the paper it is written on is only fit for wiping one's bottom. (Such papers were also known as *arse-wisps*.) In the English judicial system, an officer who specialized in apprehending debtors was called a *bum-bailiff*, from the notion that he grabbed you from behind. As for *Bumstead*, best known as the surname of Blondie and Dagwood, it's likely unrelated to the *bum* that means *buttocks*, deriving instead from *bump* and *stead*, that is, a hill-stead or hill-place.

More synonyms for the buttocks appeared in the Early Modern period of English, between 1500 and 1800. For example, in the mid sixteenth century, *prat* emerged, a word that is now most familiar in a compound first recorded in 1939, *pratfall*, literally meaning *a fall on the arse*. The origin of *prat* is unknown; there was, from the eleventh century, another *prat* that meant *trick* or *prank*, but it's hard to see how such a word could have come to mean *arse*. Also in the sixteenth century, the word *breech* came to denote the buttocks. Earlier on, dating back to the eleventh century, *breech* had referred to a garment similar to a loincloth;

by the fourteenth century, however, this garment had been extended down to the knees, and the fact that it now covered the upper legs led to the word being used in the plural, *breeches*, just as we now refer to a pair of trousers or a pair of pants, not to a trouser or a pant. Eventually, by the end of the sixteenth century, the name of this garment was transferred to the part of the body that it covered, an extension of meaning that occurred around the same time that *seat* – as in the seat of the pants – came to be used as a euphemism for the buttocks. Another semantic extension that occurred at the end of the sixteenth century was the application of the facial *cheeks* to the two *glutei maximi*. Strangely, however, this use of *cheeks* appears to have gone underground during the eighteenth and nineteenth centuries: the *Oxford English Dictionary* cites one instance of buttock *cheeks* in 1600, but provides no other examples of this sense of the word until 1922. During those intervening centuries, it might have been considered indecent – or cheeky – to imply a resemblance between the human face and the human arse. Incidentally, *cheeky* dates back to the mid nineteenth century and originated, much like the synonymous *lippy* and *mouthy*, from the fact that the cheeks help to produce the words that form an impudent answer.

The seventeenth and eighteenth centuries saw the appearance of more arse words, all of which were polarized into either vulgarities or euphemisms. The euphemisms tended to be words like *stern, posterior, derriere, behind, rear* and *bottom*, which implied the buttocks by alluding to their rear location on the human body, rather than by baldly naming them. With *stern*, prior to its acquiring an *arse* sense in the early seventeenth century, it denoted the hindmost part of the ship. In turn, this part of the ship had come to be known as the *stern* because it was where the steering apparatus of the vessel was located; *stern*, in other words, developed from a Germanic source that meant *to steer*, which also developed into the verb *steer* itself. Even earlier, the Indo-European source of these *steering* words was *sta*, a root that we previously encountered as the source of *stud*. The Indo-European *sta* meant *to stand*, and it developed into a Germanic word meaning *to steer* because steering a ship means keeping it upright, or standing, in the water. The same source even developed into the noun *steer*, a word originally denoting any large, bovine creature, and now the name of one that has been castrated. Here, the semantic connection was perhaps that cattle and buffalo spend most of their time standing – they can even sleep standing up, thanks to their lockable knees, which is why youngsters are able to sneak up on a dozing cow and tip it over. Although it might not seem plausible that an animal would be named after its mere ability to stand, consider that the rooster acquired its name from its tendency to roost.

The word *posterior* came to be used as a euphemism for the buttocks at almost the same time as *stern*, that is, in the early seventeenth century. The first recorded instance of this sense of the word was in a comment by playwright Ben Jonson, who lambasted the writer John Owen as a "poor pedantick schoolmaster, sweeping his living from the posteriors of little children" – that is, making his living from spanking bottoms. In origin, *posterior* derives from the Latin preposition *post*, meaning *behind*. It was another hundred and fifty years before more euphemisms for the buttocks appeared in English, but when they did it was in a flurry: *derriere, rear* and *bottom* all appeared near the end of the eighteenth century. Of these three words, *derriere* derives – like *posterior* – from a Latin preposition, or rather from two Latin prepositions: *de*, meaning *from*, was combined with *retro*, meaning *backwards*, to form the Latin word *deretro*, meaning *behind*. This word evolved into the French *derrière*, which English then adopted. The word *rear* is a cousin of *derriere* in that it too derives from the Latin preposition *retro*; in this case, however, *retro* was combined with the Latin preposition *ad*, meaning *to*, which formed the Vulgar Latin *adretro*, which became the Old French *ariere*, meaning *behind* or *backward*. When adopted into English, *ariere* became *arrear*, which was later shortened to just *rear*. The earliest meaning of *rear* was militaristic: it denoted the hindmost division of a moving army (which is why the Navy includes a rank of *rear admiral*). The word *arrears*, denoting an overdue debt, derives from the same source as *rear*.

In Shakespeare's play *Measure for Measure*, one of the characters is called Pompey Bum. It's seems likely that Pompey's surname is intended to evoke the buttocks: he works as a pimp, and one of the other characters tells him that "your bum is the greatest thing about you." On the surface, it might seem that Shakespeare is making a similar joke in *A Midsummer Night's Dream*, where a weaver named Bottom gets turned into an ass. However, just as *ass* had not acquired its *buttocks* connotation in Shakespeare's time, neither had *bottom*. The word *bottom* is first recorded with that anatomical sense in 1794, in a proto-evolutionary treatise written by Erasmus Darwin, the grandfather of Charles Darwin. Two centuries later, *bottom* itself underwent an evolution of sorts, as it came to denote the submissive partner in a male homosexual relationship. For some reason, too, the word *bottom* – and especially the alliterative phrase *bare bottom* – has come to be associated with spanking to a greater degree than any of the other synonyms for *buttocks*. On the Internet, a search for the phrase *bare-bottom spanking* returns 11,600 hits, whereas *bare-ass spanking* returns 3,390 hits; *bare-buttocks spanking* returns a paltry eleven hits, and *bare-rump spanking* returns no hits at all.

The preposition *behind* came to be used as a noun denoting the arse in the first half of the nineteenth century. The word derives from a compound formed from the preposition *be*, meaning *by*, and the Old English *hindan*, meaning *at the back of*. Related words include the *hind* of *hind-quarters*, as well as the verb *hinder*, which literally means *to keep back*. Another relative is the *hinter* of *hinterland*, a word denoting a country's remote regions – its "behind," so to speak. (A somewhat similar line of thought prompted American soldiers, in the 1970s, to dub far-off destinations as *Bumfuck* or *Buttfuck*, as in "We're heading off to Buttfuck, Iraq.") The use of *behind* to denote the buttocks might also have inspired the appearance of another arse word in the first decade of the twentieth century: *heinie*, a variation on the last syllable of *behind*. A few years later, *heinie* also became an ethnic slur applied to Germans, a usage

> Our language, one of our most precious natural resources, deserves at least as much protection as our woodlands, streams and whooping cranes.
>
> *James Lipton*

facilitated by the fact that the Germans had been disparaged as Huns since the late nineteenth century. In the 1930s, another idiom involving *behind* arose: sodomy was sometimes referred to as *behind the behind*.

In addition to the many euphemisms for the buttocks that were invented in the seventeenth and eighteenth centuries, numerous vulgar terms also emerged. Many of these vulgar synonyms were first recorded by Francis Grose in his 1785 *Dictionary of the Vulgar Tongue*, though they undoubtedly were current in spoken English long before he compiled them. Grose included *nock* (which probably arose as a corruption of *notch*, the cleft of the cheeks being like a notch); *double jug* (descriptive of the two cheeks of the buttocks); *fun* (an abbreviation of *fundament*); *brother round mouth* (Grose adds that the idiom *brother round mouth speaks* means "he has let a fart"); *blind cheeks* (as opposed to the other cheeks, set below one's eyes); *blind cupid* (traditionally, Cupid was often depicted as being blindfolded and bare-bottomed); *wind-mill* (an allusion to the "wind" produced from the buttocks); *Robby Douglas with one eye and stinking breath* (a humorous idiom equating the buttocks to a man, the anus to an eye, and flatulence to halitosis); *dilberry maker* (dilberries were small pieces of excrement clinging to hairs around the anus, also known as *fartleberries*; much later, in the 1950s, the word *dingleberry* arose to denote the same feculent phenomenon); *gooseberry grinder* (similar to *dilberry maker*, with the emphasis on the unplucked "gooseberries" being ground between the cheeks of the buttocks); *cooler* (perhaps adapted from the previously mentioned *cul*); and *moon* (from the resemblance of that luminous and cratered orb to the pale and pockmarked Anglo-Saxon arse). The last of these words, *moon*, also became a verb in the 1950s, meaning *to expose one's buttocks to an unsuspecting onlooker.*

In the twentieth century, a handful of words denoting the buttocks emerged and became sufficiently current that they now appear in most standard dictionaries. *Fanny*, for example, emerged around 1928, and is now a familiar, albeit quaint, euphemism for the buttocks. The word *fanny* might have been inspired by John Cleland's 1749 erotic novel, *Memoirs of a Woman of Pleasure*, the protagonist of which, Fanny Hill, is frequently exposing her bottom. (*Fanny* has also been used to refer to the female genitals, which might make a connection to Fanny Hill even more feasible.) Another possibility is that *fanny* derives from *fantail*, a nautical term denoting a boat stern that sticks out unusually far. More recently, *fanny* has been incorporated into several compounds, including *fanny batter* (vaginal secretions), *fanny flange* (the clitoris), *fanny rat* (the penis), and *fanny pack* (a pouch strapped around the waist), all of which emerged in the 1990s.

Around the same time that *fanny* emerged in the late 1920s, the word *keister* also came to denote the buttocks. Earlier on, dating back to around 1913, this word had been used to denote a safe or strongbox, and before that, dating back to the 1880s, it had referred to a satchel or valise. The application of this word to the buttocks was prompted either by a perceived resemblance in shape between a satchel and the human buttocks, or by the fact that the human arse is, like a satchel, a kind of container. In origin, *keister* derives from the German *kiste*, meaning *box*. In the 1940s, a similar analogy prompted the invention of another arse word; namely, *zatch*, which is simply a corruption of *satchel*. Also in the 1940s, the word *quoit* came to mean *buttocks*, at least in Australia. Much earlier, since the fifteenth century, *quoit* had denoted a ring made of rope or iron, about six inches in diameter, which was used in a throwing game similar to horseshoes. The connection of this word to the buttocks was simply that a quoit, like the human arse, is round with a hole in the middle. In the 1960s, three more arse words appeared in English: *buns, tush* and *kazoo*. The first of these, *buns*, was inspired by the round shape of a baked bun, though the usage must also have been facilitated by the resemblance in sound of *bun* and *bum*. What is most surprising, perhaps, is that this sense of *buns* did not arise much earlier than it did. As for *tush*, it derives from *tochus*, which had been used since the early twentieth century to denote the buttocks; in turn, *tochus* developed from the Yiddish *tokhes*, which can be traced back to the Hebrew *tahat*, meaning *beneath*. As the name of a musical toy, *kazoo* has been current since the 1880s, but it was only in the 1960s that it was extended to the buttocks. The inspiration for this sense development was probably the simple fact that the kazoo, like the human arse, is a wind instrument.

In contemporary English, dozens of synonyms for buttocks

> "Must a name mean something?" Alice asked doubtfully. "Of course it must," Humpty Dumpty said with a short laugh. "My name means the shape I am – and a good handsome shape it is, too. With a name like yours, you might be any shape, almost."
>
> *Lewis Carroll*

have appeared over the last fifteen or so years, but most of them remain slang terms, on the extreme fringes of standard English. Most of them, too, seem to be rather self-conscious synonyms – that is, they seem to be synonyms that are invented because the inventor takes delight in the humour or verbal ingenuity that the new words embody. As such, these synonyms are more interesting from a socio-linguistic perspective than an etymological perspective: they reveal, in other words, how humans use language as a creative tool, and how people tend to conceptualize certain subjects in certain terms. For instance, one subset of contemporary slang words for the buttocks manifests a dough motif, as demonstrated by this partial list: *biscuits, loaves, cupcakes, dutch dumplings, English muffins, hot cross buns* and *poundcake*. To this list we might also add a nineteenth-century synonym for buttocks, *duff*, which arose as a dialect pronunciation of *dough*. This cluster of synonyms demonstrates that there is a tendency, at least among anglophones, to conceive of the human arse as a bakery item.

Another cluster of contemporary arse synonyms are those that construe that body part in terms of its function, or rather its two functions. The first function is simply to provide something to sit on, as reflected in the terms *sitters, cushion, flesh-cushions, saddle, parking place* and *rumble seat*. (The latter term is borrowed from the world of early-twentieth-century automobiles, but *rumble* is also apropos of noisy eructations.) The other function implied by another cluster of recent arse synonyms is that of digestion, as in *change machine* and *change register*: the buttocks make change in that they expel the waste products that result from the process of metabolizing food. The slang term *money maker* might have arisen from the same analogy, though it's possible that that idiom is more literal, and originally referred to the cash paid to prostitutes or strippers. Still another thematically-linked cluster of recent synonyms are those that allude to the location of the buttocks. These words are similar to the much older *derriere* and *posterior*, except that they are more metaphorical. Some of them – such as *caboose, mudflaps, basement* and *spare tire* – refer to things that are positioned at the end or on the bottom of a larger structure. Others, such as *southern exposure, south side* or *western end* make use of the connotations evoked by directions. The south is conventionally located at the "bottom" of a map, and sundown – the "end" of the day – occurs on the western horizon. *After parts, hinterland* and *the low countries* likewise invoke the posterior location of the buttocks.

$$\approx$$

In the early stages of English, some words for the buttocks, like *fundament*, did double duty by also denoting another locus of sexuality, the anus. However, that intestinal aperture also developed its own unique lexicon over the centuries, ranging from the Old English *baec thearm* to the Modern English *yingyang*, with dozens of terms in between.

In Old English, the compound *baec thearm* was made up of two words, the first being the ancestor of our word *back*, and the second being a word that meant *intestine*. Your *baec thearm* was therefore your back intestine or, more idiomatically, your anus. Earlier on, the Old English *thearm* developed from an Indo-

European source – *ter* – that meant *to pass through*. The word *through* derives from the same Indo-European source, and so does the word *thrill*: that latter word originally meant *to make a hole* or *to pierce through*, but in the late sixteenth century it came to mean *to pierce with excitement*. The original *hole* sense of *thrill* was employed in the eleventh-century compound *aers therl*, the word *therl* simply being a variant spelling of *thrill*. Likewise, just as an *aers therl* is an arsehole, a *nostril* is etymologically a nose thrill or nose hole. One more word that derives from the Indo-European *ter*, and which is therefore related to *thearm*, *through*, *thrill* and *nostril*, is the Sanskrit word *avatar*: in Hinduism, an avatar is a god who leaves a divine realm and "passes through" to an earthly one.

In Middle English, several terms arose to denote the anus, including *tewel*, *vent* and *bore*. The first of these, *tewel*, developed from a French source that meant *pipe*, which is why that word, in the fourteenth century, was used to denote not only the anus, but also a chimney, a kind of pipe that directs smoke from a fireplace to the outdoors. Less charming is the fact that *tewel* was also used, in the fifteenth century, to refer to the hole in the middle of a pastry crust from which steam escapes, a kind of "pie anus." The fourteenth-century poet Geoffrey Chaucer, whose literary genius included a zest for flatulence, used the word *tewel* in his *Summoner's Tale*, the story of a greedy Friar who receives a gift that an irritated and bed-ridden man has supposedly stashed down his bed-clothes:

Now thanne, put in thyn hand doun by my bak,
Seyde this man, and grope wel bihynde.

Bynethe my buttok there shaltow fynde
A thyng that I have hyd in pryvetee.
Ah! thoghte this frere, that shal go with me!
And doun his hand he launcheth to the clifte,
In hope for to fynde there a yifte.
And whan this sike man felte this frere
Aboute his tuwel grope there and heere,
Amydde his hand he leet the frere a fart,
Ther nys no capul, drawynge in a cart,
That myghte have lete a fart of swich a soun.

A Modern English rendering of the passage is easier to read, but
it loses the nuances:

Now then, put your hand down my back,
Said this man, and grope well behind.
Beneath my buttock there shall you find
A thing that I have hid in privity.
Ah, thought this friar, that shall go with me!
And down his hand he plunged to the cleft,
In hopes of finding there a gift.
And when the sick man felt this friar
Grope around his asshole here and there,
Onto his hand he gave the friar a fart.
There is no horse, drawing a cart,
That could have cracked a fart of such a sound.

Hole and *bore* were also used to denote the anus in Middle
English, and in fact those two words appear side-by-side – "my

blak hoill bore" – in a fifteenth-century play based on the biblical story of Cain and Abel, part of a larger sequence of religious dramas known as the Wakefield Pageants. That play begins with Cain's servant coming out to warn everyone what will happen if they don't stop jangling, that is, if they don't be quiet:

> Bot who that janglis any more,
> He must blaw my blak hoill bore,
> Both behynd and before,
> Till his tethe blede.

In other words, noisy janglers will have to blow the servant's arsehole or, as we might say nowadays, kiss his arse. (There is, in fact, plenty of invitational analingus in this six-hundred-year-old play, such as when Cain angrily tells Abel to "Com kis myne ars" and twice tells him to do the same to the arse of the devil: "Kys the dwillis toute" and "Com kys the dwill right in the ars.") The *anus* sense of *bore* obviously developed from its earlier use as a verb, meaning *to drill* or *to pierce*. That *pierce* sense of *bore* might also have inspired the use of *bore* to mean *mentally tiring*, as in "He bored me to tears." This usage of *bore* might have arisen in a way analogous to how *thrill* came to mean to excite: a tiresome person's words "bore" into one's ears

Nincompoop: an eighteenth-century name for a man who has never seen his wife's genitals.

and mind in piercing, albeit not thrilling, manner. As a synonym for *anus*, the word *hole* was often linked with another word, as with *hoill bore* or *back hole* or *arse hole*. The latter term was in use by the early fifteenth century, though the American variant, *asshole,* did not appear until the mid 1930s. Since the late fourteenth century *hole* was also used all by itself to identify the anus, and was even employed in that sense in a children's nursery rhyme that dates back to at least the mid eighteenth century: "Little Robin red breast, sitting on a pole, / Niddle, noddle, went his head, and poop went his hole." As noted earlier in a discussion of the naked word *unbehelod,* the word *hole* is related to a wide variety of words, including *hell, holster* and *hollow.* The name *Holland,* too, derives from the same source as those words, much of that nation being low-lying as if situated in a hollow.

Two other compounds that were used in Middle English to denote the anus were *nether eye* and *virel of the arse.* With the first of these, the word *nether* means *lower* as in *netherworld* or *Netherlands* (also known as the Low Countries), and thus the compound equates the anus to a kind of lower eye. Chaucer, once again, employs the term in *The Miller's Tale,* where Alisoun sticks her buttocks out a window and exploits the darkness to trick an unwanted suitor into planting his lips where he doesn't intend: "Absolon hath kist hir nether eye." The other compound, *virel of the arse,* contains the word *virel,* which originally denoted a ring of wood or bone that was placed around a wooden shaft to keep it from splintering. The word was adopted into Middle English from French, where it in turn had developed from the Latin *viriola,* meaning *bracelet.* Although *virel* is no longer used to refer to the "ring of the arse," it did develop into the Modern English *ferrule,* which denotes a metal sleeve used to join two pipes.

In Early Modern English, between about 1500 and 1800, several new synonyms for *arsehole* appeared, including *vent* and *bung*, both of which were old words that developed new anal senses. *Vent*, for example, originally denoted a variety of things, ranging from the scent emitted by a hunted animal, to an opening in the earth from which lava issues, to a doorway on a building. In the late sixteenth century, it came to denote the anus, both of humans and animals. In origin, *vent* was adopted from French, where it had evolved from the Latin *ventus*, meaning *wind*. Earlier on, that Latin word had developed from an Indo-European source that also gave rise to the words *weather*, *wind* and *window*. (A window is literally a *wind-eye*, that is, an aperture through which the wind can enter; the word *window* replaced the older *eyethurl*, meaning *eye hole*.) Surprisingly, *vent* is even related to the middle syllable in the word *nirvana*; that Sanskrit word denotes the extinction of self that precedes enlightenment, and literally means *a blowing out*. The word *bung* has denoted the anus since the late sixteenth century, but prior to that it referred to the hole in a cask through which wine or beer was drawn, and also the stopper used to plug that hole. In the nineteenth century, the word *bung* was extended from the hole in the cask to the person who controlled that hole – that is, the proprietor of a tavern came to be known as the *bung*. As a synonym for *anus*, the word was sometimes combined with *hole*, as in Randle Cotgrave's 1611 French-English dictionary where he defines *Cul de cheval* as "a small and ouglie fish, or excrescence of the Sea, resembling a mans bung-hole." Around the same time, Shakespeare put the word into the mouth of Doll Tearsheet, who uses it to excoriate Pistol: "Away, you cut-purse rascal! You filthy bung, away!"

Belonging to an entirely different register of language than *bung* were the medical terms *podex* and *anus*, which appeared in the late sixteenth and early seventeenth centuries respectively. *Podex* was adopted directly from Latin, where it also denoted the anus. Earlier on it developed from the Latin verb *podere*, meaning *to fart*, which evolved into the French *péter*, also meaning *to fart*. From this French verb the word *petard* developed, the name of an explosive munition, now most familiar in the idiom "Heft by his own petard." The Indo-European source of this cluster of fart words was *perd*, which evolved into the Greek word *perdix*, a bird's name that eventually became the English *partridge*. The fowl acquired this name due to the fact that when it is flushed from a field, its wings make a distinct whirring sound, reminiscent of a fart. As for *anus*, it too was adopted directly from Latin; much earlier on, the Latin word had evolved from the Indo-European *ano*, meaning *ring*. The similar-sounding woman's name, *Eunice*, derives from a different source, a Greek compound meaning *happy victory*.

Acomoclitic: a preference for hairless genitals.

In Late Modern English, two slang terms for the anus emerged, as evidenced in Francis Grose's *Dictionary of the Vulgar Tongue*. The first, *Holland*, probably arose as a humorous pun on *hole-land*. The second term also has an indirect connection to Holland: that country, from the seventeenth to the twentieth centuries, controlled the Spice Islands, whose name was ironically applied to the anal area. Located in Indonesia, the Spice Islands were named after the cloves and nutmeg that were harvested there. The word *ballinocack* was another anus synonym employed in the nineteenth century. The word was a compound formed from the Irish *baille*, meaning *town*, and *cack*, meaning *shit*. A ballinocack, therefore, is a *shit-town*, which is apropos of the anus insofar as feces reside in that orifice.

The twentieth century has seen the emergence of dozens of new names for the anus. Some, like *bum hole* or *butt hole*, are merely variations on older words. Others, like *cornhole*, are more allusive, gesturing perhaps to the resemblance in shape between a corncob and a human turd. Some recent epithets have been inspired by the crinkled appearance of the sphincter, such as *barking spider*, *daisy* and *rosebud*, while others have focused on the "ring" aspect of the anus, such as *doughnut* and *hoop*. A cluster of other synonyms allude to the function of the anus, including *crapper*, *poop chute*, *turd cutter* and *loaf pincher*. A bevy of other words imply the resemblance of the anus to an eye, an analogy that extends back to the Middle English *nether eye* mentioned earlier: *back eye*, *mud eye*, *buck eye*, *blind eye*, *dead eye*, *brown eye*, *red eye*, *round eye* and *third eye*; likewise, the word *winkle* has been applied to the anus, perhaps prompted by the notion of winking. Roads and highways, too, have inspired another whack of anus words, sometime combined with names of foods, as with *fudge road* and *Hershey highway*. Some of the contemporary terms are puns on pre-existing phrases, such as *servant's entrance*, *the road less taken* or *ars musica*, the latter being a Latin phrase meaning *musical arts*. While some recent anal appellations seem designed to shock – like *man pussy* – others have achieved a kind of avuncular acceptance, such as *where the sun doesn't shine*. Finally, a few recent synonyms for the anus seem to have arisen as nonsense words, words that are invented out of thin air, though that doesn't mean that they don't conform to certain linguistic patterns. *Bazoo* and *wazoo*, for example, have been used to denote the anus, perhaps inspired by the older *kazoo*, which denotes the buttocks. *Geegee, foofer* and *yingyang* also seem to be nonsense formations, although they all manifest a linguistic pattern known as reduplication, in which a word is created through the exact or almost exact repetition of a syllable.

Three other words that often appear in the Anal Pleasures chapter of sex manuals are *sphincter, rectum* and *perineum*. All three of these words have Latin origins because they were coined by Renaissance physicians and anatomists, who drew upon the classical languages for their medical vocabulary. The earliest, *rectum*, appeared around 1541 to denote the final section of the lower intestine; the word derives from the Latin word *rectus*, meaning *straight*, an origin that implies a contrast with the rest of the intestine, which twists and turns like a bowl of spaghetti. Earlier on, the Latin source of *rectum* derived from the Indo-European *reg*, meaning *to move in a straight line*. *Reg* evolved into numerous English words, including *rectangle, correct, erect* and *rectify*, all of which clearly relate to the notion of *straightness*. Ironically, the Indo-European source of *rectum* also evolved into a number of titles for political leaders, that is, for people who ostensibly lead their subjects in the right direction, including the English *ruler* and the Latin *rex*. Also related are the Hindi *raj* and the German *reich*, which denote not a ruler, but his or her realm. (Even *realm* is cognate with all these words.) All told, almost a hundred words in English derive from the same source as *rectum*.

Sphincter appeared shortly after *rectum*, around 1578, to denote not just the band of muscle that closes the anus, but a band of muscle that closes any bodily orifice. The word is still used in this manner, which is why, during your next eye exam, your optometrist may remark upon your sphincter, meaning the circular muscle that causes your pupil to constrict in bright light. In Latin, the word *sphincter* evolved from the Greek verb *sphingein*, meaning *to squeeze* or *to bind*. The name of a mythical creature known as the *sphinx* might also derive from the same Greek source: that monster plagued the citizens of Thebes by strangling – that is, by squeezing the throat – of anyone who could not answer its riddle. When Oedipus finally came up with the correct solution, the sphinx destroyed itself.

The *perineum*, like Canada's Maritimes, is a rather vaguely defined region. Most medical texts describe it as the area between the anus and the genitals. The word was adopted from Latin in 1632, and in turn Latin derived it from a Greek compound formed from a word meaning *near* and a word meaning *to empty out*. The perineum, in other words, is near the emptying out place of the human body.

~~~

In the beginning, male and female fetuses are anatomically identical; it's only a sudden torrent of testosterone in the eighth week of gestation that causes males to develop a penis and scrotum, thus differentiating their genitals from those that develop in a female fetus. These anatomical differences are, of course, reflected in the language through words denoting the penis, the vagina, and so on. First up, however, are the words that denote the undifferentiated sex organs of men and women, the generic genitals, as signified by words like *privates* or – a thousand years ago – *gesceapu, gecyndelic, geweald* and *getawa*.

It takes no great acumen to see that the previous four words all begin with *ge*. In fact, those two letters form a common prefix in Old English, one that was sometimes used to indicate the past tense, but which had no inherent meaning of its own. Accordingly, if we momentarily remove that prefix, we end up with four forms that begin to sound almost familiar: *sceapu, cynde, weald* and *tawa*. The modern counterparts of these words are, respectively, *shape, kind, wield* and *tool*. It's hard to tell how euphemistic or metaphorical these four Old English words were. Referring to your genitals as your *shape* certainly sounds euphemistic to a modern ear, reminiscent of a timorous parent asking his three-year-old daughter about the rash on her "special place." Then again, the use of the word *shape* – or rather *gesceapu* – could have been merely descriptive. After all, it is the shape of the genitals, whether they form a penis or a vagina, that distinguishes the two sexes and thus contributes to one's identity. The use of the word *kind* – or rather *gecynde* – was likely fairly neutral, neither euphemistic nor lurid. The genital sense of this Old English noun is congruent with its broader meaning of *that which is natural*. Indeed, a parallel usage arose in the sixteenth century, with the phrase *natural parts* being used to denote the genitals. In the thirteenth century, the word *kind* also came to describe benevolent words or deeds, thanks to the sanguine belief that treating people with respect is intrinsic to human nature – that is, that humankind is kind. An example of the words *gesceapu* and *gecynd* in action can be found in King Aelfric's tenth-century translation of the Book of Genesis. In a passage previously mentioned in my discussion of naked words, Noah gets drunk and falls asleep in the buff. When Cham, Noah's son, wanders by, he "geseah his gesceapu unbeheled" – that is, he "saw his genitals uncovered." Finding this display to be rather unsightly (after all, Noah was over six hundred years old at the time), Cham and his brother "beheledon heora faederes gecynd," that is, they "covered their father's genitals."

As for the Old English *geweald*, it was also used to signify the genitals, but it literally meant *power*. The *weald* root of the word is, in fact, related to the Modern English *wield*, denoting the ability to use or manipulate a weapon or to exercise authority – in short, to wield power. This association of the genitals with power is paralleled to some extent with the word *potent*, which literally means *powerful* but is also used to signify a man's ability to complete an act of sexual intercourse – if not, then he is *impotent*. The Indo-European root from which *geweald* and *wield* evolved was *wal*, meaning *to be strong*, which also developed into the Latin *valere*. From this Latin verb numerous words pertaining to strength and power have sprung, including *value*, *valid*, *valour* and *invalid*. Through the Germanic language branch, several personal names also developed from the same Indo-European source, including *Walter*, *Oswald* and *Ronald*.

The final Old English word for the genitals was *getawa*, which seems to have derived from the verb *tawian*, meaning *to prepare for use*. How such a verb could develop into a synonym for *genitals* becomes clearer when you realize that it also developed into the noun *tool*, a word employed in modern slang to denote the penis. It therefore seems likely that *getawa* came to mean *genitals* from the notion that the sexual organs are the tools or implements of copulation and generation. Similarly, in Middle English, the word *harness* was sometimes employed to denote the genitals. This word, which now primarily denotes the leather gear strapped around the head of a horse, had a much broader meaning in the fourteenth century: it referred to gear of all sorts, ranging from the tackle of a ship to the sexual "equipment" of men and women. In John Wycliffe's 1382 translation of the Book of Genesis, he describes how Cham, wandering by the naked and dozing Noah, sees "the privey herneis of his father." A little more than a decade later, in 1395, a revised version of Wycliffe's translation changed "privey harness" to another Middle English synonym for the genitals, namely, "schameful membris."

Defining the sexual members in terms of their supposed shamefulness was nothing new. The ancient Greeks, for example, referred to the genitals as *aidoia*, a word that derives from *aidos*, meaning *shame*. (The Modern English word *edea*, used by the medical community to denote the sex organs, derives from this Greek source.) Moreover, as we'll see in Chapter Nine, the word *pudendum* also derives from a word meaning *shame*, and even the phrase *private parts* implies something shameful, something that needs to be hidden. That modern euphemism *private parts* evolved from the fourteenth-century *privy parts*, which existed alongside similar terms such as *privy members* and *privy chose*, the word *chose* being French for *thing*. The latter phrase was employed by an English vicar known as John of Trevisa, who translated a Latin encyclopedia of natural science in 1398. "The female ape," he wrote in the section on comparative anatomy, "is like to a womman in the privy chose." An early instance of the use of the synonymous *privy member* appears in a statute from 1482, recorded in the Rolls of Parliament, which legislated the proper length of certain garments: "That no maner of persone wear any Gowne or Cloke, but if it be of such lengh, as hit shall cover his prevey membres and buttokks." Somewhat later, in 1555, William Towrson used the phrase *privie parts* in his description of the peoples he encountered after sailing to the west coast of Africa: "They goe all naked except some thing before their privie partes, which is like a clout." By the eighteenth century, *privy parts* had become *private parts*, as in Francis Grose's tongue-in-cheek definition of *commodity*, a cant word denoting a woman's genitals: "Commodity...the private parts of a modest woman, and the public parts of a prostitute."

The single word *privities* was also used in Middle English to denote the genitals. Nicholas Trevet, for example, employed that word in the early fourteenth century in a tale about a wicked king who exiles his admirable wife. When the people of England learn of this evil deed, they express their outrage by essentially mooning the king:

Chyldren and oolde folke crying and revylyng the kyng
and caste foule harlotrye opon hym with grete stones
ayenst hys breste. And men, wemen and chylderen
despoyled themself naked for despyte and shewed to
hym ther pryvytees behynde.

Privities evolved, of course, into our modern word *privates*, which also came to denote low-ranking officers in the military.

Shakespeare puns on both meanings of *privates* when Rosencrantz and Guildenstern tell Hamlet that they've had indifferent luck, residing neither on the cap of Fortune nor at the soles of her shoes:

Hamlet:	Then you live about her waist, or in the middle of her favours?
Guildenstern:	Faith, her privates we.
Hamlet:	In the secret parts of Fortune? O, most true; she is a Strumpet.

Two other words were also used in Middle English to denote the genitals, or at least the genital area – *groin* and the word *genital* itself. The oldest of these is *genital*, which was adopted from Latin in the late fourteenth century. The Indo-European source of the word was *gene*, meaning *to beget*, which is obviously also the source of words like *generation, genealogy* and *gender*. Through the Germanic branch, this Indo-European source also became *kin, kindred* and the first syllable of *kindergarten*, literally meaning *children garden*. More surprisingly, an alternative name for Santa Claus – *Kris Kringle* – also derives from the same Indo-European source. The original name of that Christmas figure was *Christkindlein*, a German compound meaning *Christ child*. When German immigrants introduced the tradition of the *Christkindlein* to the U.S., the name was corrupted to *Kris Kringle*, and the figure was fused with St. Nicholas, also known as *Santa Claus*, thus managing to transform the baby Jesus into a bearded old man. As for the word *groin*, in the fifteenth century it came to signify the area where the thigh joins the abdomen. At that time, however, the word was spelt *grynde*, a form it retained until the sixteenth century when it came to be spelt *groin*, probably to make it more closely resemble *loin*. Later on, this mistaken connection to *loin* probably helped the word to acquire a more erotic sense: for example, in the seventeenth century *groin* was sometimes used to mean *sexual desire*. The early history of *groin* – or rather *grynde* – is somewhat unclear, but it's possible that it emerged as a semantic extension of the Old English *grynde*, meaning *abyss* or *valley*.

Where I grew up, a badly thrown football didn't hit you in the genitals, nor in the privates or groin. Instead, it hit you in the *crotch*, a word that was sufficiently vague in reference – rather like *lap* – that it could be safely uttered in front of Mrs. Anderson, the grade-six teacher in charge of Play Day. The acceptability of *crotch* might have arisen from the fact that etymologically it denotes an area, not a thing: that is, it refers to the place where the legs come together, not to the sex organs that reside there. When the word appeared in English in the early sixteenth century, it denoted a large fork, one used for digging in a field. By the mid sixteenth century, it had been extended to trees – the place where two branches diverged was a crotch – and by the end of that century it was being applied to the human body. In origin, the word likely arose as a variant

> A word is not a crystal, transparent and unchanging; it is the skin of a living thought and may vary greatly in color and content according to the circumstances and time in which it is used.
> *Oliver Wendell Holmes*

of *crutch* or of *croche*, the latter being the name of a shepherd's crook, an implement whose hooked end was used to snag sheep. (A crochet needle is a mini-version of a shepherd's croche.) The Indo-European source of these words also evolved into a host of other words denoting crookedness of some sort: *crouch, crank, cramp, crimp, crumple* and *crotchety*. The latter word arose from the notion that a cantankerous person is one who "bends" from the norm – someone who is socially crooked or, to use an etymological cousin, cranky.

Chapter Eight

THE LONG AND THE SHORT OF IT

Words for the Penis and its Attendant Parts

ACCORDING TO THE BOOK of Genesis, after God created Adam he paraded in front of him all the other beasts to see what he would call them – "and whatsoever Adam called every living creature, that was the name thereof." The biblical passage does not go on to say whether the first human was also responsible for naming the parts of his own body, including his spanking-new penis (or, since he presumably spoke Hebrew, his *zayin*). Adam's descendents, however, certainly have gone to town when it comes to inventing names for the male member, as evidenced by the numerous phallic sobriquets that have been produced in English over the last thousand years, including *Aaron's rod, accordion, ace poker, Adam's dagger, Adam's whip, agate, all-beef sausage, amblyopic organ, angle, animated ivory, anteater, apparatus, appendage, appropriate member, arbor vitae, arm, arm of love, armored division, arrow, arse worm, arse-opener,* arse-wedge, artillerie de cupidon, artillerie de venus, auger, baby beef, baby maker, baby's arm, baby-grinder, bacon, bacon bazooka, baculum, badger, bagadga, bag-filler, baggette, bald man, baloney, baloney pony, bamboo stick, banana, band-member, banger, banjo string, bar, barge pole, bat, baton, battering ram, battlefat, bauble, bazooka, beak, bean, bean pole, bean-shooter, bean-tosser, beard-splitter, beating tool, beaver cleaver, beaver lever, bed flute, beef bayonet, beef bayo with extra mayo, beef jerky, beef stick, beef whistle, beef, beer can, bell, bell-rope, bell-swagged, belly ruffian, belt buster, best friend, best leg of three, best part, bicho, big bamboo, big ben, big bird, big bite, big brother, big daddy, big dipper, big fella, big head, big one, big red, big wand, bilbo, billy club, billy, bingey , bird, bishop, biteful, black limo, black pencil, black snake, blackjack, blade, blanket stiff, blind bob, blind buckler, blind piece, blood-breaker, blow pop, blow stick, blowtorch, bludgeon, blue thimble, blue-veined custard chucker, blue-veined hooligan, blue-veined junket pump, blue-veined piccolo, blue-veined steak, blue-veined throbber, blue-veined trumpet, blunt end, bobby-dangler, bobstay, bobtail, bodkin, body's captain, bone phone, boneless appendage, boneless fish, boneless stiff, boner, boneroni, bonfire, botuliform genital pendant of the male, bow, bowsprit, boy, boy toy, branch, brat-getter, broom handle, broomstick, brown joe, bruiser, brush, bubbly jock, bucking bronco, buckinger's boot, buddy, buffing stick, bug-fucker, bugle, bullish, bum tickler, bun puncher, bun spreader, burrito, bush beater, bush whacker, buster, butcher, butt basher, butt smasher, butterfinger, button buster,

belly ruffian

button mushroom, buttonhole worker, button-short, canary, candle, candy, candy cane, candy stick, cannon, captain, Captain Hightop the love commander, Captain Hogseye, Captain One-eye, Captain Picard, carnal member, carnal part, carnal stump, carrot, cartes, carts, cartso, casey, cazzo, cavity probe, chanticleer, charger, charles the bald, chaud, dangling participle *cheesy bunnet, cheesy wheelbarrow, cherry birch, cherry picker, cherry splitter, chibi, child-getter, chimney-stopper, chingus, chink-stopper, choad, chode, chooza, chopper, christener, chub, chull, chum, chunky monkey, chutney ferret, cinnamon stick, clava, club, cluster, cobra, cock, cock of death, cockaroony, cockroach, cocktus erectus, cocky, codpiece, compass of the Netherlands, concern, coral branch, corker, corned beef cudgel, corpuscle, corsican, cory, coupler, coupling bat, crab ladder, crack hunter, cracking tool, cracksman, crank, crankshaft, cranny hunter, cream-stick, cremorne, crimson chitterling, crok, crook, crotch cartilage, crotch cobra, crotch rocket, crowbar, crowd pleaser, crumpet-trumpet, cuckoo, culty-gun, cum slinger, cunny-catcher, cunt-stabber, cunt-sticker, cunt-stirrer, custard-chucker, cutlass, cyclops, daddy longdick, daddy mack, dagger, dang, dangle, dangle-dong, dangler, dangling participle, dart of love, dear morsel, dearest member, delight of women, derrick, devil, diamond cutter, dibble, dick, dick butkiss, dickery-dock, dickie and the boys, dickie, dick-tator, dicky, diddly-whacker, dill, dilly-whacker, dimple-dick, ding, ding-a-ling, dingbat, ding-dong, dinghy, dingle, dingle-dangle, dingo, dingus, dingy, dink, dinky, dinosaur, dipstick, dirk, dobber, do-funny, dog, dohinger, dojigger, dojohnnie, dolly, donaker, dong, donger, donniker, donut holder, doodad, doodle, doodle-flap, doohicky, doover, doowhackey, dopper, dork, down-led, drain pipe, dribble-cock, driving post, drudge, drumstick, ducky-bird, dummy, dust cover for the cunt, dydus, eager pleaser, eel, eggwhite cannon, ejac vac, eleventh finger, Elmer Pudd, end, enemy, engine of love, engine, enob, erectile urogenital appendage, everlasting gobstopper, extra digit, eye dropper, eye-opener, family organ, fanny ferret, fat frank, fat peter, father-of-all, ferret, fiddle bow, fiddlestick, finger puppet, first leg of three, fish stick, flap-doodle, flapper, flesh pencil, flute, foaming beef probe, fool-sticker, foot long, foreman, fornicating engine, fornicating member, fornicating tool, fornicator, fountain pen, Fred, frigamajig, fruit for the monkey, fuck muscle, fuck pole, fucker, fucking stick, fucking tool, fuck-meat, fuck-rod, fuckstick, fud packer, fun bone, fun-stick, funk-stick, funmaker, gadget, gadso, gap-stopper, gardener, gargantuan organum virile, gator, gaying instrument, gear, gearstick d'amour, generating tool, genital coupler, genital forefoot, genital pound of flesh, genital reamer, genital shaft, genital staff, genital tentacle, gentle fist, gentle tittler, gentleman, gentleman's appendage, gherkin, giggle stick, giggling pin, girl catcher, girlometer, glory pole, glow rod, glow stick, gnarled root of love, goat, gobstopper, god's revenge on a woman, goober, good foot, gooser, goose neck, goot, gooter, goy toy, gravy-giver, gravy-maker, grinding tool, gristle, gristle-stick, guided missile, gully-raker, gun, gut-stick, hacker, hair divider, hair splitter, hairless wonder, hairy banana, hairy sausage, ham howitzer, hambone, hamilton wick, hammer,*

giggle stick

hampton wick, handle, hand-staff, hang-down, hard salami, hardhat harry, hard-on, harpoon, hat rack, heat seeking missile, heat seeking moisture missile, Herman the one-eyed German, hermit, he-thing, hickey, his majesty in purple cap, hissing sid, hock, hodge dog, hoe-handle, hog, hogger, hole puncher, holy poker, holy pole, honorable prick, hopping bug, hose, hot dog, hot member, hot rod, hotchee, hugen, human enema, humpmobile, hunk of meat, husbandman of nature, ice cream machine, id, idol, inch, inch instrument, instrument, instrumentum erectum, intromittent organ, it, jack, jackalope, jackhammer, jacktool, jakey, jammy, jang, jean tent, jellyroll, jenny, jerking iron, jezebel, jigger, jigging bone, jiggle bone, jig-jag, jig-jigger, jim dog, jimbo, jimbrowsky, Jimmy, jing-jang, jizz jemmy, jock, jockum, John Thomas, John Thursday, John Tom, John Willie, Johnny come lately, Johnson, joint, jolly member, jolly red giant, jolly roger, jolly stick, joy prong, joy stick, joyknob, Julius Caesar, jungle meat, junior, kazoo, key to heaven, key, kickapoo, kidney wiper, kielbasa, king-member, king's iron, knitting needle, knob, knobster, knocker, lad, ladies' delight, ladies' lollipop, ladies' plaything, ladies' treasure, lamp of life, lance, lance of love, langer, lanoola, lazarus, leather cigar, leather dresser, leather stretcher, lever, libido bandido, licorice stick, life preserver, limb, limbless erast, lingam, lipstick, little brother, little buddy, little dick, little dipper, little Elvis, little engine, little finger, little friend, little head, little man, little Peter, little pinkie, little sliver of flesh, little willy, liver turner, lizard, loaded gun, lob, lobcock, log,

husbandman of nature

lollypop, long dong silver, Louisville slugger, love bone, love dart, love gun, love handle, love length, love machine, love meat, love muscle, love pick-lock, love pump, love sausage, love scepter, love stick, love tool, love torpedo, love trumpet, love truncheon, love-rod, love's battering ram, love's dribbling dart, love's engine, love's sensitive truncheon, love-wand, lower male proboscis, lung disturber, lust bone, lust shaft, lust sword, machine, mad mick, maggot, magic wand, main vein, male begetting organ, male genital dispenser, male genital organ, male genital probe, male genital teat, male gladiolus, male interfemoral infidel, male intruder, male member, male monolith, male netherland, male organ of generation, male organ of reproduction, male organ, male organon, male pendant, male poker, male pound of flesh, male pudendal trifler, male satisfier, male sex organ, male sinker, male urogenitial horn, maleness, mallet, man root, man steel, man, manbone, manhood, man-meat, man's third leg, marrow-bone, masculine part, master member, master of ceremonies, master tool, masterpiece, mating meat, mating tool, matrimonial peacemaker, maypole, means of generation, meat, meat and two vegetables, meat axe, meat cleaver, meat dagger, meat flute, meat puppet, meat whistle, meat-seeking pissile, meatus longus, member, member for cockshire, membrum virile, mentula, merrymaker, mickey, middle finger, middle leg, middle stump, mighty meat, milk bone, milkman, millimeter-peter, missile, missile of venus, mister fuzzy, modigger, moisture missile, mole, monkey, most precious part, mouse, Mr. Big, Mr. Bluevein, Mr.

Friendly, Mr. Happy, Mr. Pokey, Mr. Wiggly, Mr. Wong, muff missile, muscle of love, mutinous rogue, mutton bayonet, mutton dagger, mutton gun, mutton musket, mutton, my body's captain, nameless thing, natural member, nature's scythe, naughty toy, nearsighted, Nebuchadnezzar, needle, nervous cane, nether proboscis, night stick, nightcrawler, nimrod, nine iron, nippy, nob, nubbin, nudger, nutrageous, oak tree, obelisk, old red, old Adam, old baldy, old blind Bob, old Damocles, old faceful, old faithful, old faithless, old goat-peter, old one-eye, old slimy, old warty cod, Omar the tentmaker, one-eyed whale, one-eyed Bob, one-eyed brother, one-eyed demon, one-eyed monk, one-eyed monster, one-eyed pants mouse, one-eyed snake, one-eyed trouser snake, one-eyed wonder, one-eyed worm, one-eyed zipper snake, organ of reproduction, organ, organum virile, Oscar Meyer, Oscar, pantilever, pants philistine, pants python, pants worm, passion pole, Pat and Mick, pax wax, peace maker, pecker wood, pecker, pecnoster, peculiar member, Pedro, pee-dee, peenie, peep, pee-pee, peewee, peezel, peg, pego, pen, pencil, pendulum, penicillus, penie, penis, peppermint stick, perch, percy, pestle, pet snake, Peter, phallating club, phallating stick, phallic cleaver, phallic pencil, phallic pendant, phallic prod, phallic quencher, phallic scratcher, phallus, piccolo, pichita de oro, pickle, picklock, piddler, piece of meat, pike, pikestaff, piledriver, pilgrim's staff, pillicock, pillock, pimple-prick, pin, pinga, pink bus, pink cadillac, pink oboe, pink torpedo, pinkler, pintel, pioneer of nature, pipe, piss handle, pisser, piss-pipe, pissworm, pistol, piston rod, piston, pitch a tent, pixie stick, pizzle, pizzler, placket-racket, plaything, plonker,

one-eyed Bob

plug, plug-tail, plunger, p-maker, pocket fisherman, pogo-stick, point, pointer, poker, polyphemus, pood, poontanger, pooper, poperin pear, popsicle, popsicle stick, pork, pork dagger, pork enema, pork sword, porridge gun, portable pocket rocket, potato finger, potent regiment, priapus, prick, prickle, pride and joy, Prince Everhard of the Netherlands, princock, privy limb, prod, pronger, pud, pudding, pudendal intruder, pudendal trifler, pump action mottgun, pump handle, pump, puny prick, pup, puppy, purple helmeted yogurt thrower, purple lollipop, purple-headed avenger, purple-headed custard chucker, purple-headed love truncheon, purple-headed meat puppet, purple-headed monster, purple-headed warrior, purple-veined tonsil-tickler, pus-rod, pussy diver, pussy feeder, pussy fodder, pussy pleaser, pussy plunger, pussy-fucker, pussy-poker, pussy-sticker, putz, pylon, python, quickening peg, quiff-splitter, quim-stake, quim-stick, quim-wedge, rabbit, ram charger, rammer, ramrod, randy, ranger, rat, raw meat, rector of females, redcap, red lobster, Richard, rig, rock formation, rocket, rod, rodger, rodney, Roger, Roger the lodger, rolling pin, roly-poly, rooster, root, rosy red reproductive rod, roto-rooter, rubigo, rudder, ruffian, rumpleforeskin, rump-splitter, rupert, salami, salty dog, salty yogurt slinger, sausage, schlong, schmeegle, schmekel, schmuck, schnitzel, schwantz, schwantzschtupper, schwanz, scorz, screwdriver, scurvy end, semen shooter, Senator Packwood, sensitive plant, sensitive truncheon, serpent, sex bone, sex meat, sex organon, sex stalk, sexing piece, sexocet missile, sexual trocar of the male, shaft of delight, shaft, shamefaste, shit

silky appendage

stabber, shit stick, shlong, shmendrik, shmok, shooting iron, shooting stick, short arm, short leg, shove-straight, shrimp, shriveller, shtick, silent flute, silky appendage, silver penny, Sinbad, Sir Richard, skin flute, skinclad tube, slug, slurpee, small arm, small person, smeat, snake, snatch pointer, snorker, snotty, solicitor general, spear, spermapositor, sperm gun, spike-faggot, spindle, spit, spitfire, spitter, spitting cobra, split-mutton, spooge gun, spout, spunky, stag, stalk, Stanley the power drill, steak, steamer, stick, sticker, stickshift, sticky finger, sticky spud gun, stiffy, sting, stinger, stocking stuffer, stormy dick, stothe, stout warrior, strap, stretcher, stud meat, stud, stump, sugar stick, superdick, swack, sweet meat, swipe, swizzle stick, sword, tackle, tadge, tadger, tail pike, tail pin, tail tackle, tail, tail-line, tallywag, tallywagger, tallywhacker, tannhauser, tan-trouser snake, tarse, tarzoon, tassel, teapot, teenie-weenie, tenant-in-tail, tender tumour, tent, tent peg, terror of virgins, the bishop, thing, thing-a-ling, thingamaling, thingummy, thingy, third leg, thistle, Thomas, thorn in the flesh, three-card trick, three-inch fool, throb knob, thumb of love, thumb, tickle faggot, tickle tail, tickle-gizzard, tickler, tickle-toby, tiddelly pod, tiki-tiki, tit-bit, tittle-bat, todger, Tom Thumb, Tommy, tom-tom, tong, tonk, tonsil wrench, toobsnake, toobsteak, tool of pleasure, tool, toot meat, tootsie roll, torch of cupid, **trouser ferret** *tosh, tossergash, touch-trap, towel rack, toy, trap stick, tricky dicky, trifle, trigger, trombone, trouser ferret, trouser mauser, trouser snake, trouser trick, trouser trout, trouser trumpet, trouser truncheon, trouser worm, trumpet, truncheon, trypan, tube, tube of meat, tube-steak, tug muscle, tummy banana,* *tummy-tickler, turkey baster, turkey neck, twanger, tweeterfrank, twiddle-diddler, twig, ugly little dog dick, uncle dick, uncle, under par, underpant eel, unemployed, unit, unruly member, up, upscope, urinary petcock, urogenital tailpiece, useless, vaginal dilator, vegetable stick, vein-laden meatpipe, veiny bang stick, veiny salami, verge, vip, virile member, virilia, vomer, voorsch, wab, wag, wammer, wand, wang bone, wang, wangdoodle, wanger, wang-tang, wank stick, wanker, wankrod, warder, ware, water pistol, water spout, wazoo, wazzock, weapon, wedge, wedge bone, wee, wee-man, wee-wee, welt, whacker, whammer, whang bone, whang, whangdoodle, whanger, whatsis, whatsit, whatsus, whatzis, wheezer, whip whistle, whip, whisker splitter, whistle, white owl, whoopie stick, whore pipe, wick, wicked willie, wiener, wienie, wife's best friend, wigga-wagga, wild rogue, wilde oscar, willie, willy the burping worm, willy, wingdoodle, winkie wankie woo, winkle, winny-popper, wire, wishbone, wistle, womb broom, womb bruiser, womb brush, womb cannon, womb ferret, women pleaser, won ton, wong, wonger, wonk, woodrow, woody, woofer, wooter, wop, worm with a nazi helmet, worm, wriggling pole, wriggling stick, wurst, yack, yang fella, yang, yard, yardage, ying-yang, yosh, yoyo, yum-yum, yutz, zab, zap, zipperfish, zoob, zoobrick, zubb, zubrick, zucchini* and *3-4-2-5*.

Admittedly, most of these 1,300 penis words are slang terms that have appeared since 1900, but that may simply reflect the fact that our record of the vulgar register of language is more complete for the last hundred years than for previous centuries, thanks to technological advances such as the invention of audio recordings, television and the Internet, and thanks to social changes such as the slackening of obscenity laws that once bridled the publishing industry. It's entirely possible that earlier centuries had hundreds of other slang names for the penis that existed only in the mouths of our linguistic ancestors, barred from the printed page and thus now forever lost.

Perhaps the oldest word for *penis* in the English language is *tarse*, first recorded in an eleventh-century book of wort-cunning, that is, a medical treatise explaining the use of various herbs or worts. Apart from the fact that the word developed from a Germanic source, little is known about the origin of *tarse*, and it essentially vanished from the language by the early sixteenth century. It was, however, well-used in a late-fifteenth-century ballad known as "A Talk of Ten Wives on their Husbands' Ware," in which ten women compare – and complain about – the tiny size of their spouses' penises. For example, in the middle of the poem, the fifth wife insists that no man can have a worse tarse than that of her husband:

Now ye speke of a tarse!
In all the warld is not a warse
Than hathe my hosbond.

Likewise, the eighth wife laments that when frosty weather comes, the tarse of her husband – or as she ironically calls him, her "sir" – shrinks or "lesys" into non-existence:

When the froste fresys.
Owre syris tarse lesys,
And all-way gose a-way.

The same ballad also employs another penis word that originated in Old English and that survived until the sixteenth century – *pintle*. The pintle of the third wife's husband, for example, is so short that it doesn't protrude beyond his pubic hair, and she adds that when her husband's breeches are torn, his penis peeps out like a warbrede, that is, like a mere worm:

> Owre syre breche, when hit is torn,
> Hys pentyll pepyth owte be-forn
> Lyke a warbrede.

The ninth wife also employs the word *pintle* in her complaint. First she acknowledges that her husband has a very long penis – about a foot, she gestures – but then she bemoans that it is not strong or hard enough to do her any good:

> Here is a pyntell of a fayre lenghte,
> But he berys a sory strenghte.

The *le* ending of *pintle* suggests that it might have arisen as a diminutive of a Germanic word – for example, in Old Frisian the word for penis was *pint*, unrelated to the name of the liquid measure. *Pintle* might also be distantly related to the word *pin*, which is another word used in Middle English to denote the penis. The seventh wife in the ballad, for instance, literally belittles her husband when she refers to "that sory pyne that schuld hengge bytwen his leggis," and goes on to suggest that when her husband sits naked, the juxtaposition of his body with his tiny penis and his normal-sized testicles makes him resemble a hen sitting on two rotten eggs.

Yet another wife refers to her husband's penis with the word *meat*, the earliest recorded instance of a slang usage that has thrived all the way up to the present-day: recent variants include *meat flute* and *meat puppet*. Unfortunately for this wife, her husband's *meat* – or *mett*, as she pronounces it – is the size of a shell-covered slug:

> I knowe the mett well and fyne,
> The length of a snayle.

Several wives have still not spoken. When the second wife does so, she calls her husband's penis a *lome*, a usage that was current through the fifteenth and sixteenth centuries. "By Saynte Peter owte of Rome," she swears, in reference to her husband's sexual organ, "I see never a wars lome, / Stondyng opon mone" – that is, she never saw a worse penis standing upon a man. Although you might suspect this *lome* to be related to *limb*, it's not; instead, it's actually identical with *loom*, a word that had been used since the tenth century to denote any kind of implement. It still exists as the name of an implement used in weaving, and also in *heirloom*, originally an implement or piece of equipment that one inherited.

One other penis word in the ballad is *ware*, which appears both in the song's title and in the sixth wife's comment that even though her "hosbondys ware / Is of good a-syse" – that is, of a good size – he is unable to get an erection. This sexual sense of *ware* is simply an extension of its usual meaning of *merchandise*, a sense still familiar from words like *warehouse* and *housewares*. A modern parallel to the fifteenth-century penis sense of *ware* is the use of phrases such as *nice package* or *the goods* to refer to a man's genital area.

Closely allied to the *loom* and *ware* metaphors are words that identify the penis with implements of war, that is, with weapons. For example, the word *weapon* itself was used to denote the penis in Middle English, as it had been in Old English, dating back to the eleventh century. The word occurs with that sense in a medieval dream vision called *Piers Plowman*, in a passage where the allegorical figure of Wit advises Piers on how to best deal with youthful horniness: "Whiles thow art yonge and thi wepene kene, Wreke thee with wyvynge." In other words, while you are young, and have an eager penis, satisfy yourself by getting a wife. Two hundred years later, Shakespeare punned on the sexual sense of *weapon* in *Romeo and Juliet*, in the opening scene where two servants make bawdy jokes about cutting off maidenheads instead of heads. "Draw thy tool," says one servant to the other, meaning his sword and implying his penis. "My naked weapon is out," his friend replies. The names of specific weapons were also applied to the penis in Middle English. *Arrow*, for example, was used with this sense in the fourteenth century, as was *lance* from about 1500 onward. In the 1960s, *lance* became a slang verb meaning *to copulate*, which was also the meaning of a phrase that arose in the 1980s, *to get your lance waxed*. Likewise, the word *warder*, a kind of medieval billy club, was used near the end of the Middle English period as a synonym for *penis*. For instance, an untitled treatise published around 1500 warned its readers against the sin of lechery, advising that "Thy warder, that was wonte for to be mighty and sadde and grene in his laboure" will eventually become weary "of superfluite" – in other words, your once mighty penis will get tired out.

The tendency to use the names of weapons to denote the penis continued on into Early Modern and Late Modern English. For example, in the early seventeenth century, the pike, a kind of iron-pointed staff, had its name bestowed on the penis, as did the ramrod in the early nineteenth century, the latter being a tool used for ramming the charge down the barrel of a gun. (Incidentally, the word *pike* is related to several other words that also derive from the Indo-European *speik*, which denoted a sharp-billed bird: cognates include *picket*, *pique*, *pickerel*, the *pie* of *magpie*, and even the *pie* that denotes a pastry, a usage inspired by the habit of the magpie – aptly known as a thieving bird – to fill its nest with pilfered bits and scraps, much as a baker fills a pastry shell with apples or berries.) In the twentieth century, the penis was sometimes denoted with the names of modern military munitions such as *howitzer* and *bazooka*. (Before *bazooka* was borrowed as the name of an American rocket launcher, it denoted a musical instrument invented by comedian Bob Burns, who derived its name from *bazoo*, a nineteenth-century word meaning *mouth*.) However, the twentieth century also invented or inherited phallic synonyms that drew upon more traditional weapons, such as *gun*, *pistol*, *bludgeon*, *dagger*, *truncheon* and even the *cutlass*. (The latter

Koro: a Japanese word denoting the delusion that one's penis is shrinking into one's body.

term denotes a kind of sword whose name, by coincidence, sounds like *cut lass*, which might explain why such an archaic word was revived as a modern slang term.)

As for another recent penis term that alludes to an obsolete weapon, *mutton musket*, its existence might be explained by alliteration, while unalloyed absurdity might have been the inspiration of *heat seeking missile* and its even bawdier variant, *meat seeking pissile*. All in all, over the last thousand years, the number of words that have equated the penis with something dangerous – that is, with something designed to puncture, cudgel or explode – is striking. Nor is English alone in applying weapon words to the penis; the ancient Romans, for example, referred to it as *clava*, meaning *club*, and as *gladius*, which means *sword* and from which we derived the word *gladiator* and *gladiolus*, a plant with sword-shaped leaves. Indeed, the weapon metaphors are implicit even in otherwise innocuous words, such as *ejaculate*. That word derives from the Latin *jaculum*, meaning *javelin*, a kind of spear. Social commentators often deplore the linkage of sex and violence in novels and movies, but they are also often linked at the more fundamental level of language itself.

Still, not all of the words used in Middle English to denote the penis were taken from the battlefield. Many were extensions of words that simply denoted items that were phallic in shape – things that were long and skinny. The word *yard*, for example, was originally a synonym for *stick*, a meaning that extended back to at least the mid tenth century. Around the year 1000, it developed a more narrow sense of a stick that is three feet in length, and four centuries later it became a name for the penis, a usage that persisted until the mid nineteenth century. In fact, throughout the Middle English and Early Modern English periods, *yard* was probably the standard word for penis, as evidenced by its frequent use in medical treatises. *Yard* was also combined with numerous other terms to form anatomical names for sub-parts of the penis: the foreskin was called the *yard end*, the glans was called the *head of the yard*, the urethral meatus was called the *eye of the yard*, the urethra itself was called the *pipe of the yard*, and a man who had not been circumcised was said to have *wholeness of yard*. A medical manuscript produced in Glasgow in the early fifteenth century employed the term in an insightful explanation of venereal disease: "A man is summe time seke in his yerde be cause of a foule womman."

The word *verge* was also used in Middle English to denote the penis, and it too appeared in medical treatises, including one from the mid fifteenth century that rendered its prescribed treatments in rhyme. It advises, for example, that if a man burns his penis, the physician should take linseed,

And boylyn it in mylke and wyn
And don it hoot in a letheryn hoodkyn
And late his verge hange ther-in.

In other words, boil the linseed in milk and wine, pour it while it's still hot into a leather pouch, and then hang the penis in it. In origin, the word *verge* derives from the Latin *virga*, meaning *rod*, which explains why the word came to denote the penis. However, *verge* also came to denote a special kind of rod, a sceptre or staff that symbolized one's judicial authority. By extension, the name of this sceptre also became the name of the geographical area over which a person wielded such authority; in the early sixteenth century, for example, the verge of the Lord High Steward was an area that extended twelve miles around the court of King Henry VIII. Any person who lived within that area was subject to its laws, and anyone who lived outside of it was not – such a person was, literally, *beyond the verge*. Eventually, this phrase also prompted the use of *verge* as a verb, as in "She's verging on leaving him."

Two other Middle English words that denoted stick-like objects, and which also became names for the penis, were *stooth* and *tent*. The first of these denoted a vertical beam used in the construction of a wall; nowadays, carpenters refer to such a beam as a *stud*, a word that derives from the same source as *stooth*. This word applied not just to human penises, but animal ones as well. An early-sixteenth-century manual known as "The Properties of a Horse" explained that the best horse is one with a "bygh Rowmpe, a longh stote and smale stonys in his qodd" – that is, a big rump, a long penis, and small testicles in his scrotum. As for the word *tent*, you might assume that this word is identical with the *tent* that denotes a camping structure made from poles and fabric. That camping *tent* is, in fact, employed in a recent synonym for *penis*, one that gestures toward the blanket-raising abilities of the male member: *Omar the tent-maker*. However, the *tent* that denoted the penis in Middle English is an entirely different word. Whereas the *tent* in *pup tent* derives from a Latin *tendere*, meaning *to stretch*, the penis *tent* derived from the Latin *temptare*, meaning *to probe* or *to test*. That Latin word became the familiar verb *tempt*, but it also became *tent*, a probe used by medieval physicians to examine the depth and nature of a wound. The word was used in a bawdy song from the early fifteenth century in which a woman has such a voluminous vagina – her "hall" – that rats reside within it, and only a man with a fifteen-inch penis and leather testicles can give such vigorous "swappes" as to drive the varmints away:

> May no man slepe in youre halle
> For rattys, Madame, for rattys, Madame,
> But gyf he have a tent of xv enche
> Wyt letheryn knappes
> To dryve awey the rattys, Madame.
> Iblessyd be suche knappes
> That gyveth such swappes
> Under my lady lappes
> To dryve awey the rattys, Madame.

In Early Modern English another host of penis words emerged, many of which are still current. *Tool*, for example, appeared in the mid sixteenth century as yet another word that equated the penis with an implement. Shakespeare employs the word with this sense in *Henry VIII* in a scene where a huge crowd gathers outside the palace to witness the christening of Princess Elizabeth. The mob is so large and clamorous that the Porter wonders whether the women have come to gawk at a man from the Indies, a region where males were thought to be well-endowed: "Have wee some strange Indian with the great toole come to court, the women so besiege us? Bless me, what a fry of fornication is at dore!" Shakespeare also used many other words to signify or imply the penis, ranging from mechanical words such as *instrument* and *pipe* to organic ones such as *carrot*, *stalk* and *poperin pear*. (The latter, a variety of pear, derives its name from a town in Flanders called Poperinghe, but the English spelling of the name facilitated a sixteenth-century pun on the phrase "pop her in.") Another penis word appears in *Henry IV Part 1*, where Lady Percy warns her husband that she will break his "little finger" if he isn't forthcoming with her. This euphemism might have been inspired by a passage from 1 Kings, where Rehoboam is counselled to tell the Israelites that "My little finger shall be thicker than my father's loins," meaning that he will be an even more severe ruler than his father.

It might come as a surprise that the Immortal Bard, the "Sweet Swan of Avon" as Ben Jonson called him, also employs the word *dildo*. It appears in *The Winter's Tale*, where a servant announces that a ballad-pedlar is at the door, ready to sell "the prettiest love-song for maids" with "delicate burdens of dildos and fadings." Shakespeare was probably alluding to the fact that *dildo* had, in the late sixteenth century, become a by-word in the bawdy refrains or "burdens" of popular ballads. It's used, for example, in a song known as "Dainty Darling, Kind and Free," first published in 1601:

> Prettie, wittie, sit mee by,
> Feare no cast of anie eye,
> Wee will plaie so privilie,
> None shall see but you and I;
> What I will doe with a dildo,
> Sing doe with a dildo.

Early on in its history, *dildo* – which probably derives from the Italian *diletto*, meaning *delight* – came to denote artificial penises, as well as real ones, as suggested by a 1598 reference to "a dildoe of glasse." By the late seventeenth century, this sense had come to dominate the word, as evidenced by a late-seventeenth-century lampoon written by John Wilmot, Second Earl of Rochester, in which a dildo is allegorized as an Italian stranger, recently come to town:

> The good Lady Suffolk thinking no harm,
> Had got this poor stranger hid under her arm:
> Lady Betty by chance came the secret to know,
> And from her own mother, stole Signior Dildo.

Incidentally, *dildo* acquired a rival in the late nineteenth century when *godemiche* was adopted from French as the name of an artificial penis. In French, the name probably developed from the Latin phrase *gaude mihi*, meaning *please me*.

It was also in Shakespeare's lifetime that the word *prick* came to denote the penis. Since the tenth century, *prick* had denoted the act of piercing something, and since the fourteenth century it had also signified the act of inciting or stimulating someone into action. (The latter sense is still familiar thanks to the King James version of the Book of Acts, where a voice from the heavens tells Saul, "It is hard for thee to kick against the pricks" – that is, it is hard for you to resist the pangs of your conscience.) Probably both of these earlier senses inspired the development of a *penis* sense of the word in the late sixteenth century: a penis physically pierces the vagina (or, even more literally, the hymen), and it also (ideally) sexually stimulates the woman who is being pricked. Interestingly, in the early sixteenth century, before *prick* acquired its *penis* sense, it was also used as a term of endearment. It continued to be so used into the seventeenth century, although naturally its rival *penis* sense caused it to fall into some disrepute. For example, writing in 1671, one author noted that some people are troubled when an "immodest maid soothing the young man, calls him her Prick." The author went on to suggest that anyone who is so troubled "instead of *my Prick*, let him write *my Sweetheart*." Most people, it would seem, heeded this advice, so that by the eighteenth century, *prick* was considered a very vulgar word. In fact, when Francis Grose used that word in his 1785 *Dictionary of the Vulgar Tongue*, it was printed as *p***k*, whereas other words in his dictionary such as *arse*, *piss*, *dildo* and *fart* were printed in their entirety.

The *penis* sense of *prick* has persisted to the present-day, as has another penis word that arose in the early seventeenth century, *cock*. That word had, of course, existed in English before it came to denote the penis. Since at least the ninth century it had been used to identify a male domestic fowl. The extension of the word from bird to penis might have been inspired by several things. First, when a rooster – or cock – becomes excited or aggressive, the wattles and caruncles and comb on its neck and head fill with blood, causing those fleshy lobes to swell and brighten in colour. A penis, as you may have witnessed or experienced, responds in a similar manner when the man to which it is

Ape-galle: a fifteenth-century name for an inflammation of the penis, also known as balantis.

attached becomes aroused, which might have prompted the transference of the name from rooster to organ. Alternatively, the word might have been transferred in a more indirect manner: first, the name of a spout found on barrels came to be known as a *cock*, or *stop-cock*, due to the fact that the top of such spouts were often shaped like a cock's comb so that they could be grasped and turned off or on. The resemblance of such a spout, pouring forth beer or wine, and the human penis, pouring forth what used to be beer or wine, might have inspired the extension of the barrel *cock* to the male member.

Many of the other *cocks* in present-day English derive from the same source as the penis *cock*. For instance, the stance in which a rooster crows – with its neck arched and head tipped back – prompted the word *cock* to develop the verb sense found in phrases such as *to cock your head* or *to cock your hat*. As well, the hammer of a gun came to be known as the *cock*, either because it is pulled back like a crowing cock's head or because it sticks up like a cock's comb; when such a gun fired accidentally, it was said to go off *half-cocked*, a term that was later extended to impulsive behaviour. *Cocktail*, too, is likely a relative of all these *cocks*. According to one theory, horses of mixed-parentage – that is, non-thoroughbreds – were identified as such by having their tails cropped, which caused them to cock up – that is, to become cock tails. Over time, the nickname of these "mixed" horses was presumably transferred to the mixed drink. One more cognate is *Cockney*, the name of a dialect of London. *Cockney* literally means *cock's egg*, which denoted a small or misshapen egg, the kind of addled egg that a cock, rather than a hen, would lay if it were somehow possible for male fowl to produce eggs.

In the early seventeenth century, this term was applied to city slickers on the analogy that people who live in cities are small and misshapen in comparison with big, strapping country folk. Later on, the word narrowed in meaning, as it came to denote not any city slicker, but one who resided in the city of London in particular. In contrast, *cockroach* has nothing to do with roosters, penises or even Londoners. The name of that insect derives from the Spanish *cuca*, meaning *caterpillar*. Nor, for that matter, is *cock* related to the word *cockles*, the chambers of the heart that are metaphorically warmed by a loved one. Instead, *cockles* derives from the Greek *konche*, the name of a kind of shellfish. As for *pillicock* – a synonym for *penis* that arose in the fourteenth century and vanished by the late seventeenth century – it's uncertain whether it's related to *cock*. The last half of *pillicock* might have simply arisen as a kind of verbal hiccup, a nonsense syllable that was added to *pill*, a word that meant *penis* in a dialect spoken in northern England. Other words, certainly, have had playful but meaningless syllables added to them from time to time, including *thing*, which became *thingamajig*, and *gabble*, which became *gobbledygook*.

When we get to the seventeenth century, we see the appearance of two penis words that were adopted from classical languages, *phallus* and *penis*. When the first of these, *phallus*, was adopted from Greek in 1613, it was not used to denote flesh-and-blood penises but only their symbolic representations, such as the erotic carvings carried during the festivals of Dionysius in ancient Greece. It was not until 1924 that *phallus* was used to denote a real live penis. In origin, the Greek *phallus* derives from an Indo-European root, *bhel*, meaning *to blow*, which evolved into numerous words descriptive of round or swollen objects including *ball, bowl, boulder, balloon* and *bollocks*. Even the word *ballot* can be added to this list, since that word originally denoted a small ball that an individual dropped into a jar in order to register a vote. As for the word *penis*, it was adopted from Latin in 1676 as a learned counterpart to another long-standing penis word. That older word was *tail*, which had been used since the fourteenth century to denote not just the female pudendum but also the male penis. Likewise, *tail* is what *penis* means in Latin, which is why it was adopted as a name for the male sex organ, and also why it was used as the source of two other English words. The first, dating back to the fifteenth century, is *pencil*, which originally referred to a kind of paintbrush – in other words, to a stick with a hairy tail on one end. It was not until the early seventeenth century that *pencil* also came to denote a writing implement made by encasing charcoal, lead or graphite in a wooden cylinder. The second word, which dates back to the early twentieth century, is *penicillin*, so named because the microscopic spores of the fungus from which that antibiotic is derived look like little paintbrushes.

Fifty years after the adoption of *penis*, English also borrowed the term *membrum virile* from Latin, literally meaning *virile member*. The *virile* part of this term derives from the Latin *vir*, meaning *man*, which also developed into the word *virtue* thanks to the confused notion that being manly is synonymous with being virtuous. The passage that the *Oxford English Dictionary* cites as the earliest recorded instance of *membrum virile* is perhaps the strangest quotation in all of its twenty volumes. The passage is taken from a collection of travelogues published by

Awnsham and John Churchill in 1732, one of which describes an event witnessed by Philip Skippon: "A Frenchman, that seeing the postboy fall down dead with the extremity of cold, opened his codpiece, and rub'd his membrum virile with snow, till he recovered him." (St. John's Ambulance does not endorse that first-aid treatment.) Further back, the Latin *vir* evolved from the Indo-European *wiro*, which developed via the Germanic language branch into the Old English *wer*, meaning *man*, which is still represented in *werewolf*, literally a *man-wolf*. The Old English *wiro* also developed into the word *world*, a place originally defined by the presence and civilization of men; etymologically, it's impossible to have a world without men. As for the word *member*, many people assume that it is related to the word *remember*, as if the act of remembering is a re-membering, a putting back together of discrete members. In fact, however, the word *member* derives from an Indo-European word that meant *flesh*, whereas *remember* derives from an entirely different source. That source, the Indo-European *smer*, developed via the Italic branch not just into the word *remember*, but also into *dismember* and *memory*, and also, via the Germanic branch, into the word *mourn*.

A learned term such as *membrum virile* clearly arose as a euphemism, as did the word *shaft*, which was first recorded as a synonym for *penis* in 1719. That year also marks the first recorded instance of someone employing the word *pudding* to denote the penis, a usage that was eventually shortened to just *pud*, which still survives in the phrase *to pull your pud*, meaning *to masturbate*. The original application of *pudding* to the penis is easier to understand when you know that puddings were not originally milk-based dessert items served in bowls, but rather a section of intestine stuffed with ground meat. In other words, puddings were a kind of sausage, one of the most phallic-shaped foods you'll ever eat. Around the same time that *pudding* came to denote the penis, the word *pego* emerged as another name for the male member. The origin of this slang word is uncertain, but it might simply have arisen as a variation on *peg*, a kind of stumpy dowel or wooden pin. The word appears to good effect in a rollicking burlesque poem by Edward Ward, where the speaker's unruly pego threatens to launch a coup d'etat when he meets his innkeeper's comely daughter:

> Her Lips so melting soft and tender,
> They did so sweet a Kiss surrender,
> That Pego, like an upstart Hector,
> Finding how much I did affect her,
> Would fain have Rul'd as Lord Protector:
> Inflam'd by one so like a Goddess,
> I scarce could keep him in my Codpiece.

A few years after Edward Ward published his poem, the name *Roger* also came to denote the penis. This was, in fact, the first of several male given names to be bestowed on that part of the male anatomy – *Thomas* followed in 1811, *Dick* in 1891, *Peter* in 1902 and *Willie* in 1905. To some extent, the application of these names to the penis occurred simply because those names were considered typically male, the kind of name that Joe Blow or any Tom, Dick or Harry might have. Indeed, since the mid sixteenth century, the name *Dick* has often been used to mean *fellow*, especially in alliterative phrases such as *dapper Dick* or *desperate Dick*. (The same thing happened with *guy*, which shifted from a personal name to a collective noun because of Guy Fawkes, the man who tried to blow up England's House of Lords in 1605. The effigies of Fawkes that were annually burned came to be known as *guys*, a usage which was later extended to any man, and still later to any person, male or female.)

With *Peter*, however, there may be an additional reason why it came to denote the penis: that name derives from the Greek *petros*, meaning *stone*, a material whose hardness might recall the firmness of an erection. The word is still used with that stony sense in the name *saltpeter*, a chemical compound that was once given to young men and soldiers to reduce their sexual ardour. Recently, the name *Stanley* has also sometimes been used to identify the penis, a humorous usage prompted by the fact that *Stanley* is the brand name of a power drill. Last names, too, have been bestowed on the penis, such as *Johnson*, which dates back to the mid nineteenth century but has recently gained wide currency. The word *jock* is also used to denote the penile area, but that *jock* – as in *jockstrap* – is probably not related to the *Jock* that is a variant of the name *Jack*. When the genital *jock* first appeared in the late eighteenth century, it originally denoted the private parts of both men and women, which makes the male name *Jock* or *Jack* an unlikely source for the word. Incidentally, some of these penis names have also developed into verbs: *roger* has been used to mean *to copulate* since the early eighteenth

Bareback: A term invented in the 1950s to denote the act of having sex without a condom.

century, and *dick* has been used since the 1960s to mean *to dither*, as in "Please stop dicking around!"

At the end of the eighteenth century, Francis Grose recorded a number of then-current synonyms for *penis*, all of them in common use among the so-called canting crowd made up of London's thieves, prostitutes and beggars. Most of these terms were compounds, such as *whore pipe, tickle tail, sugar stick* and *hair splitter*, as are the vast majority of the 1,300 penis names in the list presented near the beginning of this chapter. This technique of creating a new word by combining two old ones is, of course, ancient: in Old English such formations were called kennings, and they ranged from *hron-rade*, which literally meant *whale-road* and thus denoted the ocean, to *word-hord*, which literally meant *word-hoard* and thus denoted one's vocabulary. Not all of the penis words recorded by Grose, though, were compounds. For instance, he mentions that *doodle* denoted a child's penis, a usage that might have arisen from an earlier use of *doodle* to denote a simpleton, just as nowadays people sometimes make a distinction between a man's *big brain* and his *little brain*, the latter tending to get the former into oodles of trouble. Alternatively, *doodle* might have arisen as a play on *noodle*, a phallic-shaped pasta whose name was introduced to England not long before the emergence of the penis *doodle*. A third possibility is that *doodle* was prompted by *cockadoodle*. Since the first part of that word, *cock*, denoted the penis, people might have felt that it would be humorous, or even euphemistic, to use the last part, *doodle*, to do likewise.

Although it might seem like a stretch to suppose that *doodle* arose as a euphemism for *cock* due to their juxtaposition in *cockadoodle*, bear in mind that the word *rooster* came into existence in the late eighteenth century mostly because prudish Americans needed a way to refer to a male fowl without using the word *cock*. That word, as you recall, had acquired a bawdy sense in the seventeenth century, one that eventually hijacked the word, especially in the U.S. Writing in 1921, Henry Mencken – the author of the groundbreaking *The American Language* – claimed that nineteenth-century Americans were fervent in their creation of euphemisms for words that were perceived to have sexual implications. The word *bull*, for example, was considered by some to be indelicate, perhaps because of its association with *cock* in the phrase *cock and bull*, an idiom denoting a long and preposterous story, often about two anthropomorphized animals, the kind of tale that is now called a *shaggy dog* story. (The term *bullshit* is not recorded till 1921, so it's unlikely that *bullshit* gave *bull* its indelicate connotation.) According to Mencken, euphemistic substitutions for *bull* included *cow-creature*, *male-cow*, and even *gentleman-cow*.

The mania for euphemisms went so far that even the names of undergarments became taboo, and words like *corset* were banned from polite company. Certain body parts acquired euphemistic new names, so that *belly* was eclipsed by *stomach*, which in turn was clipped and softened into *tummy*. On a human, the *leg* became a *limb*, and on a chicken it became a *second wing*. (The terms *dark meat* and *white meat* were also popularized in the nineteenth century so that the words *leg* and *breast* would not have to pass the lips of anyone at the dinner table.) In 1839, in his *Diary in America*, the English novelist Frederick Marryat mocked the Americans he had met on his tour through the U.S.

who were so punctilious that they even avoided referring to the legs of furniture: "I am not so particular as some people are, for I know those who always say limb of a table, or limb of a piano-forte." The same attitude prompted the invention of little skirts that were modestly draped over the legs of offending pieces of furniture.

Like *doodle*, the word *dink* probably originated as a euphemism when it first appeared around 1888, as is suggested by its ancestry. Its earlier form was likely *dinkus*, which in turn seems to have developed from *dingus*, which was also used in the late nineteenth century to denote the male sexual organ. Even further back *dingus* probably evolved from the Dutch *dinges*, which was synonymous with *thing* or *whatchamacallit*. To call a penis a *dingus* or *dinkus* or *dink* was therefore to dub it a *thing*, the kind of word that's euphemistically used when you can't bring yourself to pronounce something or someone's real name, like your sister-in-law, for instance. For some reason, the word *dink* apparently became much more popular in Canada than in the U.S. As late as 1961, Eric Partridge, the author of a seminal etymological work known as *A Dictionary of Slang and Unconventional English*, claimed that *dink* belonged exclusively to Canadian English. Even today, the continued Canadian provenance of *dink* is borne out by the fact that commentators at American tennis tournaments don't seem at all flustered when they describe a sneaky tapping shot as a *dink*.

Partridge claimed that *dong*, another penis word, was also a Canadianism. However, if *dong* did originate around 1900 as a primarily Canadian term, it has subsequently penetrated the slang vocabulary across North America, both as a synonym for *penis* and for *dildo*. A quick search of the Internet for the phrase *double-headed dong* results in hundreds of matches, mostly on the web pages of U.S.-based sex-toy stores. (Interestingly, most of these stores have two colours of double-headed dongs in stock: black and "natural.") The *Oxford English Dictionary* suggests that as a name for the penis, the word *dong* was borrowed from a poem by Edward Lear, a nineteenth-century painter and humorist. In that poem, entitled "The Dong with a Luminous Nose," a creature known as the Dong constructs a huge, glow-in-the-dark proboscis, the better to seek his long-lost sweetheart:

> Playing a pipe with silvery squeaks,
> Since then his Jumbly Girl he seeks,
> And because by night he could not see,
> He gathered the bark of the Twangum Tree
> On the flowery plain that grows.
> And he wove him a wondrous Nose, –
> A Nose as strange as a Nose could be!
> Of vast proportions and painted red,
> And tied with cords to the back of his head.

Alternatively, *dong* might simply have been inspired by the word *dangle*.

The first half of the twentieth century saw the emergence of few penis euphemisms, but many more vulgar synonyms, such as *pisser* in 1901 and *pecker* and *rod* in 1902. The word *pecker* had existed in English in the late sixteenth century, but it then referred to a kind of hoe; without knowledge of this earlier sense, modern readers of a Virginia travelogue written by Thomas Harriot in 1587 would be puzzled (or intrigued) by his description of women with short peckers, ones measuring "a foot long, and about five inches in breadth." In the mid nineteenth century, *pecker* also came to mean *courage*, as in the idiom *Keep your pecker up*. This sense was probably inspired by the observation that a bird holds aloft its pecker – that is, its beak – when it is chipper, and drops it when fatigued or dozing. (The semantically similar *Keep your chin up* did not appear until the 1930s, and was a metaphor drawn from the boxing ring.)

The word *wiener* was applied to the human penis around 1910, only five years after the word emerged as a name for a kind of food. Earlier on, the word had been known only as part of the compound *wienerwurst*, which dates back to 1889 in English. That name means *Vienna sausage*, Vienna being the city where that style of sausage was popularized. Even earlier, the name of that city developed from a Celtic phrase, *vindo bona*, meaning *white fort*.

The year 1922 was a very good one for penis words, witnessing the appearance of both *tube* and *middle leg*. Ten years later, *putz* was also adopted as a slang word for penis. In Yiddish, from whence it was adopted, *putz* literally meant *ornament*, and thus its anatomical application implied that the human penis is more decorative than functional. *Putz* also existed in German, a language closely related to Yiddish, and in that language the *ornament* sense of the word prompted it to be adopted, near the beginning of the twentieth century, as the name of a nativity scene, the kind placed under Christmas trees. Thus, for much of the twentieth century, *putz* denoted both the male member and the holy manger of the Christian saviour. Incidentally, the word *schmuck* – or rather *shmok* – also denoted the penis in Yiddish, and also literally meant *ornament*, but when it was adopted into English in the 1890s it lost this sexual sense, and instead simply came to denote an obnoxious person. A similar loss of sexual meaning occurred when *yang* was adopted into English in the eighteenth century. In Chinese that word denotes the force of masculine sexuality in the universe, just as *yin* denotes the corresponding force of female sexuality. The compound *yang ju*, for example, literally means *the organ of yang*, and thus denotes the penis. However, after they were adopted into English both *yin* and *yang* lost most of their sexual force, though they are still commonly understood to represent complementary masculine and feminine cosmic impulses.

Another word of Yiddish origin that appeared in the 1930s was *schlong*. In Yiddish, *schlang* means *serpent*, which anticipates numerous penis synonyms that arose in the later twentieth century, such as *one-eyed trouser snake* and *tube-snake*. The alteration of *schlang* to *schlong* probably occurred as men sought to make the word more closely resemble the adjective *long*. Also in the 1930s the word *whang* appeared, now usually spelt *wang*. This penis word might have been formed from *whangdoodle*, a word of fanciful invention that dates back to the mid nineteenth century. The fact that *doodle*, as mentioned above, had been used to denote the penis since the early eighteenth century may have inspired some speakers to transfer the *penis* sense from the *doodle* of *whangdoodle* to the *whang* of *whangdoodle*. If so, then the following complex paternity might be reconstructed: *wang* came from *whang*, and *whang* came from *whangdoodle* thanks to people using the first half of the word (*whang*) to stand in for the second half (*doodle*, which already meant *penis*), and *whangdoodle* was created as a fanciful expansion of *doodle*, and *doodle* came from *cockadoodle* thanks to people using the last half of that word (*doodle*) to stand in for the first half (*cock*, which already meant *penis*). A simpler explanation for *wang* exists, but when it comes to word histories, and how people use language, simplicity is not necessarily a guiding principle. Nonetheless, it's possible that the noun *wang* simply developed from the verb *wank*, which had meant *to masturbate* since the late nineteenth century. In turn, *wank* might have formed as a humorous conflation of *whack* and *spank*. It's conceivable that *wank* also developed into the penis word *winkle*, which dates back to the 1940s. As for *dork*, which is first recorded in 1961, it probably arose as a variant of *dick*, with the vowel change perhaps being influenced by *dong* and *cock*.

≋

If your pet chihuahua suddenly grew rigid and quadrupled in size every time your sister-in-law came to visit, you would no doubt invent a unique name for your dog when it was manifesting that turgid condition, a whimsical name such as *corndog* or perhaps a quasi-clinical one such *rigor canis*. The same is true for the human penis: what it's called when it emerges from a cold shower often differs from what it's called when it's glimpsed *in flagrante delicto*. In the former case, the shrivelled member has recently acquired sobriquets such as *dead soldier*, *Mr. Softy*, *half a cob*, *wet noodle* and *Sleeping Beauty*. In the latter case, the tumescent organ has been known by numerous names, or described with sundry adjectives, many of which date back hundreds of years. The adjective *tumescent*, for example, dates back to the late nineteenth century, where it was formed from the Latin *tumere*, meaning *to swell*, from which the word *tumor* also developed. Further back, the Latin *tumere* evolved from an Indo-European source, *teue*, also meaning *to swell*, which developed via the Germanic language branch into the first syllable of the word *thousand*. That word derived from the Old English *thusi hundi*, literally meaning *swollen hundred*. The Indo-European *teue* also became the Old English *thuma*, which became the modern word *thumb*, thanks to the notion that the thumb is a "swollen" finger. Finally, the Indo-European *teue* evolved via the Hellenic language branch into the Greek word *turos*, meaning *cheese*, on the analogy that cheese is a "swollen" form of milk. The word *turos* was then combined with the Greek word *bous*, meaning *cow*, to form *bouturon*, which evolved into our word *butter*.

Gonorrhoea: a venereal disease whose name literally means "seed flow," from the mistaken belief that the discharge of mucous caused by the illness was semen.

Nowadays, a tumescent penis would normally be called an *erection*, a usage that dates back to at least the early fifteenth century. That word derives, like *rectum* and *rectangle*, from the Latin *rectus*, meaning *straight*. Even earlier, going back to the fourteenth century, the words *rising* and *stonding* were both employed to denote an erect penis, the latter name simply being a variant of *standing*. In a medical treatise authored around

1475, Gilbertus Anglicus observes that "In a mannes yerde ther ben diverse grevaunces" – in other words, in a man's penis there may be many diseases – and he goes on to describe one of them as "to moche stonding, that is clepid satiriasis" – in other words, too much erection, which is called satyriasis. The good doctor then explains the cause of this condition: "Satiriasis cometh of a greet boistrois hoot wynde that makith the yerde to arise" – in other words, satyriasis results from a great, boisterous, hot wind that makes the penis rise. This word, *satyriasis*, denoting an erection that won't go away, was formed from *satyr*, the name of a creature from Greek mythology that was commonly depicted as having the torso and head of a man combined with the legs, tail, ears, and horns of a goat. Satyrs were notoriously lecherous creatures. In Book III of Edmund Spenser's *The Faerie Queene*, published in 1590, a cuckold named Malbecco can only watch from the bushes as his unfaithful wife has sex nine times in one night with a single satyr:

> At night, when all they went to sleepe, he vewd,
> Whereas his lovely wife emongst them lay,
> Embraced of a Satyre rough and rude,
> Who all the night did minde his joyous play:
> Nine times he heard him come aloft ere day,
> That all his hart with gealosie did swell.

The disease of satyriasis was also known as *priapism*, a name also derived from Greek mythology. Priapus was a god of procreation, and he was originally worshipped at Lampsacus, where asses, which symbolized fertility, were sacrificed in his honour. Statues of Priapus were often placed in gardens, both because his procreative abilities were thought to foster plant growth, and also because he functioned as a scarecrow, thanks in part to the huge penis that he traditionally sported. Since the early seventeenth century, the word *priapus* itself has also been used as a synonym for *erection*.

Another Middle English word that denoted a relentless (and therefore painful) erection was *prickpride*, which dates back to at least the fifteenth century. Writing around 1550, William Thomas said that when a man suffers from prickpride "the yard is stretched out in length and breadth, nothing provoking the pacient to lust or desire." He added that sometimes the condition is accompanied with "beating and panting," by which he probably meant that the erection would throb and ooze fluid. In the fifteenth century, the word *pride* was also used, all by itself, to denote a normal erection, that is, one that came and went. *Pride* is still used this way in at least one late-twentieth-century idiom, *morning pride*, the name bestowed on an erection that is already full-blown upon waking. In the eighteenth century, that morning phenomenon was known as *piss-proud*, the notion being that such an erection resulted from a superfluity of urine. *Piss-proud* also came to denote an old man who married a young woman: the label implied that the only erection he would be able to muster would be one prompted by his bladder.

In Early Modern English, three new synonyms for *erection* appeared, two of them learned formations and one of them slang. The learned terms were *tentigo* and *surgation*, the first of which was derived around 1603 from the Latin *tendere*, meaning *to stretch*. The adjective *tense* derives from the same source, the notion being that when people are tense they feel "stretched" – and, in fact, they may even look drawn, another word that implies being stretched. The other learned synonym for *erection* was *surgation*, which was adapted around 1681 from the Latin *surgere*, meaning *to rise*. Further back, *surgere* was formed from the prefix *sus*, meaning *up*, and *regere*, which is the infinitive form of the Latin *rectus*, meaning *straight*. More literally, therefore, the word *surgere* means *to go straight up*, and its connection to *rectus* means that it is also related to the cluster of words represented by *rectum*, *rectangle*, *correct*, *erection* and so on. The slang term *horn* also appeared in Early Modern English at the end of the eighteenth century, a usage prompted by the resemblance of an erect penis to the bony protuberance on the head of a cow or goat, and also by the associations of horns with sexuality, as discussed previously in Chapter Four, devoted to words denoting sexual desire.

In Late Modern English, the words *hard-on*, *boner*, *stiffy*, and *woody* appeared. The oldest of these, *hard-on*, dates back to 1888, followed by *boner* in 1966, *stiffy* in 1980 and *woody* in 1990. The term *woody*, however, might have arisen from a much older term: back in the 1920s, the phrase *wooden spoon* was used to denote an erect penis. (Even earlier, in the late nineteenth century, *wooden spoon* signified a dim-wit, a wooden spoon being the traditional booby prize presented annually to the undergraduate who received the lowest mathematics mark at Cambridge.) As for *boner*, before it came to denote an erection, it meant *blunder*; thus, one of the books on my shelf, published in 1953 and entitled *World's Biggest Boners*, is not filled with astonishing photos of well-endowed men, but rather is a compilation of mistaken (and humorous) claims drawn from student essays. The word *baculum* has also been recently used to denote an erection, though this is a misuse of the technical sense of the word. Strictly speaking, a baculum is the bone that runs through the penis of many mammals, including dogs but not humans.

Not just stiffness but size has also been used to distinguish penises. Recent slang names for a penis whose erect length significantly exceeds the 5.77 inch average, a statistic established in 2001 by the makers of Lifestyle Condoms, include *whopper, whalebone, cucumber, longhorn, ten-pounder* and *choker*. One term that is significantly older is *lobcock*, which dates back to the late eighteenth century. Even older is the use of *well-hung* to denote a large penis, a usage that dates back to the early seventeenth century. At that time, however, *well-hung* could also refer more generally to any organ that was large and pendulous; in fact, the first recorded use of *well-hung*, from 1611, is in reference to a man with well-hung ears. Incidentally, it's a mistake to describe a man dangling from a gallows as well-hung; rather, such a person is well-hanged, assuming that the execution went off to everyone's satisfaction. A somewhat more recent learned synonym for *well-hung* is *mentulate*, which first appeared in a medical dictionary in 1890. Physicians created that word from the Latin *mentula*, one of several words the ancient Romans employed to denote the penis, which in turn might have developed as a diminutive of

Herpes: a disease that can afflict the genitals, and which takes its name from the Greek *herpein*, meaning to creep.

the Latin *mentum*, meaning *chin*. If so, then a word that literally meant *little chin* became a Latin word for *penis*, which in turn became an English word describing a large penis.

~~~

While you've probably known the word *penis* since you were a child, you might not be familiar with the names of that organ's various parts, such as *glans, corona, frenulum, urethral meatus* and *prepuce*. The first of these words, *glans*, denotes the head of the penis (though on a woman it can also refer to the head of her clitoris). The word *glans* was adopted in the mid seventeenth century from Latin, where it means *acorn*, a nut that resembles the penis head in both shape and size. (The Latin *glans* is also the source of the word *gland*.) The nut metaphor lies behind several other words that have been used to denote the head of the penis. For example, *acorn* itself is a contemporary slang name for the glans, and *nut* was used from the mid sixteenth to the mid eighteenth century; likewise, *balanus*, which derives from the Greek word for *acorn*, was current from the early fifteenth to the late nineteenth centuries. A derivative, *balanitis*, is still used as a name for an inflammation of the penis head, whether in men, dogs, or horses. Other contemporary slang names for the glans include *cock knuckle, cockhead, German helmut, mushroom tip, turnip* and *radish*.

In the tip of the penis there is, or better be, an opening known as the *urethral meatus* through which urine and semen are discharged. The first word in this name derives via Latin from the Greek *ourein*, meaning *to urinate*, while the latter word is simply the past participle of the Latin verb *meare*, meaning *to pass*. More interesting is the name bestowed upon this penile opening in the early fifteenth century: *miter*, so called because the headdress worn by a bishop – his miter – is fashioned with a deep cleft, somewhat resembling the opening or cleft in the tip of a penis. Modern slang names for the urethral meatus include *eye of the Bishop*, *Jap's eye* and *pee-pee hole*.

The back part of the upper side of the glans – the ridge where the glans meets the shaft of the penis – is known as the *corona*, a usage that dates back to the mid eighteenth century. In Latin *corona* means *crown*, and thus the word has also been applied to the upper region of other parts of the body, such as the corona of a tooth. In the early eighteenth century, *corona* also referred to a crown-like string of blotches that sometimes appeared across the forehead of individuals afflicted with syphilis. On the underside of the *penis*, where the glans meets the shaft (or what was called, in Middle English, the *root*), is a membrane that attaches the foreskin of the penis to the shaft of the penis. This membrane is called the *frenulum*, a word that was created as a diminutive of the Latin *frenum*, meaning *bridle*. This small piece of tissue helps to harness the foreskin to the penis, much as the frenulum under your tongue keeps that muscle from lolling about.

The *foreskin* of the penis has been known by that name since the early sixteenth century, but even older is *prepuce*, first recorded in a late-fourteenth-century travelogue that explains how an angel "gave the prepuce of oure Lord" – for Jesus, being Jewish, was circumcised – to Emperor Charlemagne, so that the shrivelled bit of skin could be revered as a holy relic. The first part of the word *prepuce* clearly seems to be the preposition *pre*, meaning *before*, but the last syllable is more puzzling. Some etymologists have suggested that it must have developed from an unrecorded Vulgar Latin word for *penis*, a form that probably evolved from the Indo-European root *put*, meaning *to swell*. Other etymologists have proposed that the last syllable of the word is connected to the Latin *putere*, meaning *to stink*, which is also the source of *putrid*. In the early fifteenth century, the prepuce was also known as the *husk*, a word that extends the nut metaphor represented by *glans*. One late-fifteenth-century surgical treatise also refers to the foreskin as the *tuffa*, a word that likely derives from the Latin *tufa*, a kind of crest applied to a helmet. The word *tuft*, as in a tuft of hair or trees, also derives from this source. Current slang names for the foreskin include *banana skin*, *curtains*, *turtleneck* and *snapper*.

Of course, not every male has a foreskin, thanks to the marvellous invention of circumcision. Among Jews that custom dates back thousands of years, though occasionally it fell into disuse and had to be revived. According to the Old Testament, the practice arose when God commanded Abraham to circumcise himself and all of his descendents as a token of the covenant between the Almighty and the Israelites. (In Judaism, the circumcision ceremony is called a *bris*, which derives from the Hebrew word *berith*, meaning *covenant*.) In the Book of Genesis, the Lord warns that the consequences of refusing to doff your foreskin are considerable: "the uncircumcised man whose flesh of his foreskin is not circumcised, that soul shall be cut off from his people." Although circumcision did not become widely popular in England and North America until the 1870s, the English language has possessed names for that surgical procedure for more than a thousand years because of its biblical importance. Among the oldest words meaning *to circumcise* are the Old English *ymbceorfan* and *ymbsnithan*. With both of these words, the first three letters form the preposition *ymb*, meaning *around*. Thus, *ymbceorfan* meant *to carve around* (the Modern English *carve* derives from *ceorfan*), and *ymbsnithan* meant *to cut around* (*snithan*, meaning *to cut*, became obsolete by the thirteenth century, although its cognate *snode*, denoting a morsel of bread, survived until the fourteenth century, and its participle *snithing* continued to be used up until the late nineteenth century to describe a cold or "cutting" wind).

In early Middle English, synonyms for *circumicise* included *umbesheren* and *umbeclippen*, both of which appear in manuscripts written near the beginning of the thirteenth century. Here, the *umb* that begins both words represents the later form of the Old English *ymb*; thus, *umbesheren* means *to shear around*, and *umbeclippen* means *to clip around*. In the mid thirteenth century, the word *circumcise* itself appeared, deriving via French from the Latin *circum*, meaning *around*, and *caedere*, meaning *to cut*. (The Latin *caedere* is also the source of the words *scissors* and *decide*, a decision being something that cuts through an issue.) The word *carve* continued to be used to denote circumcision into the fifteenth century, although that word was also used to signify castration, which might have led to some regrettable miscommunications.

Also in the fifteenth century, the removal of the prepuce was sometimes described as being *skinned*, and the resulting penis was said to be *hoodless*. The *hood* notion is also present in the medical term *acucullophallia*: the *cucullo* part of that word derives from the Latin *cucullus*, meaning *hood*, so *acucullophallia* means *without the hood of the phallus*. Another word used by the medical community to describe the state of being circumcised is *apellous*, which derives from the negating prefix *a* and the Latin word *pellis*, meaning *skin*, from which we derive the word *pelt*. More imaginative are some of the contemporary slang names for being circumcised, such as *snipped, clipped, lop cock, kosher-style, Canadian bacon, Principal Skinner* and *bald-headed hermit*. In newspaper personal ads, the term *cut* has been employed since the 1980s, and even more recently the phrase *not intact* has come to be used by groups advocating the abolition of circumcision. Incidentally, one of the reasons put forth by those in favour of circumcision is that it prevents an accumulation of *smegma*, a cheesy secretion that appears on the glans of the penis. Ironically, the name of that substance is a direct adoption of the Greek *smegma*, meaning *soap*, which derives from the verb *smekhein*, meaning *to clean*.

≈

One of the strangest words in this book is *rantallion*, first recorded at the end of the eighteenth century by Francis Grose in his *Dictionary of the Vulgar Tongue*. According to Grose, *rantallion* denotes a man whose scrotum is so relaxed as to be longer than his penis. Grose adds, drawing on a firearm metaphor, that such a man's shot pouch – that is, his bag of bullets – is longer than the barrel of his musket. The word *rantallion* is strange not because of its etymology, which is unknown, but simply because of its existence. What social circumstances would necessitate the invention of a word that describes a phenomenon that is hidden from public view, that has no impact on sexual function, and that occurs (based on my casual observation in saunas and locker rooms) rather infrequently? The English language has certainly managed to do without words for many other seemingly insignificant phenomena. Some men, for example, have ring fingers that are longer than their index fingers, a condition that lacks a name. (However, this may change if it turns out, as some scientists have recently claimed, that long ring fingers are correlated to high testosterone levels and high sperm counts.) Perhaps the existence of the word *rantallion* points toward the fact that the scrotum and the testicles it contains enjoy a privileged place in the construction of male identity. They have, after all, been dubbed the *family jewels*, and for many males they are synonymous with manhood. Not surprisingly, therefore, the scrotum – and its testicles – have acquired many names over the centuries.

One of the oldest names for the scrotum is *cod*, which dates back to at least the eleventh century. The word, in its original sense, meant *bag* and probably developed from an Indo-European source that meant *rounded* or *curved*. That Indo-European source also developed into *cove*, the name of a small and rounded bay; into *cubby*, as in *cubby-hole*; and into *cot*, a kind of small shelter, roughly round in shape, from which the word *cottage* later developed. (The *cot* that denotes a portable bed developed from an unrelated Hindi source.) The scrotum *cod* may also be related to the fish with the same name: it's possible that the fish was named after its bag-like appearance. As a name for the scrotum, *cod* was often used in medical contexts, as in one fifteenth-century "leechbook" that advised that "the swellynge of a mannes codd is amendid with a pleistre," that is, with the application of a plaster. The word was also used in Middle English etiquette books, such as *The Book of Carving and Nurture* written by John Russell in the late fifteenth century. At the dinner table Russell sagely advises, "Put not youre handes in youre hosen, youre cod-ware for to clawe" – in other words, while you're eating, don't stuff your hands down your pants in order to scratch your scrotum.

Today, the *cod* that meant *scrotum* is known only in the compound *codpiece*, the name of a pouch that covered the genitals of gentlemen in the sixteenth century. The codpiece was originally just a triangular piece of fabric that was sewn on one side over the crotch, so that it could be flipped back when the man needed to urinate. Although not much to look at, this patch of cloth was an improvement over earlier times, when the rising hemlines of tunics, coupled with a lack of underwear, led to frequent exposure of the penis and scrotum, especially when sitting on a bench or on horseback. The parson in Chaucer's *Canterbury Tales*, for example, decries the "scantnesse of clothyng that covere nat the shameful membres of man." The garments of some men, he goes on to say, reveal their "horrible swollen membres" and also their buttocks that poke out like the "hyndre part of a she-ape in the fulle of the moone." The invention of codpieces helped to prevent such displays, but over time they became more elaborate, and their shape was influenced by fashion and by the realization that they could be padded and stuffed. By the middle of the sixteenth century, some codpieces resembled a loaf of bread in size and shape. Henry VIII even had a steel codpiece hinged onto his suit of armour. Although these sartorial symbols of virility fell out of fashion near the end of the sixteenth century, they are echoed by the modern necktie, a fashion accessory that points, like an arrow, toward a man's genital area.

Other words that were used in Middle English to denote the scrotum include *purse, pocket, leather* and *oceum*. The first of these, *purse*, was often used in conjunction with an adjective, as with *nether purse* or *ballock purse*. Medieval medical treatises often used *purse* with this sense, as in one treatise from the early fifteenth century that explained how to treat an inguinal hernia: "Make an hole thorugh the purse of the ballokes with a launset and drawe out the water." The word *purse* was also used to mean *scrotum* in the medieval idiom *by the top and by the purse*, literally meaning *by the head and by the scrotum*, and figuratively meaning *completely* or *from top to bottom*. In origin, the word *purse* derives from the Latin *bursa*, meaning *pouch*, which in turn developed from an Indo-European source that meant *skin* or *leather*. The Latin *bursa* was also adopted into English as the name of a fluid-filled pouch positioned between muscles and tendons in order to diminish friction. Moreover, *bursa* also developed into the word *bursar*, originally the name of an officer who looked after pouches of money, which in turn prompted the word *bursary*. The word *leather* denoted the scrotum in Middle English compounds such as *ballocks leather*, which might be rendered into Modern English as *testicle skin*. Like *purse*, this word was also employed by medieval physicians, who seem to have spent an inordinate amount of time writing about hernias. "Whanne a mannes bowels fallith into his ballokis letheris," wrote one doctor at the beginning of the fifteenth century, "it is clepid hernia intestinalis." As for *oceum*, that scrotum word appeared in the early fifteenth century, and in form it seems a mere respelling of the Greek word *ossium*; that Greek word, however, means *bone*, so it's difficult to see why it was adopted as the name of a soft and jiggly pouch. Nonetheless, the word was indeed used as a synonym for *scrotum*: one fifteenth century physician, for example, employed the word when he was speculating on the "divisioun of the oceum." He decided that "the ballocke codde is parted in two" so that "if ther felle enye disese to the one partie of the codde, the tother partie migte abiden hole and unhurt."

Somewhat more recent than any of these terms is the word *scrotum* itself. That word first appeared in English at the end of the sixteenth century, having been adopted directly from Latin. Earlier on, the ancient Romans had derived their word *scrotum* from another Latin word, *scrautum*, meaning *quiver*, a tube-shaped pouch for holding arrows. This word, in turn, had evolved from the Indo-European *skreu*, meaning *to cut*, from which a host of other words developed, such as *scroll* and *shred*, as discussed earlier in relation to the collective noun *shrew*. The semantic connection between the Indo-European *skreu* and the Latin *scrautum* was probably that arrow quivers were cut from leather. Much more recently, probably dating back only to the 1970s, the word *scrotum* has been abbreviated to the slang word *scrote* or *scrot*.

> The limits of my language are the limits of my mind. All I know is what I have words for.
> *Ludwig Wittgenstein*

Other modern slang names include *bag* and *sack*, which date back to the late nineteenth century and 1930s respectively. In the 1990s, *bozack* emerged, presumably a conflation of *ball sack*.

〜〜

The reason the scrotum hangs outside the male body is that the testicles it contains prefer a slightly cooler than body-temperature environment. Thus, on a scorching summer day the testicles dangle low, perhaps even rantallion-like, while on a frosty winter morning they pull up close to the loins, snuggling together like two shivering puppies. The sensitivity of testicles to heat and cold is interesting considering that orchids, which derive their name from the Greek *orkhis*, meaning *testicle*, are also sensitive to temperature changes. That flower, however, takes its name not from the fact that it thrives or wilts as the mercury fluctuates, but from the resemblance of its tuberous root to the human testis. The etymological connection between the plant and the gonad is evident in the medical term *monorchid*, used to describe a man with a single testicle. Further back, the Greek *orkhis* evolved from an Indo-European source, *ergh*, meaning *to mount*, the connection being that the testicles, or at least the testosterone they produce, are what prompt a man or male animal to mount a female: snip off the testicles, and sexual desire wanes. The Indo-European *ergh* also developed into the Greek *orkheisthai*, meaning *dance*, the connection either being that dancing arose in symbolic imitation of sexual movements, or else that dancing was performed on a raised or "mounted" platform. In English, the Greek *orkheisthai* became the word *orchestra* and was transferred to the musicians who supplied music for the dance performance. The size and shape of the testicles has also prompted their name to be extended to things other than orchids, too. The word *avocado*, for example, derives from the Nahuatl word for *testicle*, Nahuatl being the language of the Aztecs. Similarly, a plant known as *salep* takes its name from an Arabic phrase meaning *fox's testicles*, thanks to the resemblance of that plant's tuberous root to the gonads of that canine.

In English, one of the earliest names for the testicles was *ballocks* – or, as it was often spelt in Old English, *bealluc*. By the fourteenth century, this word was being spelt *ballocks*, and by the 1930s the slang form *bollix* had emerged, which was also used as a verb meaning *to bungle*. If you bollixed a plan, you screwed it up. On the surface, this verb usage of *bollix* or *ballocks* is puzzling: there's no obvious connection between testicles and bungling. Likely, however, the usage was inspired by the word *balls*, which had been used to denote the testicles since the fourteenth century, and which came to mean *to bungle* in the late nineteenth century. Here, the connection between balls and bungling is more clear: some forms of equipment, like a long rope or a hose or a fishing line, are rendered temporarily useless when they become so tangled that they form a ball instead of a length. This notion of a thing getting literally balled up developed a more figurative sense, which was then transferred – via the testicle sense of *balls* – to the word *ballocks*. In origin, *bealluc*, the Old English ancestor of *ballocks* was a Germanic source that simply meant *ball*, which in turn evolved from the Indo-European *bhel*, meaning *to blow* or *to swell*. As mentioned earlier, *phallus* also derived from that same Indo-European source, which means that *phallus* is the Greek cousin to the Germanic *bollocks*. Another word that was employed in Old English to denote the testicles was *herthan*, often used in the compound *herthan-belig*, meaning *testicle bag*, that is, the scrotum. Likewise, the Old English *sceallan*, meaning *shells*, was also used as a synonym for *testicles*, an interesting parallel to *nuts*, a testicle synonym that dates back to the mid nineteenth century. The Old English *sceallan* and the Modern English *nuts* were likely inspired not just by the resemblance in size between the human testicles and most nuts (barring the coconut), but also by the fact that nuts and testicles are both the seed-bearing organs.

In Middle English, the word *stones* became the usual name for the testicles, as evidenced by the number of phrases in which it appeared: *privy stones, precious stones, stones of gendure* (that is, stones of engendering) and *stoned at full* (a phrase meaning *possessing large testicles*). Moreover, the native English name of the salep plant, mentioned above, was *dogstones*. Back then, in the fourteenth and fifteenth centuries, the ovaries were thought to be essentially like testicles, and thus *stones* was sometimes used in reference to women. For example, an early-fifteenth-century translation of Guy de Chauliac's *Grande Chirurgie* says that "the prive stoones of wommen ben withynne." The word *genitras* was also employed in Middle English to mean *testicles*, as it was in a late-fourteenth-century account of what happened to the mythological Uranus when he was overthrown by his own son, Cronos: "His owne sone geldid him, and his genytras weren i-throwe into the see." According to the Greek myth, after these severed testicles were tossed into the sea, they grew into Aphrodite, goddess of love. Other Middle English words that denoted the testicles included *hangers, clogs, knappes, cullions* and *jewels*. The first of these, *hangers*, is employed in Thomas Malory's fifteenth-century romance, *Morte D'Arthur*, where Alisaunder learns that the wicked Morgan Le Fay intends to keep him prisoner so that she can have sex with him at will. "O Jesu defend me," replies the horrified Alisaunder, "I had liefer cut away my hangers than I would do her such pleasure." The notion of something hanging also lies behind the use of the word *clogs* to signify the testicles: a clog was a chunk of heavy wood that was tied to an animal (or person) to slow its gait. *Knappes*, on the other hand, likely arose as a variant of *knop*, which referred to various kinds of protuberances, ranging from ornamental knobs on candlesticks, to the seedcases of flowers, to the elbows and kneecaps of a person. *Cullion* derived from the Latin *culleus*, meaning *bag*, and was employed in Chaucer's *Canterbury Tales* where the Host, offended by the Pardoner's offer to sell him some holy relics and saint icons, angrily threatens him:

I wolde I hadde thy coillons in myn hond
In stide of relikes or of seintuarie.
Lat kutte hem off, I wol thee helpe hem carie;
They shul be shryned in an hogges toord!

The threat of castration also underlies the earliest recorded instance of *jewels* as a synonym for *testicles*. That usage dates back to the medieval morality play known as *Mankind*, where the protagonist strikes an allegorical enemy named New Guise with a shovel, prompting him to cry out, "Alas, my jewellys! I schall be schent of my wyff"; in Modern English the passage might be rendered as "Crap! Right in the nuts! Now I'll be a laughingstock to my wife!" The variant *family jewels* did not appear till the early twentieth century.

Unlike *hangers, knappes, clogs, cullions* and *jewels*, the word *testicle*, which also emerged in Middle English, was a learned rather than a slang or argot word. *Testicle* was formed as a diminutive of the Latin *testis*, which also denoted each of the two ovoid organs contained by the scrotum. Earlier on, the Latin *testis* had meant *witness*, as suggested by the derivatives *testify* and *testament*. The anatomical sense of this word was prompted by the notion that the testicles are a *witness* to a man's virility – in other words, they are evidence of his manliness, his machismo, his spunk, his mojo. In ancient times, the "witnessing" associations of the testicles prompted them to be employed in judicial contexts. When a man provided evidence or made a promise, he grabbed either his own or another man's testicles and didn't let go until he was done speaking, a custom described in the Book of Genesis:

> And Abraham said unto his eldest servant of his house,
> that ruled over all that he had, Put, I pray thee, thy
> hand under my thigh: And I will make thee swear by
> the Lord, the God of heaven, and the God of the earth,
> that thou shalt not take a wife unto my son of the
> daughters of the Canaanites, among whom I dwell.

Even further back, the Latin *testis* evolved from the Indo-European *trei*, meaning *three*: the semantic connection was that a witness was a third-party, someone who could testify from an unbiased perspective. Thus, the words *testicle*, *testify* and *three* are, in a sense, etymological triplets. In Early Modern English, numerous slang names for the testicles appeared, many of which were simply metaphorical extensions of older words: *bullets*, for example, was used by Shakespeare in *Henry IV Part 2* where the aptly-named Pistol tells Falstaff what he plans to do with their buxomy hostess: "I will discharge upon her, Sir John, with two bullets." Likewise, the word *baubles*, which dates back to the early fourteenth century as the name of a trinket or child's toy, was extended to the testicles in the eighteenth century. (It's curious that the testicles have been equated both with valuable jewels and with worthless baubles – clearly, one man's trash is another man's treasure.) A cluster of polysyllabic words also came to denote the testicles in the eighteenth century, including *twiddle-diddles*, *whirligigs*, *thingumbobs* and *tallywags*. The first of these, *twiddle-diddles*, seems to be a combination of *twiddle*, meaning *to twirl* as in *twiddle your thumbs*, and *diddle*, which in the eighteenth century meant *to shake*. The term *twiddle* is slightly masturbatory in connotation, implying that a bored man might just as well fondle his testicles as twiddle his thumbs. The onanistic notion of twirling is also apparent in *whirligigs*, which originally signified a child's top. As for the word *thingumbobs*, it's exceptional in being a double diminutive: it appeared in the mid eighteenth century as a diminutive of *thingum*, which in

> When I feel inclined to read poetry, I take down my dictionary. The poetry of words is quite as beautiful as the poetry of sentences.
>
> *Oliver Wendell Holmes*

turn appeared in the late seventeenth century as a diminutive of *thing*. The more recent *thingumabobs* continues this process by adding a fourth syllable, though even it is outdone by its five-syllable synonym *thingumajiggers*, a word that has also been used to signify the testicles. The origin of *tallywags* is unknown, though one might speculate that it was a fanciful word created by fusing *tail* with *wag*.

Late Modern English saw the emergence of dozens of testicle words, starting with *knackers* in the mid nineteenth century. That word probably developed as a diminutive of *knack*, which had meant *trinket* since the sixteenth century, a sense still familiar in *knick-knack*. In 1932, Ernest Hemingway introduced the word *cojones* to the English language in his rhapsody on bullfighting, *Death in the Afternoon*. Hemingway borrowed the word from Spanish, where it also meant *testicles*. The word *nuts*, as mentioned earlier, came to denote the testicles in the mid nineteenth century, and probably inspired the later extension of *conkers*, a word that originally denoted a game in which boys took turns striking chestnuts against one another till one of them broke into pieces. The name of the game, which probably arose as a corruption of *conquer*, was transferred to the chestnuts themselves, and then to the anatomical "nuts" of the men who had once competed, many years before, to see who had the mightiest conkers.

In the 1940s, testicles came to be known as *rocks*, a usage that probably developed from the earlier usage of *jewels*: the word *rock* had been used to denote a precious stone, especially a diamond, since the opening years of the twentieth century. Similarly, *agate*, the name of a semi-precious stone, was also used in the 1940s as a slang synonym for *testicle*. In the 1950s the term *eggs* came to denote the testicles, a usage paralleled by the much more recent adoption of the Spanish *huevos*, which also means *eggs*. Late-twentieth-century names for the testicles include *doodads*, *clappers* and *kanakas*. The first of these is simply a nonsense word, similar to *doohickey*, which was applied to the testicles much like the earlier *thingumbobs*. The second term is probably a metaphorical extension of the *clapper* found within a large bell, with its dangling position and swinging motion supplying the semantic connection to the testicles. The third term arose in Australian English, having been derived from the Hawaiian word *kanaka*, meaning *human*. This Hawaiian word was introduced Down Under when indentured labourers from the Pacific Islands were shipped to Australia in the nineteenth century. The word's recent shift in meaning, from *human* to *testicle*, was probably prompted by its accidental resemblance to the previously-mentioned *knackers*. In the 1960s, the novel *A Clockwork Orange* popularized the word *yarbles* as a name for the testicles. In that novel, the dialect of the wicked hooligans is called Nadsat, and author Anthony Burgess invented much of its lexis by fusing English and Russian words; *yarbles*, for example, appears to be a conflation of the Russian *yaytsa*, meaning *egg*, and the English *marble*.

Two other recent testicle names manifest a technique known as rhyming slang: *Jackson Pollocks* and *Sandra Bullocks*. Because the surnames of that abstract painter and that film star rhyme with, or at least sound like, the word *bollocks*, they have been co-opted as bawdy synonyms for *testicles*. Moreover, what often occurs with rhyming slang is that the part of the phrase that actually completes the rhyme is eventually dropped; in this case, it would mean that *Jacksons* and *Sandras* would become new names for the testicles. Finally, several testicles names have been borrowed from the kitchen. When the testicles of critters are prepared for the dinner table they are known by the generic name *animelles*. Specific kinds of cooked testicles also have unique names: those of a deer are called *doucets* (from the French *douce*, meaning *sweet*), those of a ram are called *lamb fries*, and those of a bull are called *prairie oysters*. All of those culinary names have served as humorous nicknames for human testicles, even when they are uncooked and still attached to the man in question.

When your testicles get detached, what you become depends on what you were to begin with: a chicken becomes a *capon*; an ox becomes a *steer*; a horse becomes a *gelding*; a boar becomes a *barrow*; a deer becomes a *havier*; a cat becomes a *gib*; a ram becomes a *wether*; and a man becomes a *eunuch*, or a *spado*, or – if he sings in the Roman Catholic Church – a *castrato*. Of the latter three terms, the word *spado* is the oldest, dating back to the early fifteenth century where it was adopted directly from Latin. The ultimate ancestor of the Latin *spado* was probably the Indo-European *spe*, denoting a flat piece of wood. This Indo-European source developed into the names of various implements and weapons, such as *spade*, *spatula* and *épée*, the latter being a kind of sword that one might use when turning a man into a spado or when spaying a cat. The word *eunuch* also dates back to the early fifteenth century. That word derives, via Latin, from the Greek *eunouchos*, meaning *castrated man*, which was created as a compound from *eune*, meaning *bed*, and *echein*, meaning *to keep*. Eunuchs, therefore, are literally *bed keepers*, an etymology that reflects their original function. In Middle Eastern courts they guarded the bedchamber of the sultan's wife (or wives), the assumption being that a man without testicles would not be tempted by the lovely ladies cavorting around him.

In Europe, pre-pubescent boys had their testicles removed, or at least had their spermatic cords severed, for a very different reason. The goal was to produce a *castrato*, a soloist whose voice had the pitch of a woman and the timbre and power of a man. Such voices were prized by the Roman Catholic church from the late sixteenth century onwards, reaching a peak in the eighteenth century when up to four thousand boys were put to the knife each year. The practice persisted well into the nineteenth century, with the last Vatican-sponsored castrato dying in 1922 at the age of sixty-four. In origin, the words *castrato* and *castrate* derive from the Latin *castrare*, which not only meant *to cut off the testicles* but also *to prune*. Earlier on, that Latin source derived from the Indo-European *kes*, meaning *to cut*, which also developed into the word *castle*, a fortified place which is cut off from the surrounding area. Likewise, the word *chastity* also developed from the same Indo-European source, the notion being that chastity is the condition of cutting yourself off from sin and desire.

Nowadays, castration is performed only as a last resort treatment for testicular cancer, a procedure that the medical community refers to as an *orchidectomy*. Earlier centuries used other names to describe the same operation, the earliest being *geld*, which appeared in the early fourteenth century. The word is still current, but since the seventeenth century its application has primarily been toward animals with four legs rather than two. In the late thirteenth century, the word *lib* also emerged with the sense *to castrate*. This word appears to be related to the word *left* in that both derived from a Germanic source that meant *weak*. Castration results in diminished muscular development and the left hand is, for most people, weaker than the right hand. In the early seventeenth century, *lib* was corrupted in pronunciation and spelling to the verb *glib*, which is the word Antigonus uses in Shakespeare's *The Winter's Tale* when he cries, "I would rather glib myselfe, than they should not produce faire issue." In other words, he would rather cut off his balls than have his daughters give birth to bastards. Shakespeare also uses *glib* in reference to characters who seem insincere and flattering; this *glib*, however, derives from a different source, one that meant *slippery*. Shakespeare could also have made use of a third unrelated *glib*: since the early sixteenth century, that word had denoted an Irish hair style – namely, a thick mat of hair that hung over the face. The earliest references to this *glib* are in statutes forbidding the Irish to wear their hair in this manner, the fear being that the glib prevented English authorities from telling one peasant from another.

Near the beginning of the seventeenth century, three new castration words appeared: *unstone, eviration* and *emasculate*. The first of these simply means to remove the "stones" or testicles of a man or beast. (A learned counterpart to the folksy *unstone* appeared in the late nineteenth century with the invention of

> England and America are two countries separated by the same language.
> *George Bernard Shaw*

the Latinate *extesticulate*.) As for the word *eviration*, it was formed from the Latin prefix *ex* and the noun *vir*, meaning *man*, and thus literally means *to take the man out*. The word usually denotes castration, but can also be used more loosely to signify other ways by which manhood can be lost. For instance, if a man is forced to dress as a woman, he is *evirated*. Similarly, the word *emasculate* literally means *to take the male out*. It's curious that these two words – *evirate* and *emasculate* – are parallel in formation, in meaning, and in date of origin, and yet the latter word has far surpassed the former one in use.

In the middle of the seventeenth century, the word *swig* came to denote a particular method of castrating an animal: the testicles were tightly looped round with a string, presumably until the lack of blood supply caused them to grow numb, at which point the snipping began. This *swig* is probably not related to the *swig* that means *to take a drink*, but it likely is connected to *swag*, as in swag lamp, a lighting fixture with a kind of looping cable. In the mid nineteenth century, the technique of attaching a string to the soon-to-be-lopped-off testicles came to be known as *twitching*, a usage prompted by the sudden tug or twitch that would pull the cord tight. In contrast with the graphic image evoked by the word *twitching* are two abstract euphemisms for castration that appeared in the early twentieth century, *doctor* and *de-sex*. Writing in 1902, one feline specialist demurely advised her readers "to have your male cat doctored when he arrives at years of discretion," a phrasing which makes Snowball seem more like a wise grandfather than a randy house pet.

♒

Within the testicles, sperm is produced, a substance whose name derives from the Greek *sperma*, meaning *seed*, which in turn developed from the Greek verb *speirein*, meaning *to sow*. The word *diaspora*, which denotes the scattering of a people who have been forced to leave their homeland, also derives from this Greek word. Further back, the Greek *speirein* evolved from the Indo-European *sper*, meaning *to strew*, a sense which is clearly evident in the derivatives *spray*, *spread*, *sprawl* and *spritz*. The botanical word *spore* also comes from this Indo-European source, and it in turn gave rise to the word *sporadic*, literally meaning dispersed like spores. In English, the word *sperm* dates back to the late fourteenth century; it was used, for example, by a medieval herbalist who prescribed a cure for men who were "polluted" by wet dreams: "Who-so is ofte in slepe polute thorw his sperme, ete he this herbe." Of course when a fourteenth-century herbalist was referring to sperm, he wasn't actually thinking of the two hundred million sperm – or rather sperms – that are rocketed through the urethra when a man ejaculates. Sperm cells are among the smallest cells in the human body, and the microscope wasn't invented until the early seventeenth century. Thus, early instances of the word *sperm* are synonymous with the word *semen*, the fluid which carries the sperm. In English, the word *semen* is about as old as *sperm*; it's used, for example, in a late-fourteenth-century work possessing the rather vague title of *On the Properties of Things*, where the author advises that one of the properties of lettuce is that it "multiplieth milk in wommen and semen in men." English adopted the word *semen* directly from Latin, and that Latin word is also the source of the word *seminary*, an institution for training priests. While you might suppose that seminaries acquired their name from the nocturnal activities of the young men cloistered within their walls, the word *seminary* actually arose from a horticultural context. In the mid fifteenth century, a seminary was a plot of ground where seedlings were sown and grown until they were fit to be transplanted; by the late sixteenth century, the word had developed a figurative sense, signifying an institution where young scholars were reared into the priesthood. Further back, the Latin *semen* evolved from an Indo-European source, *se*, meaning *to sow*, which also developed into the words *sow* and *season*, the latter word originally denoting the part of the year when sowing took place. The word *seed* also derives from this same Indo-European source, and it too has been used since the thirteenth century to denote the seminal fluid. Surprisingly, the word *virus* was also used in Middle English to denote semen. When that word was adopted from Latin, where it denoted any slimy liquid, it was used to signify various substances, ranging from "the humour that cometh out of mankynde" – that is, semen – to the venom discharged by an asp or viper. The current use of *virus* as a generic name for infectious organisms did not begin to emerge until the early eighteenth century.

In Early Modern English, three words that denoted courage all developed a sub sense of *semen*. The first of these was *spirit*, which in the thirteenth century referred to a non-physical entity such as the Holy Ghost, and then came, in the sixteenth century, to denote courageous resolve, as in the phrase "That's the spirit!" Shortly after, *spirit* was equated with semen thanks to the notion that semen was the physical essence of manliness and therefore of manly courage. Shakespeare puns on the various senses of *spirit* in one of his sonnets, where the speaker bitterly exclaims that lust is nothing but an "expense of spirit in a waste of shame." (In this passage, there is also a pun on *waste*, which suggests both something that has been squandered and also the waist or genitals of his paramour.) For similar reasons, in the late eighteenth century, semen came to be described as *mettle*, a word that had already meant *courage* for the previous two hundred years. Even earlier, *mettle* arose as a variant of *metal*, the notion being that courage and resolve make a person strong just as metal can reinforce a shield or a structure. The same metaphor is implicit when we say, "She steeled herself for the bad news." This *semen* sense of *mettle* is also evident in the eighteenth-century idiom *to fetch mettle*, which meant *to masturbate*. The third word that denoted both courage and semen is *spunk*; when this word first appeared in the sixteenth century, it meant *spark*, a sense that can be clearly seen in a 1669 religious treatise called *The Fullfilling of the Scripture*: "That little spunk now under ashes must assuredly revive and blow up to a flame." By the mid eighteenth century, *spunk* had come to denote one's inner spark, that is, one's courage, and by the late nineteenth century its sense had extended further to *semen*.

In Late Modern English, the word *jism* was also used to mean both *courage* and *semen*, but the two senses emerged so close to one another that it's difficult to tell which one actually came first. The earlier history of the word, too, is unclear. Some etymologists have speculated that *jism* derives from a West African source such as the Kikongo word *dinza*, meaning *life-force*. Equally unclear is whether *jism* is, as some etymologists have claimed, the source of the word *jazz*, first recorded in 1913 with the sense of *spirit* or *energy*, and recorded three years later, in 1916, with its current musical sense. One year later, in 1917, *jazz* is also recorded with the meaning *nonsense talk*, and in 1918 with the meaning *to copulate*. All of these usages occur too near each other in time to establish the actual sequence of sense development, which makes it difficult to definitively trace *jazz* back to *jism*. Nonetheless, writing in the magazine *Etude* in 1924, Harry Clay Smith claimed that "If the truth were known about the origin of the word *jazz* it would never be mentioned in polite company."

The last half of the twentieth century saw the appearance of dozens of semen synonyms, most of them trying hard to be distasteful, such as *cock snot*, *man chowder* and *baby gravy*. Some show the influence of fast-food culture: *McSpunk*. Others are instances of rhyming slang: *Thelonius Monk* (appropriately, a jazz pianist). Some, like *wad*, are merely semantic extensions of older words, while others are new inventions based on already existing words: *spooge* and *splooge*, for example, seem to have been inspired by *spew*, a word that has been used since the 1990s to denote the ejaculation of semen. *Spew* might seem like an especially vulgar way of describing the expulsion of semen, but it's not that different from several much older idioms that also signified ejaculation: for example, the fifteenth-century's *pissing tarse* or the sixteenth-century's *spitting white*. Other words and phrases that were once used to denote ejaculation include the Middle English *outpassing* and *shedding nature*, both of which are fairly neutral in connotation. Other Middle English terms were more negative, such as the verb *miswaste* or the noun *pollution*, both of which denoted ejaculations that resulted either from masturbation or nocturnal emission. For example, one early-fifteenth-century text called *Fifty Heresies and Errors of Friars* said that it was worse to "mysspende" God's word than to "myswaste mannys seed." Around the same time, the author of *Form of Confession* wrote, "I crie God Merci in polucions of niht or tymes slepyng." A modern equivalent of "polucions of night" is *nocturnal emission*, first recorded in 1821, followed a few decades later by both the medical term *spermatorrhea* and the vernacular idiom *wet dream*.

As for the word *ejaculation* itself, it dates back to the late sixteenth century, and the root from which it derives is the Latin *jacere*, meaning *to throw*. The Latin *jacere* is closely related to *jaculum*, which is what the ancient Romans called a javelin, and it also evolved into numerous Modern English words, such as *subject* (meaning *to throw under*), *interject* (meaning *to throw between*), and *jettison* (which originally denoted the act of throwing goods overboard in order to save a sinking ship). In the early seventeenth century, the word *ejaculation* also came to denote a sudden exclamation of joy or anger, a usage that gradually died out in the twentieth century, as the word's sexual sense came to dominate. The *exclamation* sense of the word can be seen in numerous nineteenth-century novels, such as Charles Dickens' *Oliver Twist*, where the narrator reports that "The cook and housemaid simultaneously ejaculated" or Charles Reade's *The Cloister and the Hearth*, where we learn that "Gerard's eloquence was confined to ejaculating and gazing," or George Meredith's *Diana of the Crossways*, where "Sir Lukin ejaculated on the merits of Diana Warwick." Around 1910, the phrase *premature ejaculation* was invented to denote seminal discharge that occurs prior to sexual intercourse, a phrase that eventually replaced the earlier *ejaculatio praecox*, meaning *precocious ejaculation*. Further back, *praecox* developed from the Latin prefix *prae*, meaning *before*, and the verb *coquere*, meaning *to cook*. In Latin, the word *praecox* was originally used to denote fruit that ripened before other fruits – that is, one that was metaphorically "cooked" by the sun sooner than others. One fruit that tended to ripen early was the apricot, whose name derives – via a circuitous route through Greek, Arabic and Spanish – from the Latin *praecox*. Slang equivalents for premature ejaculation include *rabbit*, *to go off half-cocked* and *preemie*, the latter of which has also been used since the 1920s to denote premature babies. At one time, prostitutes also used *78* to denote a premature ejaculator, an allusion to the old gramophone records that spun at 78 revolutions per minute.

Chapter Nine

DOWN IN
THE VALLEY

Words for the Vagina,
the Clitoris, et alia

*M*OST WORDS PERTAINING TO female genitalia lack specificity. The word *cunt*, for example, doesn't denote just the labia or the vulva or the vagina, but rather gestures vaguely to the whole anatomical ensemble. The same is true of *snatch*, *twat*, *quim* and dozens of other terms that have been employed over the centuries to denote a woman's genital area. Even words that originally might have been more specific – such as the hirsute *beaver* or the vulvacious *slot* – tend to become generalized in their later application. Accordingly, this chapter begins by focusing on the many words that have a broad meaning of a woman's private parts, and then moves on to terms – such as *vagina*, *labia* and *clitoris* – that are anatomically more specific.

At present, there are only three words that are considered so obscene that they are sometimes alluded to only by their first letter: the *F-word*, the *C-word* and the *N-word*, standing respectively for *fuck*, *cunt* and *nigger*. The recent introduction of *nigger* to this list – evidenced by the O.J. Simpson trial, where television reporters had to devise a way of referring to Mark Fuhrman's racist epithets – epitomizes a late-twentieth-century taboo, one that demonizes words that pejoratively denote race or ethnicity. In turn, the rise of this *N-word* taboo reflects a shift in social ideology that in North America was triggered with the civil rights movement of the 1960s, though of course it can be traced back much further in history, even to the American Civil War. This new ideology assumes that a just and harmonious society is one that embraces, rather than denigrates, cultural and ethnic diversity; words and actions that subvert this ideology are therefore considered taboo, or even criminal. In contrast, a few decades ago, the word *nigger* had already developed a slightly negative connotation, but the people who used it in casual conversations or in letters to the editor were not censured. Even earlier, *nigger* was considered an essentially neutral or merely descriptive term, as in Mark Twain's 1885 novel *Huckleberry Finn* where Huck tells Tom what he's planning: "There's one more thing – a thing that nobody don't know but me. And that is, there's a nigger here that I'm a-trying to steal out of slavery, and his name is Jim."

Twat-scowerer: an eighteenth-century name for a surgeon.

With *cunt*, its current *verboten* status results from the fusion of two ideologies, one old-fashioned and one new-fangled. The old-fashioned ideology proscribes the word *cunt* because it denotes a part of the female body that has traditionally been considered shameful or menacing. Etymologically, this can be seen with the word *pudendum*, which derives from the Latin verb *pudere*, meaning *to cause shame,* and with *snatch,* which implies that a woman's genitals will grab hold of a man and devour him. The second and new-fangled ideology is the recent rejection of the long-standing chauvinist habit of construing women as sex objects; from this politically-correct perspective, there is nothing shameful about the female cunt, but there is something very wrong with reducing a woman to her sex organs. To put it another way, calling a woman a *cunt* is far more taboo than talking about her cunt.

Things were not always this way with the word *cunt.* Up until the fifteenth century or so, *cunt* appears not to have been a taboo word. In fact, for many centuries, religion, rather than sex, was the main source of profanities and oaths, such as *splood* and *marry* which were contractions of *God's blood* and *Virgin Mary.* The neutral status of *cunt* can be gauged by the fact that both London and Oxford, in the thirteenth century, had a street called *Gropecuntlane,* probably named in recognition of the brothels located there. Church records dating back to the eleventh century also reveal surnames that incorporate the word *cunt* such as *Bele Wydecunte, Godwin Clawecunte* and *Robert Clevecunt.* Presumably, these individuals – or their ancestors – were named after some anatomical abnormality or behavioural tendency. By the fourteenth century, however, the word *cunt* seems to have shifted toward the taboo. Chaucer, for example, does use that word but he consistently spells it *queynte.* "Ye shul have queynte right ynogh" is what the Wife of Bath tells one of her husbands, meaning that he doesn't need to begrudge her having sex with other men so long as he still gets his fill. Chaucer's spelling of the word could be an attempt to get some distance from its original form, which might have become too naughty even for his earthy sensibilities. Alternatively, the spelling might reflect his notion that *cunt* was derived from *quaint*, a word that could then mean, among other things, *skillfully designed* or *cunning*. Over time, *cunt* acquired even more ribald connotations, so that by the end of the sixteenth century, Shakespeare could have Hamlet make a bawdy pun on the first syllable of the word *country*:

Hamlet:	Lady, shall I lye in your lap?
Ophelia:	No, my lord.
Hamlet:	I meane, my head upon your lap?
Ophelia:	Ay, my lord.
Hamlet:	Do you thinke I meant country matters?
Ophelia:	I thinke nothing, my lord.
Hamlet:	That's a faire thought to lie between maids' legs.

A few years later, John Donne made a similar bawdy pun in his love poem "The Good-Morrow," where the speaker muses on how he and his beloved once "suck'd on country pleasures." Near the end of the seventeenth century, the word *cunt* was firmly ensconced in obscenity, as suggested by the fact that it was frequently used by John Wilmot, the Second Earl of Rochester, whose poems were considered too lewd for publication during his lifetime. He uses the word *cunt*, for example, in a poem called "The Imperfect Enjoyment," in which the speaker rails against his cantankerous penis:

Worst part of me, and henceforth hated most,
Through all the town a common fucking-post,
On whom each whore relieves her tingling cunt
As hogs do rub themselves on gates and grunt.

By the late eighteenth century, the word *cunt* was sufficiently shocking that it appeared in Francis Grose's *Dictionary of the Vulgar Tongue* only as *c__t*, which he noted was a "nasty name for a nasty thing." When the word needed to be alluded to elsewhere in his dictionary, he consistently referred to it as *the monosyllable*, a rather elliptical euphemism. Grose also reported that some of his contemporaries were even more squeamish about the word, going so far as to alter the word *constable* to *thingstable* in order to avoid, as he put it, "the pronunciation of the first syllable in the title of that officer, which in sound has some similarity to an indecent monosyllable." We, like Grose, might consider this avoidance of a harmless syllable "a ludicrous affectation of delicacy," and might dismiss it as an eccentricity of a bygone age. However, even today most contemporary versions of the Bible use the term *acacia wood* at Exodus 25:5 and thus avoid the *shittim wood* that appears in the King James version. Similarly, I know of at least one person who is uncomfortable referring to shitake mushrooms, and I recall a producer at CBC radio stressing that the name of the seventh planet should be pronounced *ura-nus* not *ur-anus*. Modern dictionaries, too, have long been reluctant to include the word *cunt* in their pages: the *Oxford English Dictionary* did not include the word until it published a supplement in 1972, though it had included *prick* and *cock* in the twelve-volume edition published in 1933.

The word *cunt* has similar-sounding counterparts in other European languages, including the French *con*, the Spanish *coño* and the German *Kunte*. Some etymologists have suggested that *cunt*, like its French and Spanish equivalents, derives from the Latin *cunnus*, which denoted the vaginal region. In turn, the Latin *cunnus* might have developed from the Latin *cuneus*, meaning *wedge*, from a supposed resemblance in shape. Alternatively, *cunnus* might have developed from the Greek *konnus*, meaning *beard*. On the other hand, *cunnus* might have developed from the Greek *kusos*, which in turn evolved from the Sanskrit *cushi*, meaning *ditch*. It's even possible that *cunnus* might have developed from the Indo-European *skeu*, meaning *to conceal*. Germanic sources of *cunt* have also been suggested, such as the Old English *cynd*, which meant numerous things, ranging from *origin* to *birth* to *race*. It's plausible, too, that *cunt* is related to the word *quaint*, as implied by Chaucer's spelling of the word; as mentioned previously, *quaint* was used in the thirteenth century to mean *skillfully designed*, and in origin *quaint* developed from the Latin *cognitum*, meaning *known*. Even the Arabic *khunt*, meaning *femininity*, has been put forth as a source for *cunt*, though it's hard to imagine why thirteenth-century anglophones would turn to such an exotic source in order to name such a familiar thing. In short, no one really knows the ulterior origin of *cunt*.

In contrast, the more recent developments of *cunt* are easily traced. For example, the word was first used to denote a vile person, whether female or male, around 1860, which is about the same time that *cunt-struck* appeared, applied to a man who is overwhelmed by his horniness for a woman. Also in the 1860s, *cunt-sucker* was invented, denoting someone who performs cunnilingus, followed in 1916 by the synonymous *cunt-lapper*. In the same year, another compound, *cunt-eyed,* is first recorded, denoting someone who tended to squint. In the late 1950s, *cunt hair* emerged as an informal unit of measurement: a military pilot might drop a bomb within a cunt hair of the target. Around 1967, mustaches were sometimes vulgarly called *cunt ticklers,* and although none of my slang dictionaries record this usage, I recall the terms *cunt-faced* and *cunted* being used in the 1980s to mean *exceedingly drunk*.

Chaucer's Wife of Bath twice refers to her *queynte*, but she also employs another word to denote her genitals. "In wyfhod," she says, "I wol use myn instrument / As frely as my Makere hath it sent." In other words, in marriage she will use her vagina as freely as God gave it to her. Elsewhere, she also refers to her pudendum as her *bel chose*, a French euphemism meaning *beautiful thing*, and in fact she uses the word *thing* itself to refer both to her own, and her husband's, genitals. This anatomical sense of *thing* persisted for many centuries. For example, in *Othello*, Emilia tells her husband, Iago, "I have a thing for you," meaning the handkerchief she has taken from Desdemona. Iago, however, pretends to misunderstand his wife and replies, "A thing for me? It is a common thing," implying that Emilia has been so unfaithful and promiscuous that her private parts have become public property. She has become a *common woman*, a phrase that has meant *harlot* since the fourteenth century. The Wife of Bath could also have used the word *tail* to allude to her private parts, since the pudendum sense of that word dates back to the mid fourteenth century, and has survived to the present-day. Shakespeare, again, plays on this bawdy sense of *tail* in *The Taming of the Shrew* where Petruchio willfully misunderstands Kate, and then feigns outrage that she has apparently invited him to put "my tongue in your taile."

In Early Modern English a number of slang synonyms for *cunt* emerged, one of the strangest of which was *et cetera*, a Latin phrase that literally means *and the others*. The best known instance of this use of *et cetera* occurs in the First Quarto version of Shakespeare's *Romeo and Juliet*, where Mercutio says, in reference to the sweetheart Romeo had before he met Juliet, "O that she were / An open *et caetera*, thou a pop'rin peare!" Some twentieth-century editors of that play have assumed that *et caetera* – which is merely a variant spelling of *et cetera* – was inserted into the line by a printer who feared that the original word was too vulgar to be printed. The original word, according to those editors, was *arse*, and thus many modern editions of the play amend the line to "O that she were / An open arse, and thou a pop'rin peare!" However, it seems more likely that *et cetera* was, in fact, what Shakespeare wrote, and that when Mercutio employs that Latin phrase he is mocking those who used it as a genuine euphemism. Randle Cotgrave, for example, uses it as a euphemism in his 1611 bilingual dictionary, where he defines the French word *con*, which means *cunt*, as "a womans &c." (The *&c* was a conventional abbreviation for *et cetera*.) Further,

Syphilis: originally the title of a Latin poem published in 1530, which recounted the story of the first sufferer of venereal disease, a shepherd named Syphilis.

in a seventeenth-century poem that was actually entitled "Et Caetera," the speaker says "On Corinna's Breast I panting lay, / My right Hand playing with Et Caetera."

Only a few lines before the passage from *Romeo and Juliet* just mentioned, Mercutio makes another lewd joke when he suggests that the lovesick Romeo will

> sit under a medlar tree,
> And wish his mistress were that kind of fruit
> As maids call medlars, when they laugh alone.

The joke here is that *medlar*, the name of a fruit, was used in the sixteenth century as a slang synonym for *vagina*. The usage was probably prompted by the fact that the medlar has a deep depression at its top resembling the vaginal cleft. That morphological feature is probably also why the original English name of the fruit, dating back to the eleventh century, was *open-arse*. The vaginal sense of *medlar*, however, might also have been facilitated by the fact that the unrelated but similar-sounding verb *meddle* had been used since the fourteenth century to mean *to copulate*. Thus, a person who *meddled* was a *meddler*, a homonym for *medlar*.

From the late sixteenth century, the word *scut* was also used to denote a woman's genital area. That word originated in the sixteenth century as the name of a short tail, the kind found on a rabbit or deer, unlike the long tail found on cows or most dogs. Also in the late sixteenth century, Shakespeare employed a variety of words to metaphorically, and often humorously, evoke what his character Posthumus, in *Cymbeline*, calls the "dearest bodily part." For example, in one of Shakespeare's sonnets, the speaker addresses his beloved and says that his flesh is content "to stand in thy affaires, fall by thy side"; the flesh, of course, is his penis, which will first "stand" and then "fall" after occupying the "affaires," or vagina, of his mistress. In *Othello*, the jealous protagonist uses the word *corner* to imply that his wife's privates are a place where many men have lurked. "I had rather be a Toad," Othello says, "Than keep a corner in the thing I love for others' uses." In *The Merry Wives of Windsor*, the grammatical term *case* is used to suggest a woman's genitals. *Case* denotes grammatical categories such as subjects and objects, but it can also refer to a vessel or sheath, such as the vagina. Moreover, it's not just any case, but the genitive case, the word *genitive* denoting both the possessive case in Latin, and also implying the reproductive word *generative*. One of the characters then recites the three genitive forms of a Latin pronoun, *horum*, *harum*, *horum*, which another character mistakes for the word *whore*. The ribald and complex punning is dizzying. The word *case* was also used in the sixteenth century as a name for a brothel. This sense of *case* might have been inspired by the *vagina* sense of the word, or it might have arisen as a corruption of the Spanish *casa*, meaning *house*.

In the early seventeenth century, *mons veneris* was also created as a name for a woman's genital area, though strictly speaking it refers to the slight prominence located over the pubis bone or, as *Blancard's Physical Dictionary* put it in 1693, "the upper part of a Womans Secrets, something higher than the rest." The phrase *mons veneris* is Latin, and literally means *mountain of Venus*, so-named in reference to the Roman goddess of love. Other English words that have been derived from the Latin *Venus* include *venereal* and *venerate*; also closely related is *venom*, which developed from the Latin *venenum*, meaning *love potion*. In origin, this cluster of words developed through the Italic branch from the Indo-European *wen*, meaning *to desire*. However, the Indo-European *wen* could also mean *to strive for*, and it was this sense of the word that developed into the Latin *venari*, meaning *to hunt*, from whence English developed *venison*, meaning *deer meat*. In the Germanic branch of Indo-European, the word *wen* evolved into the words *wish* (to desire), *win* (to achieve what you desire), and *winsome* (to possess the ability to inspire desire).

Around the same time that scholars invented the term *mons veneris*, the word *lap* also developed a pudendum sense, as seen in a 1615 anatomical treatise called *Microcosmographia*, where the author explains that "the clitoris is a small body, not continuated at all with the bladder, but placed in the height of the lap." A few decades later, another term arose that still seems strikingly contemporary, even though it has been in use for more than 350 years: *slit*. This word was no doubt extended to the pudendum because of a perceived resemblance, but its usage might also have been prompted by the fact that *slit*, when used as a verb, implies a violent and bloody action. Throats, for example, get slit. This savage undertone is evident in a bawdy poem published in 1648 by Robert Herrick, a former chaplain. In that poem, a husband threatens to slit his wife's nose as punishment for her infidelity, to which his wife replies,

> Stability in language is synonymous with rigor mortis.
> *Ernest Weekley*

> Good sir, make no more cuts i' th' outward skin,
> One slit's enough to let adultery in.

Slit was only the first of many words and phrases to equate the female pudendum with a wound. Others include *everlasting wound* and *gash*, which appeared in the mid nineteenth century, and *slash*, *axe wound*, *divine scar* and *cat with its throat cut*, which are twentieth-century innovations. In the early twentieth century, *gash* also came to be used as a pejorative collective noun for women. Some psychologists have suggested that this wound motif reflects a deep-seated fear of castration. When a young boy first glimpses the female genitalia – for instance, while watching his parents bathe his baby sister – the lack of penis and scrotum seems, in his mind, to suggest that those appendages have been snipped off. The fear and perhaps revulsion inspired by this notion manifests itself linguistically in the "wound words" that the boy later applies to the female genitals – or at least so says Freud.

These wound words may also provide a clue as to the origin of the word *twat*, which appeared in the mid seventeenth century. Etymologists have long been stumped as to where that word came from, but one possibility is that it derives from the Old English *thwitan*, meaning *to cut off*, the phallocentric notion being that the female genitals are an amputated version of the male genitals. If so, then *twat* is related to *thwaite*, which denotes an area of land where the trees have been cut down and cleared away. Although *thwaite*, as a noun, is verging on obsolescence, it is still familiar as a surname or as part of various surnames, including *Braithwaite* and *Applethwaite*, which might be loosely rendered as *broad twat* and *apple twat*.

In North America, *twat* is pronounced as if it rhymes with *lot*, whereas in Britain a pronunciation that rhymes with *cat* is not uncommon. This pronunciation can be seen in a mid-nineteenth-century poem by Robert Browning called "Pippa's Passes" where he rhymes "owls and bats" with "cowls and twats." Incidentally, Browning's strange juxtaposition of *cowls* with *twats* is due to his mistaken belief that a *twat* was a kind of headdress worn by nuns. His error probably resulted from his misreading a bawdy seventeenth-century ditty called "Vanity of Vanities," in which this passage appears:

> They talked of his having a Cardinal's Hat,
> They'd send him as soon an Old Nun's Twat.

The passage is, of course, intended as an insult, similar to someone nowadays saying, "He asked me to lend him twenty bucks, but I'd rather give him a kick in the arse." Browning, however, naively assumed that the *twat* of a nun is like the hat of a Cardinal. In England, the word *twat* has also been used since the 1920s to denote an annoying person, much as *cunt* or *dick* are sometimes used. This sense of *twat* quickly inspired a mollified form of the word, *twit*, which is not considered vulgar at all. As for *twit-twat*, an alternative name for the common house sparrow, that compound is not likely related to any of these *twat*s or *twit*s. Instead, *twit-twat* is a shortened form of *twittle-twattle*, which arose as a variant of *tittle-tattle*, which arose as a reduplicated form of *tattle*, meaning *to chatter*.

Like *twat*, the word *merkin* was also used in the seventeenth century to signify the female pudendum. However, this sense of *merkin* was soon overshadowed by an earlier and alternative meaning: since the early seventeenth century, *merkin* had denoted a kind of pubic wig or genital toupée. The need for such an accoutrement was prompted by syphilis. One of the symptoms of that venereal disease is hair loss, not just on top, but down below, too. Originally, merkins seem to have been sported only by women. In 1671, for instance, Stephen Skinner defined *merkin* in his *Etymologicon Linguae Anglicanae* as "pubes mulieris," Latin for "pubic hair of women." Likewise, a century later, Francis Grose included this definition in his *Dictionary of the Vulgar Tongue*: "Merkin, counterfeit hair for women's privy parts." Later on, the term came to denote pubic wigs for both sexes. Nowadays, *merkin* remains a word on the fringe of familiarity. It appears, for instance, as the first name of the American President in Stanley Kubrick's 1964 satirical film *Dr. Strangelove*. The bawdy surname of that President – *Muffley* – makes it clear that Kubrick was aware of the *pubic wig* sense of *merkin*. (*Merkin* is also used as a person's name in a 1962 Superman comic, where the Man of Steel tries to convince Lois Lane that her name is really Myrtle Merkin.) Still more recently, *merkin* has been proposed as a lesbian counterpart to the gay term *beard*; that is, just as a gay man pretending to have female partner is said to have a *beard*, so a lesbian pretending to have a male partner is said to have a *merkin*. In origin, the word *merkin* perhaps arose as a variant of *malkin*, a word that dates back to the thirteenth century, where it was used as a personal name for lower-class women; one medieval source implies that it's a pet form of *Matilda*. The name *Malkin* also became a common name for cats, especially in the form *Grimalkin*, meaning *grey cat.* That form of the word is still familiar, thanks to *Macbeth*, where one of the three weird sisters cries out to an unseen feline spirit, "I come, Grimalkin!"

Near the beginning of the eighteenth century, three more pudendum words appeared: *muff, tuzzy muzzy* and *quim.* The first of these words, *muff,* originally denoted a kind of fur cylinder into which one shoved one's hands for warmth. Although that garment *muff* is closely related to the pudendum *muff,* the immediate source of the latter was probably the word *muffler,* the name of a scarf worn by women in the sixteenth century. The function of that scarf – to conceal and protect – was probably seen as analogous to the function of a woman's pubic hair, and thus the sartorial *muffler* inspired the anatomical *muff.* Earlier on, *muffler* – both the garment and the automobile part – developed from the verb *muffle,* meaning *to wrap up,* which in turn might have evolved from the medieval Latin *muffula,* meaning *thick glove.* In turn, *muffula* might have developed from *mufro,* a Vulgar Latin name for a species of sheep, the kind of beast whose skin or wool was often turned into gloves. Related to *muff* and *muffler* is *muffin,* which arose in the early eighteenth century as the name of a bakery roll whose softness and shape resembled that of a muff (the garment muff).

As for *tuzzy muzzy,* that term came to denote a woman's genitals in the early eighteenth century. Much earlier, back in the mid fifteenth century, it denoted a bouquet of flowers. Such bouquets were also known as *nosegays* because their fragrance was pleasing – that is, they made the nose gay – and in fact this aromatic aspect is likely why the word *tuzzy muzzy* was extended to a woman's private parts, although the original application might have been ironic. Also in the early eighteenth century, the word *quim* arose, with the first recorded instance appearing in a ballad called "Harlot Un-Mask'd:"

Tho' her Hands they are red, and her Bubbies are coarse,
Her Quim, for all that, may be never the worse.

In the early nineteenth century, the Congressional representative for that region, Felix Walker, made a long and irrelevant speech, which he later defended by saying that he was only "talking for Buncombe." Before long, people were equating *Buncombe* – or *bunkum* – with empty words.

In his *Dictionary of the Vulgar Tongue*, Francis Grose records numerous names for the female pudendum that were current in the late eighteenth century. Among the most popular was *commodity*, a word that construes a woman's genitalia as a commercial product, something that can be bought and sold on the street or in a brothel. Other pudendum words collected by Grose also have mercantile associations, such as *ware* and *money*, the latter of which, he says, tended to be used by adults speaking to young girls: "Take care, miss, or you will shew your money." The phrase *Eve's custom house* also denoted a woman's private parts and it too implies a commercial transaction: custom houses were offices where duties were levied against products that were being imported or exported. Anthropomorphic names for a woman's genitalia were also common in the late eighteenth century: *Miss Laycock* (a bawdy compound of *lay* and *cock*), *Brown Madam* (an allusion, perhaps, to dark-coloured pubic hair), and *mother of all Saints* (since saints, like all humans, proceed from the womb). The personal name *Madge* was also extended to the pudendum, perhaps because it sounds like the first syllable of *vagina*. (Likewise, *vag* or *vadge* are currently common slang names for the vagina.) Alternatively, *madge* might have been applied to the female pudendum because barn owls were sometimes called *madges* or *madge howletts*: to an eighteenth-century wit, the connection would have been that pudendums are like owls because they only come out at night.

Another animal name that was extended to the pudendum was *bun*, short for *bunny*, parallel to the later terms *pussy* and *beaver*. Also current in the late eighteenth century were the terms *cock alley* and *doodle sack*, both of which construe a woman's genitals as a kind of penis receptacle. That same notion might also lie behind *gig*: that word denoted, among other things, a hole in the ground into which firebrands were placed in order to dry flax. Several late-eighteenth-century terms were also invented as puns or witticisms. *The miraculous pitcher*, for example, was bestowed on the vagina because, as Grose said, "it holds water with the mouth downwards." Grose also noted that the phrase *old hat* was applied to the pudendum because a hat, like a woman's private parts, "is frequently felt." (In those days, men's formal hats were commonly made from felt.) The present-day *old hat* – the one meaning *hackneyed* – developed in the early twentieth century independent of the earlier bawdy usage.

Perhaps the strangest late-eighteenth-century pudendum synonym that arose as a witticism was *Buckinger's boot*. This term was inspired by Matthew Buckinger, who in 1674 was born without hands, legs or feet; despite this handicap, he became an accomplished juggler and musician, and was thereby able to support himself. Because Buckinger lacked feet, the only limb where he could don a boot was his penis, and the only thing that donned his penis was his wife's vagina – thus, *Buckinger's boot* became synonymous with *vagina*. From our perspective, the humour seems cruel, but in the eighteenth century mocking the deformed was considered good fun. For example, in an elegy written to commemorate the death of "the little man," the poet James Caulfield made numerous jokes, saying that Buckinger was not "close-fisted," that he "never made one false step," and that "he us'd to pray, his Widow knows, / As often as he Fingers had and Toes."

Several other pudendum words from the late eighteenth century are alike in that they construe a woman's genitals as something dangerous. This is self-evident with terms such as *man trap* and *bottomless pit*, but it also underlies slang names such as *dumb glutton* and *bite*, both of which seem to embody the fear that a woman's genitals will devour a man's penis. (The word *bite*, in the eighteenth century, could also denote a cheat or a swindler, a sense that might have reinforced the perceived menace of the female pudendum.) Grose also mentions that *bumbo* denoted the female pudendum. While that word might simply have arisen as a variation on *bum*, it might also be connected to the *bumbo* that denoted an alligator, a sense that appears to have arisen in the West Indies. If so, then *bumbo* also figures the pudendum as a devouring menace.

The slang names mentioned in the previous paragraph are linguistic manifestations of the *vagina dentata*, meaning *toothed vagina*, a neurotic fantasy that was first identified by the psychoanalyst Otto Rank in his 1924 book *The Trauma of Birth*. Rank proposed that many men fear the vagina. They feel inexorably drawn to it, like a siren of Greek mythology, and yet they leave the vagina depleted of their semen, as if a vampire or lamia has sucked out their vital essence. The most familiar contemporary term that embodies the *vagina dentata* is *snatch*, which strongly implies the notion of being seized, as if by a toothed beast. This sense of *snatch* dates back to the late nineteenth century, though *snatch* had also been used, since the late seventeenth century, to denote sexual intercourse. The *vagina dentata* is also clearly evident in twentieth-century slang names for the female pudendum such as *dog's mouth, nether mouth, dick muncher* and *box with teeth*, and is also implicit in *snapper, red snapper, snapping turtle* and even *crab cove*, although the last of these also conjures up the image of the venereal parasite known as *crabs*. The image of being seized is embodied in the terms *grabber* and *gristle-gripper*, and the fear of being captured is conveyed in *venus fly trap, penis fly trap, mouse trap* and even *claptrap*, all of which have been used in the twentieth century to refer to a woman's genitalia. Grinding the penis to bits, as if by molars, is suggested in *organ grinder, meat grinder, coffee grinder, pencil sharpener* and *mangle* (the latter of which was current in the nineteenth century). Likewise, the sense of being swallowed up is evoked by *black hole, dark hole, hole of no return, the deep* and even *vacuum*, which was first equated with the female pudendum in the nineteenth century. *Vicious circle* implies the *vagina dentata* in at least two ways. On the one hand, the circle is the vaginal orifice, which viciously devours the penis. On the other hand, the vicious circle is an allegory of a man's relentless compulsion to return to the vagina. Copulation satiates sexual desire only temporarily – within a few days or even hours he will again feel drawn to the "dark hole" of a woman. This inner conflict was articulated in the late fourth century by Saint Augustine who prayed, "Lord, give me chastity and continency, but not yet!"

There are also, of course, many words that emerged in Late Modern English that do not construe the female pudendum as a toothed mouth. *Yoni*, for example, was adopted about two hundred years ago from Sanskrit as a counterpart to the Greek *phallus*. Just as psychoanalysts might describe a dream about a tower as phallic, they might also describe a dream about a dewy tulip as yonic. In Sanskrit, the word *yoni* could mean *vulva*, *source* and even *nest*. Like the Sanskrit word *yoga*, the word *yoni* derives from the Indo-European *yeug*, meaning *to unite*, which also developed via the Germanic branch into the word *yoke*, and via the Italic branch into the middle syllable of *conjugal*, meaning *yoked together*.

Somewhat less exotic than *yoni* is *pussy*, which came to denote a woman's private parts in the mid nineteenth century, just as *beaver* did in the 1920s and just as *badger* and *mink* did in the late twentieth century. As mentioned in the chapter devoted to terms of objectification, the word *pussy* was originally a common pet name for a cat, and probably emerged in imitation of the *pss-pss* sound humans make to get a feline's attention. *Pussy* also came to be a pejorative name for an effeminate or cowardly man in the 1940s, and *pussy-whipped*, denoting a man who is dominated by his wife, emerged in the 1950s. In the 1960s, police officers who specialized in apprehending prostitutes came to be known as the *pussy posse*. Similarly, the word *beaver* has inspired several new compounds, most notably *beaver shot*, from the 1960s, which signifies a pornographic photo that zooms in on the woman's pudendum. In the nineteenth century, before it acquired its genital sense, the word *beaver* denoted a man's beard, which was the object of a children's street game. The first to spot a man with a beard would shout "Beaver!" and thus accrue points. In origin, *beaver* derives from an Indo-European word that meant *brown*, which also developed into the words *bear* and *bruin*, and also the first syllable of *berserk*, originally the name of a Norse warrior who fought with the fury of a bear.

The early twentieth century saw the appearance of *minge*, a word that might have developed from the Romany *minj*, also meaning *female pudendum*. (Romany is the language of the Rom, a nomadic people once known as the Gypsies because they were thought to have originated in Egypt; in fact, the Rom have roots in northern India, although for the last thousand years they have engaged in a now-global diaspora.) Another name for a woman's genitals, *poontang* also originated in the early twentieth century, probably as a corruption of the French *putain*, meaning *prostitute*. Earlier on, *putain* evolved from the Old French *pute*, meaning *girl*, which ultimately developed from the Indo-European *pau*, meaning *little*. That same Indo-European source also developed into a number of words that all have to do with littleness, ranging from *poor*, *poverty* and *pauper* (having little money), to *pony*, *poultry*, *filly* and *foal* (the little ones, or young, of those creatures), to *Paul* (meaning *little one*), to *few* (meaning *little in number*). The jelly roll, a cylindrical pastry containing a sweetened paste, also gave its name to the female pudendum in the early twentieth century.

The word was popularized through jazz songs, which often made use of bawdy double entendre. For example, a song called "I Aint Gonna Give Nobody None of this Jelly Roll," written by Spencer Williams, was a hit in 1919, and in 1927 Peg Leg Howell wrote "New Jelly Roll Blues," which contained these lyrics:

> Jelly-roll, jell y-roll, ain't so hard to find.
> Ain't a baker shop in town bake 'em brown like mine
> I got a sweet jelly, a lovin' sweet jelly-roll,
> If you taste my jelly, it'll satisfy your worried soul.

Other pudendum words that emerged in the first half of the twentieth century include *cooz*, which is first recorded in the 1920s and is of unknown origin, and *berk*, which arose in the 1930s as a shortened form of *Berkeley Hunt*, which in turn was invented as rhyming slang for *cunt*. Around 1942, *slot* was invented as a variation of the earlier *slit*.

In the late twentieth century, hundreds more slang names for the female genitalia emerged, ranging from the quasi-erudite (such as *Pandora's box*, the mythological chest from which all evils were released), to the grotesque (such as *fur pie* and *skin chimney*), to the reduplicated (such as *hoo-hoo* and *ya-ya*, the latter having been popularized by the 2002 film *The Divine Secrets of the Ya-Ya Sisterhood*), to the typographical (such as *x* and *y*, the former suggesting *X-rated*, the latter suggesting *yoni*, and both suggesting the crotch, thanks to the intersecting lines that form each letter).

When gynecologists speak with their patients, they tend to avoid using words like *twat*, *doodlesack* and *poontang*. Not only do such words belong to a non-professional register of language, they also – as noted above – fall short in terms of anatomical specificity. A vague slang term such as *down there* is as out of place in the doctor's office as *laparohysterosalpingo-oophorectomy* is in the bedroom. (The latter term denotes the removal of the uterus, fallopian tubes and ovaries through an abdominal incision.) However, even though a gynecologist's clinical vocabulary is very specific, most of the anatomical words that he or she employs are rooted in metaphors. For example, the word *vagina*, which denotes the canal leading from the vulva to the uterus, is a Latin word: it means *sheath* or *scabbard*, a kind of holster for storing a sword. It was adopted by English in the late seventeenth century. In Spanish, the Latin *vagina* evolved into the word *vaina*, which later developed a diminutive form, *vainilla*, meaning *little sheath*. The Spanish bestowed this name on a fragrant plant because its seed pods are long and narrow like a miniature sheath, and eventually, in the mid seventeenth century, English adopted the Spanish name of the plant as *vanilla*.

Before the word *vagina* was adopted into English near the end of the seventeenth century, that genital canal was known by several other names. For example, medieval physicians invented the euphemistic phrase *hole of Venus*. They also employed the word *vessel*, a usage that seems less strange when we remember that Modern English uses the same word in the phrase *blood vessel*. As well, Middle English denoted the vagina with *valve*, a word that originally denoted a folding door; not until the mid seventeenth century did *valve* come to denote a mechanical device that controls the flow of a fluid. The phrase *matrice nekke*, literally meaning *womb neck*, was also used in Middle English; it appears, for instance, in a fifteenth-century medical treatise where the author notes that "the matrice necke is villous and rugous," that is, bumpy and wrinkled.

In the late nineteenth century, physicians took a stab at inventing a new name for the vagina, *elytron*, derived from the Greek rather than the Latin word for *sheath*. Their motivation was, perhaps, that *vagina* had become too colloquial for their lofty conversations, and thus a more rarefied term was needed. Despite this intention, *elytron* never really managed to challenge *vagina*, and is now only used by entomologists to refer to a wing-case of certain insects. A distant cousin of *elytron*, however, did manage to thrive – namely, *vulva*, which was adopted from Latin in the mid sixteenth century. Those two words, *elytron* and *vulva*, do not look much alike, but they both derive from the Indo-European *wel*, meaning *to roll*. With the Greek word, the initial *w* sound of *wel* was lost entirely, while in Latin it changed to a *v* sound. At the heart of both words is the notion that the elytron (that is, the vagina) and the vulva have been formed by rolling tissue into a sheath-like structure. This sense of rolling or turning is evident in the other derivatives of the Indo-European *wel*, including *revolve*, *involve*, *valve* and *Volvo*, the latter denoting a make of car whose name is a Latin word meaning *I roll*. The rolling sense of the Indo-European source is also evident in the derivative *volume*, which originally denoted a rolled scroll, and then came to denote a book, and then came to denote something that had the size and bulk of a book, and then came to denote size or capaciousness in an abstract sense, and then came to denote the "size" of a singer's voice, and then came to denote the loudness of any sound, especially one produced by an electronic amplifier. Other derivatives of the Indo-European *wel* include *waltz*, a dance characterized by spinning, *wallow*, meaning *to roll about*, and the noun *well*, which originally denoted a spring of rolling water. Thus, the opening sentence of my non-existent erotic novel, tentatively entitled *Forbidden Cognates*, contains six words that all

Hymen: The name of the Greek god of marriage, meaning thick skin.

descend from the same Indo-European source: "I wallowed in sorrow, and tears welled into my eyes, as I realized that she was involved with the man with whom she was waltzing, a man who had caressed her vulva in his Volvo." In the nineteenth century, another word that was bestowed on the vulva was *concha*, which in Late Latin had denoted a semi-circular structure, like an apse, that projected from a building, and which had earlier been formed from the Latin *conch*, which referred to the shell of a mollusk, such as a clam.

The *labia minora* and *labia majora* form part of the vulva, and their names mean, respectively, *smaller lips* and *bigger lips*. The singular form of the Latin *labia* is *labium*, which is a doublet of the English *lip*. Both words developed the same Indo-European source – *lep*, meaning *to lick* – with one evolving through the Italic branch and the other through the Germanic branch. You might think that *label*, a kind of sticker that sometimes requires licking, derives from the same source, but it is unrelated. From the seventeenth to the nineteenth century, the labia minora were sometimes known as *nympha*, a word that is more fully discussed in Chapter Eighteen, devoted to words pertaining to wanton behaviour. Contemporary slang terms for the labia abound, including *cunt lips, piss flaps, pink bits, dew-flaps, bacon strips, fillet o' fish* and *curtains.*

The word *clitoris* did not appear in English until the early seventeenth century, perhaps because male anatomists had trouble finding it on the women whose bodies they examined. When they did, they borrowed and respelt the Greek name for that organ, *kleitoris,* which probably arose as a diminutive of an earlier Greek word meaning *hill,* which in turn evolved from the Indo-European *klei,* meaning *to lean* or *to slope.* The last syllable of *incline, decline* and *recline* evolved from the same Indo-European source, as did the middle syllable of *proclivity,* which means *to lean toward.* Likewise, a *client* is etymologically someone who leans on you for support. The word *clinic* is also related: its immediate source was the Greek word *kline,* meaning *bed,* a place where one reclines. *Climax,* too, ultimately derives from the Indo-European *klei:* the Greek *klimax* meant *ladder,* something that leans against a wall. Sixteenth-century humanists borrowed the word *climax* to describe a series of steps in an argument, each of which is more forceful than the previous one, thus creating a rhetorical ladder that stretches up to an irrefutable apex. By the mid nineteenth century, the rhetorical apex itself had come to be identified with the word *climax,* and from there it was short hop, in the early twentieth century, to transfer the word to the peak of the sex act, the orgasm.

Long before *clitoris* emerged in English, that organ was referred to as the *kekir,* a word that might derive from the Old English *cocer,* denoting a quiver for arrows, an item similar in shape, though not in size, to the human clitoris. For example, one fifteenth-century clerk or scholar used it in a passage that described the female genitalia. "This mouth is clepid of clerkis vulva," he wrote, "and it hath in his myddil a lacertous pannicle sumwhat hangynge withoutenforth, the which pannicle summen callen it in Latyn tentigo, and in Englich it is callid in sum cuntre the kekir." (By "sum cuntre" the clerk means "some countries" or "some parts of the country," but he is surely also bawdily punning on "some cunt.") Twentieth century counterparts to *clitoris* and *kekir* include *clit, rosebud, door bell, cherry pit, love button, spare tongue, joy buzzer, female cock, bald man in a boat* and *navicula*, the latter term originally denoting an incense burner formed in the shape of a boat.

Before the uterus came to be known as the uterus, it had several names including *gecyndlim, womb, matris* and *belly*. The earliest of these is the Old English *gecyndlim*, which is closely related to the Modern English *kin* and *kind*. The word *womb*, too, is very old, dating back to the early ninth century, where it was used not only to signify the uterus, but also the abdomen, the stomach, and sometimes even the soul. Over the centuries, *womb* has been compounded with other words to form new terms, including a fourteenth-century name for the vulva, *womb-gate*, a seventeenth-century name for the placenta, *womb-cake*, and an eighteenth-century name for the fallopian tubes, *womb-trumpets*. Much more recent than *womb*, relatively speaking, is the word *matrice*, which came to denote the uterus in the early fifteenth century. *Matrice* was adopted from French, where the word had been derived from the Latin *matrix*. In the sixteenth century, the word *matrix* itself was adopted directly from Latin, and thus the two words existed as rivals until *matrice* became obsolete in the eighteenth century. *Matrix* is related to a bevy of other words, all of which evolved from the Latin *mater*, meaning *mother*, including *maternal, matricide, matron, matriculate* and *matrimony*. (For a woman, getting married – that is, undertaking matrimony – was once synonymous with becoming a mother.) More distant relatives include *material* and *matter*, both of which developed from the Latin *materia*, meaning *timber*, a substance that produces the lumber from which things are made. The Indo-European source of these Latin-based forms also developed, in Greek, into the last two syllables of *Demeter*, the goddess of fertility. (The first syllable of her name may mean *earth*, thus making her the earth mother.) The word *mother*, too, derives from the same Indo-European source, via the Germanic branch.

Somewhat later in the fifteenth century, the word *belly* also came to signify the uterus. The immediate ancestor of *belly* was the Old English *belig*, meaning *bag*, which is also the source of *bellows*, a kind of accordian-like bag which is pumped to provide a blast of air to a fire. (The Old English word for *bellows* was *blaest-belig*, meaning *blast-bag*, but the first word in this compound was dropped by the eleventh century.) Further back, *belly* and *bellows* evolved from the Indo-European *bhelg*, meaning *to swell*, which also developed into *billow*, originally denoting the ocean swell, and later any large wave. The word *budget*, too, is related: that word originally signified a leather bag, and then later, in the eighteenth century, came to denote the treasures or money that were deposited into such bags. In the sixteenth century, the word *bellibone* emerged, but it had nothing to do with the belly or with bones; instead, that term denoted a comely lass, one who was both *belle et bonne*, or beautiful and good.

In the early seventeenth century, the word *uterus* was adopted as a learned synonym for *womb*. Surprisingly, though, the word *uterine* had entered English almost two hundred years earlier to describe siblings who had the same mother but different fathers. (Such siblings might even be twins: it's possible for a woman to release two eggs in one menstrual cycle, and for one egg to be fertilized by one man, and the other by another man: the result, though rare, is fraternal twins who have different fathers.) In origin, the word *uterus* ultimately comes from the Indo-European *udero*, meaning *womb* or *abdomen*. This Indo-European word also developed into the Greek *hustera*, meaning *womb*, from whence English gets the word *hysteria*. This supposed psychoneurotic disorder was once thought to be a woman's disease, somehow caused by a disturbed uterus, and thus the adjective *hysterical*, meaning *deranged by a faulty womb*, was invented in the early seventeenth century. In the early nineteenth century, the adjective *hysterical* prompted the medical term *hysteria*, and later, in the 1960s, *hysterical* came to mean *hilarious* thanks to the notion that mental illness is funny. The Greek root of these words is also evident in *hysterectomy*, denoting the surgical removal of the uterus, a procedure that was employed in the late nineteenth century to treat women suffering from hysterical neuroses.

On each side of the uterus is an *ovary*, an organ whose name comes from the Latin *ovum*, meaning *egg*. One close relative of *ovary* is the egg-shaped figure known as the *oval*, which also developed from *ovum*. The Indo-European source of *ovum* was *awi*, meaning *bird*, which is also the source of *aviary*, the name of a large enclosure for birds, and *aviation*. Also related is the fish-egg delicacy known as *caviar*, which developed through the Indo-Iranian offshoot of Indo-European. It's even possible, though not certain, that the word *egg* itself developed from this Indo-European source through the Germanic branch. Incidentally, the next time you order eggs for breakfast, you may want to regale your companion by noting the coincidental resemblance of *ovaries* and the egg-cooking technique known as *over-easy*.

Chapter Ten

TWO OF A KIND
Words for Breasts

THE TWO SOFT PROTUBERANCES located on the upper body of women have been known as *breasts* for a long time. The word can be traced back to Old English where, in the eighth century, the singular form was *breost*. In turn, the Old English *breost* evolved from the Indo-European *bhreus*, meaning *to swell*, which is also the source of the word *browse*. That word originated as a noun denoting small twigs and shoots that swell from trees; the noun form then developed into a verb signifying the act of feeding on such shoots, as a deer or goat might do. *Browse* then developed a figurative sense in the early seventeenth century, as it came to denote a person who roamed about while focusing attention upon one thing and then another.

It's curious that in its long history *breast* has remained, for the most part, a "human" word. While it's true that you can cook chicken breasts for supper, the word *breast* – and especially the plural form, *breasts* – is not generally applied to animals. We might refer to a dog's scrotum, or penis, or vagina, or even vulva, but we are reluctant to say that a dog – or, for that matter, a cat or cow – has breasts. Instead, such animals have teats, dugs or udders. We have been reluctant to extend the word *breast* to other mammals perhaps because breasts have such deep-seated and powerful significance for us: they are, after all, the organs that provided us with nourishment and comfort as children, and to a great extent we see them, as nursing infants, not just as a part of our mother, but as identical with our mother. Given this profound emotional and symbolic significance of the breast, it's not surprising that we have not, for the most part, diminished the word by using it in reference to quadrupeds. Likewise the word *udder* is rarely applied to a woman, and if it is, it tends to be pejorative, a word that reduces the woman to a beast. The word *teat*, on the other hand, is more complicated in its application: when it arose in the tenth century, it was used in reference to both animals and women, but it denoted only the nipple, not the breast as a whole. By the seventeenth century, the application of teat had narrowed, and it tended to be used as an "animal" word. Then, in the 1920s, a dialect variant of *teat* – *tit* – came to denote not just the nipple, but the human breast as a whole, as in the 1950s idiom *tits and ass*. Thus, once again the animal *teat* was essentially distinguished from the human *tit*, though not to the same degree as with *breast* and *udder*.

Tit also appears in *titmouse*, but that word has nothing to do with breasts, nor for that matter with mice. Instead, the first part of that bird's name probably derives from a Scandinavian source meaning *small*, which is why in the mid sixteenth century *tit* came to denote a small horse, and why in the late sixteenth century it came to denote a young – and therefore small – man or woman. For example, in a 1629 play called *The Tragedy of Albovine*, a grizzled old Captain says, "I ever thought these Court-Tits / Were much taken with my smooth lookes," the court-tits being young ladies residing in the royal household. As for the expression *tits up*, meaning *dead*, it appears to have originated in Canadian prisons in the 1960s.

Almost as old as *tit* and *breast* is *mamma*, which emerged in the eleventh century as a synonym for *breast*, and which remains current in medical usage, with a plural form of *mammae*. The word was adopted directly from Latin, and is also represented in *mammary gland* and *mammal*, the latter being a class of creature that nurses its young by secreting milk. Even further back, the Latin *mamma* derived from the Indo-European *ma*, meaning *mother*, a parenting role which for thousands of years was synonymous with breast-feeding. The Indo-European *ma* obviously resembles the *ma* that some North Americans employ when addressing their mother, just as the Latin *mamma* resembles the *mamma* that is also used in reference to mothers. It would not be quite accurate, however, to say that the current use of *mamma* and *ma* as synonyms for *mother* has evolved from the Indo-European *ma*. Instead, it's probably more true to say that the ancient *ma* and the modern *ma* are independent instances of a sound that infants instinctively tend to make at a pre-linguistic stage; or, as the Indo-European scholar Calvert Watkins says, *ma* is "a linguistic near-universal found in many of the world's languages." Not surprisingly, this infantile *ma* sound – or its reduplicated form *mamma* – tends to become identified with the object that looms largest in an infant's life – the mother or her lactating breast. In written English, *mamma* is not recorded as a familiar form of address for one's mother until the late sixteenth century, though it was probably current in spoken English much earlier. The variant *mom* is not recorded until the end of the nineteenth century. Unrelated to any of these forms is the similar looking *ma'am*, which arose from the French *ma dame*, meaning *my lady*.

In 1595, Edmund Spenser wrote a poem as a wedding gift for his wife, in which he rhapsodized on her many excellent qualities, including "Her brest like to a bowle of creame uncrudded, / Her paps lyke lyllies budded." Around the same time, Thomas Lodge had written a pastoral poem in which he had this to say about the shepherdess Rosalynde: "Her pappes are centers of delight, / Her pappes are orbes of heavenly frame." Such praises were echoed by Hugh Crompton in his poem "The Glory of Women," where he compliments his sweetheart by praising "her paps with Nectar fill'd." This use of *pap* as a literary synonym for *breast* persisted into the eighteenth century, and the word continues to exist as an archaic or rustic synonym for *teat*. In origin, *pap* probably arose in imitation of the smacking sound infants make when suckling, as did the other *pap* that denotes mushed-up food served to infants and old people who are too weak to protest.

Strictly speaking, the word *bosom* denotes the breast of a human, male or female, not the breasts of a woman; a man, for example, can hold a child to his bosom, and for centuries the phrase *Abraham's bosom* has denoted the heavenly place into which the souls of the righteous are gathered. Nonetheless, *bosom* – or rather the plural *bosoms* – has been used since the early twentieth century to denote a woman's breasts. James Bond, for example, gets "a quick glimpse of fine bosoms" in 1965's *The Man with the Golden Gun*. This use of *bosoms* is undoubtedly the source of the slang term *bazooms*, which emerged in the 1920s and which later inspired dozens of variations, such as *bazumbas*, *buzwams*, *babooms* and *babaloos*. In turn, each of these variants is probably the source of many other slang synonyms for breasts: *bazumbas*, for example, begat *bazongas*, which begat *gazongas*, which begat *kazongas*, which begat *kajoobies*, which begat *jaboos*. In origin, *bosom* might derive from the Indo-European *bhaghu*, meaning *arm*, which also developed into the word *bough*, and which might also be the source of *fathom*. A fathom equals six feet, the distance between the fingertips of an adult's outstretched arms.

> When we study human language, we are approaching what some might call the "human essence," the distinctive qualities of mind that are, so far as we know, unique to man.
>
> *Noam Chomsky*

In Early Modern English, two terms that were used to denote a woman's breasts were *duckys* and *bubbies*. The first of these appears in a letter that Henry VIII wrote to Anne Boleyn. Henry wrote that he longed to be "in my sweethearts armes whose pritty duckys I trust shortly to kysse." Shortly thereafter, Anne became his wife, and three years later Henry had her executed on trumped-up charges of adultery. The word *duckys* might simply have been inspired by a resemblance between the soft, white feathers of a domestic duck and the soft, white skin of an English woman's breasts, facilitated by the coincidental resemblance of *duck* and *dug*, the latter denoting an animal's teat. As for *bubbies*, it first appeared in the late seventeenth century, and is notable because it evolved into the still-familiar *boobies*, which was shortened, in the mid twentieth century, to just *boobs*. The word *booby* has also been used since the late sixteenth century to mean *nincompoop*, as in *booby-prize* or *booby-trap*; this *booby*, however, derives from a different source, namely, the Spanish *bobo*, meaning *fool*.

In the eighteenth century, slang names for a woman's breasts began to proliferate. In his 1785 *Dictionary of the Vulgar Tongue*, for example, Francis Grose lists *diddleys*, *cat-heads*, *dairy*, *kettledrums* and *apple-dumpling shop* as then-current synonyms. He also added that the phrase *to sport blubber* was used to describe a "large, coarse woman, who exposes her bosom." The nineteenth century contributed breast synonyms such as *sweets* and *charlies*, the latter term perhaps deriving from the Romany *chara*, meaning *to touch*, and modified to resemble the more familiar name *charlie*. The word *knockers* came to denote breasts in the 1940s, thanks to a perceived resemblance between a door knocker and a woman's breast. *Bristols* appeared in the 1960s as a result of rhyming slang: *titty* rhymes with *Bristol City*, which was then shortened to just *Bristol*. The city of *Manchester* had its name turned into a synonym for *breasts* in the same way, though in its case the coincidental presence in its name of both *man* and *chest* amplified the word play. *Honkers* was invented in the 1970s, on the analogy that a woman's breasts are meant to be squeezed like an old-fashioned bicycle horn. *Honkers* might then have inspired the term *hooters*, a word whose twinned and globular vowels – oo – might have assisted in its adoption as a slang name for women's breasts.

Hundreds of other slang names for breasts were invented in the twentieth century, too many to consider each one individually. Considered collectively, however, it becomes apparent that most of those slang terms fall into a handful of categories, each category epitomizing a way in which men – for surely most of these terms were invented by men – have conceived of female breasts over the last few decades. One category, for example, comprises words that evoke the lactating function of breasts: *jugs, cream jugs, bottles, cans, milk cans, milkers, milk duds, milkshakes, butter-bags, baby dinners, baby bar, brassiere food, café la mama, jersey cities.* To this list, the term *norks* might also be added. That Australian term might have been inspired by the Norco Dairy Cooperative, which made and sold butter whose wrapping featured a cow's udder. As for *Norco,* the cooperative invented its name by taking the first few letters from the two words that make up the phrase *north coast.*

Another category includes breast words that construe breasts in terms of food items, as something to be consumed: *apples, cantaloupes, casabas, coconuts, grapefruits, grapes, guavas, jellies, loaves, peaches, mangoes, melons, oranges, potatoes, murphies, pumpkins, tomatoes, yams, niblets, cupcakes, love muffins, buns, dumplings, sweet rolls, meat loaves, meatballs, sweater meat, sweater treats, tamales, cherry-topped sundaes.* Implicit in this category are sub-groups based on breast size – the word *grapefruits,* for instance, denotes larger breasts than *grapes.* Some of these food-related terms have also inspired more fanciful formations such as *bubatoes,* a fusion of *boobs* and either *tomatoes* or *potatoes.* The shape of a breast, specifically the notion that it resembles a bag, lies behind a third category of breast words, including *fun bags, flesh bags, airbags, bean bags, beef bags, sandbags, punching bags, bags of mystery, silicon sacks* and *skin sacks.*

Not shape but position relative to a larger structure is what characterizes a fourth cluster of breast terms, all of which evoke items that either hang from on high or jut forward: *cliffs, bumpers, frontage, balcony, fore-buttocks, top-balls, shelf, top set* and *topside*. A fifth category encompasses words that gesture toward the "double nature" of a woman's breasts, that is, toward the notion that most women have two nearly identical breasts: *the pair, the twins, twin peaks, twofers, matched set, easts and wests, big brown eyes, headlamps, headlights* and *umlauts*, an umlaut being a diacritical mark that appears above certain vowels, as in *Häagen-Dazs*. Two sub-groups also exist within this category. First, there are terms that convey the notion of doubleness by anthropomorphizing the breasts into well-known duos from popular culture: *the Bobsey twins, Mickey and Minnie, Laverne and Shirley, Thelma and Louise, Wilma and Betty, Lucy and Ethel, the Pointer Sisters*. Second, there are slang words that imply the doubleness of breasts through reduplication, that is, through the repetition of a syllable, as with *chi-chis, flip-flaps, hee-haws, lulus, knick-knacks, nay-nays, num-nums, boom-booms* and *bon-bons*.

A sixth category of words equates breasts with weapons of mass destruction, such as *atom bombs, flesh bombs, torpedos, cannons, howitzers, scuds, warheads* and *bazookas*, though the latter term is probably a play on *bazooms* as well. Finally, there are dozens of recent slang names for breasts that seem to be merely nonsense formations, almost as if the very notion of breasts can transport men back to a time when they were mere suckling babes, a pre-linguistic age when they delighted in experimenting with all the sounds and syllables that their pudgy little cheeks and lips could make: *bamboochas, cadabies, chalubbies, chudleighs, chumbawumbas, chuberteens, dzwoonies, smosabs, snorbs, groodies, gubbs, baps, meguffies, noogies* and *roplopos*.

Although some of the foregoing nouns denote especially large breasts, English also has several adjectives that describe that condition, including the learned terms *macromastic* and *bathycolpian*, the latter term deriving from the Greek *bathus*, meaning *deep*, and *kolpos*, meaning *bosom*. In the fifteenth century, such a woman might be referred to as *bolstered*, a bolster being a kind of long pillow. Nowadays, she might be called *buxom*, a word that has been used to describe full-bosomed women since the late sixteenth century. In origin, *buxom* derives from an Old English word that meant *bendable*; by the twelfth century, however, the sense had shifted from something that was physically bendable to someone who would "bend over backwards" to accommodate others. Buxom or accommodating individuals were, naturally, well-liked, and so were full-figured women, so eventually *buxom* shifted from denoting a pleasing and compliant temperament, to a pleasing and large-bosomed woman. A more recent word that might be used to denote a buxom woman is *zaftig*, which was adopted in the 1930s from Yiddish, where it means *juicy*.

Two final breast words are *nipple* and *areola*. The first of these appeared in English in the early sixteenth century, and was perhaps formed as a diminutive of *neb*, which denoted the beak of a bird. As for *areola*, it came to signify in the early eighteenth century the circle of darker tissue surrounding a nipple. It was formed as a diminutive of the Latin *area*, and thus literally means *small area*. Related to *areola* and *area* is *hectare*, a unit of measurement that denotes a hundred "areas," with each of the smaller areas measuring ten meters by ten meters.

Chapter Eleven

ORGAN SOLO

Masturbation Words

*S*EX IS LESS ABOUT bodies than bodies in motion. It's not the static organs that make sex, but rather the things that are done with them (or to them). To put it another way, sex is more about verbs than nouns.

For most people, the main sex verb is *fuck*. In fact, in 1999, an entire book was published – *The F-Word* – which was devoted to that single term. However, there are plenty of actions that happen before copulation, and thus plenty of words before *fuck*, including those that refer to the auto-erotic activities that commonly coincide with the discovery of one's sexuality. *Masturbation* is perhaps the most familiar of these words, but it's not the oldest: that honour goes to *frig*, which dates back to the late sixteenth century. In origin, *frig* probably derives from the earlier verb *frike*, which derives from the Old English *frician*, meaning *to move briskly*. Nowadays, *frig* is still used as a verb denoting masturbation, but it's probably more familiar as a mild equivalent for the catch-all adjective *fucking*, as in "That frigging guy hung up on me!"

The next masturbation term to emerge in English was *the sin of self-pollution* in 1626, which construed auto-eroticism as a sinful and damaging activity, as did the term *the sin of self-abuse*, which appeared in 1728. That negative view of masturbation was fanned into a social frenzy in 1710, thanks to the publication of *Onania: The Heinous Sin of Self-Pollution, And All Its Frightful Consquences, in Both Sexes Considered, With Spiritual and Physical Advice to those Who Have Already Injured Themselves by this Abominable Practice.* The title *Onania* was inspired by the unfortunate story of Onan, whose troubles began in the Book of Genesis when his brother died and his father asked him to have sex with his widowed sister-in-law so that she would beget children. Onan initially complied, but at the last minute changed his mind and instead of impregnating his dead brother's wife, he "spilled his seed upon the ground." This willful squandering of his vital bodily essence so displeased the Almighty that he smote Onan on the spot. Several thousand years later, his name was adapted for the title of a book. *Onania* was so popular that it prompted numerous spinoffs, including *Of the Crime of Onan*, *Onania Displayed* and *Onania Examined*, all of which helped prompt the invention of the word *onanism* as a synonym for *self-pollution*. These books, and others, vividly described the debilitating effects of onanism. In a French text published in 1760, called *L'Onanisme*, Samuel Tissot reported what the auto-erotic habit had done to one of his patients:

Furtle: the act of inserting fingers into cut-out areas of pornographic photos.

I went to his home; what I found was less a living being than a cadaver lying on straw, thin, pale, exuding a loathsome stench, almost incapable of movement. A pale and watery blood often dripped from his nose, he drooled continually; subject to attacks of diarrhea, he defecated in his bed without noticing it; there was constant flow of semen; his eyes, sticky, blurry, dull, had lost all power of movement; his pulse was extremely weak and racing; labored respiration, extreme emaciation, except for the feet, which were showing signs of edema. Mental disorder was equally evident.

Naturally, such horrible descriptions terrified parents, who employed all kinds of means to dissuade or prevent their children from becoming onanists. For example, in the nineteenth century, some parents took their children to wax museums to see life-size models of terribly disfigured onanists, showed them engravings of women whose masturbatory habits had caused their noses to fall off, put them to bed with their hands safely tied to bedposts, or had their foreskin or clitoris surgically removed.

Onanism acquired a rival in 1766, when the word *masturbation* appeared in the subtitle of a yet another book about the "heinous sin." The word was borrowed from French, where it had existed since at least 1570, and where it had probably been invented by combining the Latin *manus*, meaning *hand*, with *stuprare*, meaning *to defile*; if so, then *masturbation* means *to defile with the hand*. Gradually, *masturbation* replaced *onanism* as the usual medical name for this sexual activity, so that by the twentieth century, *onanism* – while still familiar – had become somewhat archaic.

Other masturbation words emerged in the nineteenth century, such as *toss-off*, which dates back to at least 1879, and *jerk-off*, which appeared in the 1890s. Near the end of the nineteenth century, *beastliness* also came to signify masturbation, despite the fact that beasts do not masturbate: paws and hooves are not conducive to that activity. *Wank* also appeared in the nineteenth century, perhaps formed as a conflation of *whack* and *spank*. As for the familiar *jack-off*, it is first recorded in 1916, and probably arose as a variant of *jerk-off*, perhaps influenced by the second syllable of *ejaculate*. In the 1920s, the idiom *play with yourself* appeared, followed by *diddle* in the 1930s. The latter term developed from an earlier use of *diddle* to mean *to shake* or *to quiver*, which in turn evolved from the synonymous *didder*, which dates back to the fourteenth century. Related to *diddle* is *dither*, which signifies a more metaphorical vacillation, an inability to follow through on a single course of action.

In the last half of the twentieth century, innumerable slang synonyms for masturbation – or at least for male masturbation – were invented, most of which are interesting only because they collectively reveal certain sexual-linguistic patterns. One striking pattern concerns the number of slang terms that construe male masturbation as a violent attack on the penis – in other words, as a form of masochism. The most familiar of these is *beat off*, which inspired later variants such as *beat the meat*, *beat the stick*, and *beat the piss out of my best friend*. The verbs *pound* and *spank* are also featured in many masturbation synonyms, such as *pound the pork*, *pound the flounder*, *pound the pudding*, *spank the monkey*, *spank the donkey* and *spank Elvis*. Pugilism, too, appears in many of these masochistic idioms:

box the bozack, *box the bald-headed clown* and *box with Richard*. Choking and strangling are also inflicted: *choke the bad guy*, *choke the chicken*, *choke the gopher*, *choke the chipmunk*, *strangle Kojak*, *strangle Mr. Jesus* and *strangle the serpent*. Other violent metaphors include *whip the dummy*, *whack the weasel*, *torment the trouser snake*, *club the baby seal*, *bash the dummy*, *twist the turnip* and *flog your pride*.

The idioms mentioned in the previous paragraph represent only a fraction of the hundreds of violent and masochistic metaphors that have been equated with male masturbation since the middle of the twentieth century. Such metaphors might be an unconscious vestige of the long-standing belief that masturbation is both sinful and damaging: to put it another way, these idioms are metaphorical equivalents of the centuries-old phrase *the sin of self-abuse*. However, the hostility in such idioms is not always directed exclusively at the penis: many of the violent metaphors equate the penis with church officials, and thus the aggression is channelled toward the institution of the church, which construed masturbation as a negative act in the first place. One of the earliest of these idioms, dating back to at least the seventeenth century, is *to box the Jesuit and get cockroaches*, the

Sacofricosis: the technique of cutting a hole in a front trouser pocket in order to masturbate surreptitiously in public.

Jesuits being a religious order with strict and repressive attitudes toward sexuality. The parallel idiom *bang the bishop* arose in the late nineteenth century, and more recent are masturbation phrases such as *batter the bishop*, *pummel the priest*, *punish the pope*, *disobey the pope* and *conk the cardinal*.

Admittedly, there are other patterns manifested by male masturbation words that are not violent or masochistic. One cluster, for example, construes the act in terms of the sperm that is ejaculated – *cream your corn, make instant pudding, milk the chicken, hold the mayo, clear the snorkel, flush the babies* – while another cluster focuses on the onanistic role of the human hand – *hand fuck, five-finger knuckle-shuffle, five-digit disco, playing a little five-on-one* and *manual labor*. With another group of idioms, the hand is anthropomorphized into a dating substitute, as with *date Manuela, date Rosy Palms, date Palmala Handerson, date Thumbalina and her four sisters* and *make love with Mother Thumb and her four daughters*. Yet another category is made up of idioms that play on phrases borrowed from other contexts, such as *dishonourable discharge, perform an organ solo, play a flute solo, come into your own, come to grips with things* and *get a hold of yourself.* Cultural touchstones and popular icons form another cluster of masturbation idioms: *raise Lazarus, whitewash with Huck and Tom, puff the one-eyed dragon, Free Willy, Peewee's Big Adventure* and *going Hans Solo*. Many other terms simply manifest a playful use of literary techniques, such as rhyme and alliteration: *Fidget the midget, doodle the noodle, bleed the weed, yank the crank, slammin' the salmon, jerkin' the gherkin.*

In contrast with male masturbation, terms denoting female auto-eroticism – such as *pearl diving* – are few in number. All appear to be of recent coinage. None of them manifest the violent metaphors that characterize so many of the male masturbation terms, though other patterns do recur, such as rhyme with *clit twit* and word play with *hand to gland combat, mistressbate* and *jill-off.* A handful of these terms also play on phrases borrowed from other contexts, such as *tickle my fancy, part the Red Sea, squeeze the Charmin,* and *enter no man's land.* One cluster that reveals a unique pattern includes phrases that associate masturbation with the south: *explore the Deep South, enjoy a little Southern Comfort, experience Southern pleasures, have a Southern romance* and *visit the Southern Belle.* This motif may simply reflect the fact that women have a better sense of direction than men.

Chapter Twelve

AURAL SEX

Words for Wooing and Seducing

*F*OR MOST PEOPLE, ONANISTIC pleasures are eventually supplemented by onerous pleasures; masturbating gives way to romantic dating, with all its complexities, challenges and frustrations. Such relationships usually begin with a *proceptive phase*, the stage at which an individual uses non-verbal communication to broadcast his or her erotic interest in another person. It is also at that stage that individuals attempt to engage in what is technically known as *ingratiation*, that is, in forms of self-presentation that are calculated to enhance one's sex appeal: a woman might repeatedly toss her hair or lick her lips, while a man might puff out his chest or adjust the sock he's stuffed down his pants.

Nowadays, such behaviour is commonly called *flirting*, a word that first appeared in English in the mid sixteenth century. At that time, however, the verb *flirt* had no amorous connotations, but rather meant *to sneer* or *to scoff*, and perhaps arose in imitation of the contemptuous *feh* sound that often accompanies sneering and scoffing. Alternatively, *flirt* might have developed from the much older word *fleer*, meaning *to grimace*. Only a few years after *flirt* emerged with its *scoffing* sense, it came to be used as a noun denoting a giddy or petulant young woman. In his *Anatomy of Melancholy*, for example, Robert Burton refers to a "peevish drunken flurt, a waspish cholerick slut." The shift from *scoffing behaviour* to *petulant woman* might have been assisted by the fact that *flirt* sounded like the older words *flick* and *flit*, both of which suggest a kind of flightiness. By the mid eighteenth century, the word's association with petulant young women caused its meaning to shift again, and it came to signify coquettish behaviour, that is, the act of vainly trifling with a would-be lover. Oddly, while the verb *flirt* has recently lost these negative connotations, the noun form has retained them. Thus, if you tell someone you are flirting with him or her, you'll probably get a pleased smile, but if you tell the same person that you are a flirt, you'll probably get the cold shoulder.

Nowadays, the words *flirt* and *woo* mean much the same thing, though *flirt* is perhaps more sexual, while *woo* is more romantic. The words also once differed with regard to their gender application: while a flirt, as noted above, was a woman, a wooer was a man. That difference may explain why *woo*, unlike *flirt*, has never had negative connotations: it was acceptable for a man to be forward in love, but not a woman. The word *woo* dates back to the eleventh century, and might have developed from the Indo-European *weng*, meaning *to bend*. The connection was that a wooer aims to get his beloved to "bend" toward him. If *weng* is, in fact, the source of *woo*, then *woo* is related to other "bending" words such as *wink* (meaning *to bend down the eyelid*) and *wonky* (meaning *unsteady*, as if having a bent leg). The word *wench* also derives from this source. The Old English predecessor of that word, *wencel*, denoted a toddler whose legs bend this way and that as they totter along. Almost as old as *woo* is *drury*, a noun that existed from the early thirteenth century to the fifteenth century, and that denoted the act of wooing or courting. The word was also sometimes used as a name for a keepsake exchanged by lovers. In origin, *drury* probably developed from *drut*, meaning *friend*, which also became obsolete by the mid fifteenth century.

In the late sixteenth century, the word *court* emerged as a synonym for *woo*; earlier on, that verb had denoted the act of coming to Court – the Royal Court at Hampton – in order to venerate the monarch. Eventually, love-smitten men extended the *veneration* sense of the word *court* to encompass the women who were the metaphorical queens of their heart. Nowadays, the verb *court* has acquired an almost rustic connotation, and conjures up visions of a farm-hand knocking on a door with a bouquet of fresh-picked daisies in hand – "Jeb's courtin' Amy-Lou," the neighbours say, peeking out from a curtain. In origin, *court* derived via French from the Latin *cohors*, meaning *enclosure*, from whence English also gets the word *cohort*, originally denoting a company of soldiers. Earlier on, *cohort* was formed from the prefix *com* and a derivative of the Latin *hortus*, meaning *garden*. This means that *court* and *cohort* are related to *horticulture* and even to *orchard*, the first syllable of which is probably a descendant of the Latin *hortus*.

Honeymoon: the month – or moon – after a marriage during which everything seems as sweet as honey.

The word *assail* was also used in Early Modern English to denote the act of wooing and courting. In the fourteenth century, *assail* described a hostile attack. It literally meant *to jump on*, since it derived – like the previously discussed *salacious* – from the Latin *salire*, meaning *to leap*. By the early seventeenth century, however, *assail* was being used figuratively to signify a romantic "assault" on a woman's heart. The same shift in sense, from hostile attack to amorous attack, also occurred with the verb *board*, which originally denoted one ship coming alongside an enemy ship so that it could be boarded, but which later, in the mid sixteenth century, came to signify wooing. This sense of *board* can be seen in a passage from Shakespeare's *Twelfth Night*, where the dim-witted Sir Andrew Aguecheek mistakenly thinks that the name of the woman he is being urged to court is "Mistress Accost." Sir Toby Belch attempts to enlighten him: "You mistake, knight. 'Accost' is front her, board her, woo her, assail her."

Since appearing in English in the mid seventeenth century, the word *coquetry* has tended to have a negative connotation, signifying insincere and narcissistic flirting. For example, in his 1656 dictionary called *Glossographia*, Thomas Blount defined *coquetry* as "the prattle or twattle of a pert gossip or minx." Nowadays, that kind of behaviour might be ascribed to a *cock-teaser*, and there is, in fact, an etymological link between *coquetry* and *cock-teaser*: simply put, both terms derive from words denoting cocks. The word *coquetry*, for example, derives from the French *coquet*, a diminutive of the word *coq*, meaning *rooster*. The word *coquet* was used in French to describe a man who strutted about like a rooster – the English *cocky* and *cock of the walk* parallel this French sense. Earlier on, before *coquetry* had been adopted into English, the word *coquet* itself was borrowed from French as *cocket*, an adjective meaning *arrogant*. This word was respelt as *coquet* in the late eighteenth century, in order to recover its French flavour, and it also came to be used as a noun to denote someone who fancied himself a ladies' man. Throughout its early history, *coquet* referred only to men; eventually, however, the feminine form, *coquette*, emerged and it soon drove its masculine counterpart into extinction. As for *cock-teaser*, that term dates back to the late nineteenth century, where it existed alongside the synonymous *cock-chafer*. Both terms denoted women who supposedly aroused a man's cock – which is named, as discussed in Chapter Eight, after the *cock* that means *rooster* – but who then failed to sexually gratify the aforesaid cock.

Also in the late nineteenth century, around the same time that *cock-teaser* and *cock-chafer* appeared, the verb *cruise* developed a sexual sense. While *cruise* is not quite synonymous with *flirt* or *woo*, it does denote the quest for a sexual partner that precedes those proceptive behaviours. By the 1920s, *cruise* had come to be especially associated with homosexual men, a connotation it retains to the present-day. The goal of cruising is, of course, to *pick up* a sexual partner, a term that is surprisingly old: it dates back to the late seventeenth century, where it denoted an act of acquiring a prostitute. As for the term *pickup line*, denoting a snappy comment or question intended to pique someone's interest, it probably dates back to the 1970s, when Eric Weber published his best-selling *How to Pick Up Girls*. Classic pickup lines include "Gee, I didn't know angels flew so low," and "Is it hot in here or is it just you?" and "Weren't you in my wet dream last night?" In the 1970s, the proliferation of male pickup lines prompted a sub-genre of female put-down lines, including the following:

"Haven't I seen you somewhere before?"
"That's why I don't go there anymore."

"I know how to please a woman."
"Then please leave me alone."

"So what do you do for a living?"
"I'm a female impersonator."

"What's your sign?"
"Do not enter."

One other synonym for *woo* that arose in the twentieth century is *smoodge*, which dates back to around 1906. *Smoodge* probably developed from the earlier *smudge*, meaning *to caress*, a word that is not related to the *smudge* that means *to soil*. The wooing *smudge* probably evolved from *smouch*, meaning *to kiss*, a word that probably arose in imitation of the sound produced when the pneumatic seal produced by the conjunction of two sets of lips is released, and which eventually came to be spelt *smooch*.

When flirting, it's often the eyes that signal erotic interest, a fact that has not gone unnoticed over the centuries. Nowadays we refer to that form of amorous body language as *making eyes* at someone, an idiom that dates back to at least the late nineteenth century. Somewhat older is the synonymous phrase *to throw the eye*, which appeared in the mid nineteenth century, and much older, dating back to the sixteenth century, are phrases such as *to mingle eyes* and *to change eyes*, the latter phrase not meaning *to transform the eyes* but rather *to exchange glances*. Also in the sixteenth century, amorous glances were called *oeillades*, a word formed from the French word *oeil*, meaning *eye*. The seventeenth century employed the terms *the languishing eye*, *the sheep's eye* and *the whiting's eye*, the whiting being a kind of small fish. The word *ogle*, too, arose in the late seventeenth century to signify the casting of an amorous glance. The Indo-European source of *ogle* was *okw*, which also developed into the Latin word for the eye, *oculus*, represented in words such as *monocle*. The word *inveigle*, comes from the same Indo-European source, and literally means *without eye*. Nowadays, *ogle* tends to have a negative sense, having shifted from the amatory to the predatory, as has the word *leer*, which in the sixteenth century could simply denote an innocuous come-hither look. The word *leer* might have developed from an older and now obsolete *leer* that meant *cheek*, the notion being that when you leer at someone, you tend to slightly raise your cheek as if you are gazing over it. As for the phrase *come-hither look*, it dates back to the beginning of the twentieth century. (A useful but chimerical counterpart to *come-hither look* is *go-thither look*, denoting the wilting gaze directed at an unwanted beau.)

Chapter Thirteen

LIP SMACKING
Words for Kissing and Fondling

*I*F THE FLIRTING PROCESS goes off without a hitch, the proceptive phase of a relationship gives way to the acceptive phase, the stage at which sustained body contact is established, and the individuals become physically intimate. The word *intimate* derives from the Latin verb *intimare*, meaning *to make known*, which in turn derives from the Latin adjective *intimus*, meaning *inmost*. On the surface, the notion of *making known* and the notion of *inmost* might appear contradictory; however, the connection is that *intimus* was also used as a noun to mean *friend*, and to our friends we make known our inmost thoughts. Further back, *intimus* was formed as the superlative of the preposition *in* – in other words, *intimus* literally means *the most in*.

Intimate body contact often takes the form of a kiss, a word that developed from the synonymous Old English word, *cyssan*, and which appears to have no cognates in English or in any other language. Over the centuries, however, *kiss* has been combined with numerous other words to form new compounds: *kiss the cup*, arose in the fifteenth century meaning *to take a drink*; *kiss the book* arose in the sixteenth century meaning *to swear on the Bible*; and *kiss and tell* arose near the end of the seventeenth century meaning *to reveal one's sexual secrets after an affair has ended*. The insult *kiss my ass* – or rather *kiss my arse* – dates back to the early eighteenth century, while *ass-kisser* appears not to have become common till the mid twentieth century. In culinary jargon, the early-eighteenth-century term *kissing-crust* denoted a spot where one bread loaf swelled and touched another while baking, resulting in a crustless patch. In the nineteenth century *kiss the dust* came to mean *to be overthrown*, while *kiss-me-quick* became the name of a bonnet worn far back on the head, and *kisser* became a slang synonym for *mouth*. In the early twentieth century, *kiss off* emerged, meaning *to reject rudely*.

In the late fourteenth century, another word meaning *kiss* arose – namely, *ba*. Chaucer's Wife of Bath, for example, uses that word when she says to one of her husbands, "Com neer, my spouse; lat me ba thy cheke." The word *ba* probably arose as a clipped form of the Old French *baisier*, meaning to *kiss*. (Incidentally, the Old French *baisier* means something quite different from its Modern French descendent, *baiser*: in the seventeenth century that latter word shifted from meaning *to kiss* to meaning *to copulate*.) By the mid fifteenth century, *baisier* itself had been adopted into English, and by the mid sixteenth century, this word had given rise to the word *buss*. While *kiss* and *buss* denoted the same thing, they had different connotations, as suggested by Robert Herrick in his 1648 collection of poetry called *Hesperides*: "Kissing and bussing differ both in this, / We busse our wantons, but our wives we kisse." By the late eighteenth century, the term *horse buss* had emerged to denote a kiss that concluded with a loud and resounding smack. The word *smack* itself also came to denote the act of kissing in the late sixteenth century, a word that probably arose in imitation of the sound of the lips parting. By the early seventeenth century, *smacker* had emerged meaning *one who kisses*. For instance, in his 1611 French/English dictionary, Randle Cotgrave defines a *baiseur* as "a kisser, smoutcher, smacker."

The early seventeenth century also saw the emergence of a kissing sense for *lip*: Othello, for example, says that there is nothing worse than "to lip a wanton in a secure couch, and to suppose her chaste!" Around the same time that Shakespeare was penning *Othello*, the word *neb* and *bill* came to denote the act of kissing. These two words had both arisen, in Old English, as names for a bird's beak; they then became verbs signifying the act of rubbing beaks together (as is common with doves). They were then extended in the early seventeenth century to the meeting of human lips that occurs during a kiss. The word *nib*, denoting the point of a pen, arose in the early seventeenth century as a variant of *neb*. Another bird word that developed a *kissing* sense is *peck*, denoting a quick or perfunctory kiss, a sense which did not emerge until the 1960s.

The mid seventeenth century saw the appearance of two learned synonyms for *kiss* – namely, *osculate* and *suaviate*. These two words reflect two different kinds of kisses that existed in ancient Rome. The first was the *osculum*, literally meaning *little mouth*, which denoted an affectionate kiss between friends, usually applied to the cheek; Roman senators, for example, sometimes traded *oscula* at the beginning of a legislative session. (In England, in the eighteenth century, this kind of greeting kiss came to be known as a *salute*, a word that derives from the Latin *salus*, meaning *health*.)

The second kind of Roman kiss was the *suavium*, denoting a passionate kiss, similar to what is now called a French kiss. That latter term – *French kiss* – is first recorded in 1918, and is an example of the tendency of anglophones to attach the adjective *French* to things or actions that smack of hedonism. From the sixteenth century to the eighteenth century, for example, venereal disease was known as the *French pox*. In the nineteenth century, the terms *French letter* and *French safe* arose as synonyms for *condom*, followed in the early twentieth century by *French tickler*, the name of a condom furnished with a specially-designed band intended to stimulate the vagina. *French postcard* appeared in the 1920s to denote postcards printed with erotic photos, just as playing cards with similar images made up a *French deck*. In the 1930s, *French bath* was invented to signify the act of extensively licking a sexual partner's body, and *French fuck* was created to denote the act of a man rubbing his penis between a woman's breasts. Even as recently as the 1970s, the term *French handshake* arose to describe a handshake in which one individual strokes a middle finger across the palm of the other in order to signal a willingness to have sex. Rather than being gratified by these numerous compounds, the French reciprocated by creating the

Frotteur: a person aroused by brushing against others in public places, for example, on a crowded subway car.

unflattering term *le vice Anglais*, denoting a spanking fetish. Incidentally, in the eighteenth century, before the term *French kiss* was invented, the act of sinuously interweaving the tongues was known as *tipping velvet*.

In the mid eighteenth century, the letter *x* came to be jotted at the end of love letters to denote a kiss, probably because the shape of that letter – its four arms meeting in a point – resembles pursed lips. (Much more recent is the use of *x* to denote sexually explicit material, as in *X-rated*: that use of *x* arose in the 1950s probably because of the letter's presence in the word *sex* or *explicit*, though it's tempting to speculate that it represents the crossbones of the skull and crossbones symbol that has appeared on gravestones since at least the seventeenth century, and on bottles of poison since the mid nineteenth century.) More recently, the love-letter *x* that symbolises a kiss has evolved into a series of alternating *x*s and *o*s, with the circle of the *o* probably representing the hooped arms of an embrace. Since the advent of on-line chat rooms, people have also began to use the asterisk (*) to denote another puckered orifice.

In 1871 the first recorded use of *butterfly kiss* appeared in George Eliot's novel *Middlemarch*. This term signifies the act of fluttering your eyelashes against someone's cheek, and was popularized in 1997 thanks to Bob Carlisle's song, "Butterfly Kisses." The mid twentieth century saw the appearance of *Eskimo kiss*, denoting the act of rubbing two noses together, a term that has declined in use since the late twentieth century as the generic *Eskimo* was usurped by more specific names such as *Inuit*. Also in the mid twentieth century, the word *hickey* came to signify a mark left on the skin by a passionate kiss. Earlier on, dating back to the 1920s, *hickey* had denoted a mole or pimple, and before that, near the beginning of the twentieth century, *hickey* had been synonymous with *thingumabob* – in other words, a *doohickey*. The last decade or so has seen the invention of *spit swapping* and *sucking face* as synonyms for *kiss*.

Hugging often accompanies kissing, but hugging was not possible until the mid sixteenth century when *hug* emerged in the English language. Prior to that, lovers could only *clip*, *halse*, *lap* or *embrace*. The earliest of these hugging words, *clip*, existed in Old English as *clyppan*, and was commonly used in Middle English to denote the act of embracing. For example, in the fourteenth-century romance *The Parlement of Three Ages*, the allegorical figure of Youth says that he wants to spend his life with "ladys full lovely" so that he can "clyp thaym and kysse thaym and comforthe myn hert." This *hugging* sense of *clip* is now obsolete, but the verb itself still exists with the sense of *fastening together*, as with a paper clip. The *clip* that means *to cut off* – as represented in *toenail clippers* – is unrelated to the *clip* that means *to fasten together*; it's curious that those two *clip*s can co-exist, even though they mean opposite things.

The word *halse* emerged as a rival for *clip* in the fourteenth century, though it only existed for about two hundred years before dying out. *Halse* probably developed from the earlier noun *halse*, meaning *neck*, the connection being that in an embrace your arms fold around that part of your sweetheart's body. The notion of folding is also behind the verb *lap*, which was also used from the fourteenth to the sixteenth century to mean *to embrace*. For example, in the medieval romance *Le Bone Florence of Rome*, the hundred-year-old Garcy describes how the fifteen-year-old Florence shall treat him in bed: "Sche schall me bothe hodur and happe" – that is, she will both cuddle and tuck him in – "And in hur lovely armes me lappe, / Bothe evyn and mornetyde." Earlier on, the verb *lap* probably developed from the noun *lap* that denoted a fold in a garment. This *garment* sense of *lap* is now extinct, but the noun survives as a name for the "fold" in the human body that appears when one sits down, and as the name for a "fold" in a racetrack. A ten-thousand meter race, for example, might demand twenty-five laps around the track.

Embrace also emerged in the fourteenth century, though it, of course, has maintained its *hugging* sense up to the present-day. The word evolved, via French, from a compound formed from the Latin preposition *in* and the Latin noun *bracchia*, meaning *arms*; accordingly, *embrace* literally means *in arms*. The Latin *bracchia* is also the source of the word *brassiere* and thus of its shortened form, *bra*, which appeared in the 1930s. Also related to *embrace* are *bracelet* and even *pretzel*, the latter being a baked-dough snack probably named after its folded-arm appearance. Finally, in the mid sixteenth century, *hug* emerged as another word denoting the act of embracing a loved one. If the word evolved from the Old Norse *hugga*, meaning *to console*, then it must have existed in a dialect of spoken English for many centuries before it appeared in written English, since the last Viking invasions took place in the eleventh century. In the early nineteenth century, *hug* prompted the invention of the word *huggery* to denote sycophantic behaviour, especially when it's performed with a view to gaining a job or promotion. Nowadays such behaviour is called *brown-nosing*, though the idioms *sleeping your way to the top* and *the casting couch*, suggest much the same thing.

At some point, hugging and kissing slide over into fondling and groping, and the love play becomes foreplay, which implies that sexual intercourse is on the horizon. The word *foreplay* first appeared in 1929 in a book called *Sex in Civilization*. Only slightly older is the use of the verb *pet* to denote mutual digital stimulation of the sex organs, a usage first recorded in 1924. This sense of *pet* must, however, be significantly older because a contributor to the March 14, 1925 issue of the *Literary Digest* claimed that it was already passé: "*Petting* now exists only in the college novels, the more forceful, if more obscure, *necking* having taken its place to describe amorous adventures." Although it arose as a slang word, *pet* eventually came to be adopted by early sexologists. For example, writing in 1953, Alfred Kinsey claimed that "the most responsive females may be the ones who most often pet to orgasm before marriage." Kinsey might also have used the synonymous word *contrectation*, which derives from the intensifying prefix *con* and the Latin verb *tractare*, meaning *to touch*.

Other words that pertain to foreplay include *grope*, *fondle* and *fam*. The first of these, *grope*, first appeared in the ninth century, and ultimately evolved from the same Indo-European source as *grip*. Also related is *gripe*: in the fifteenth century, that word became the name of a bowel pain that feels like someone is gripping your guts; later on, in the 1930s, it came to denote any nagging complaint. As for *fondle*, it acquired its current sense of *to physically handle* in the late eighteenth century. Earlier on, dating back to the late seventeenth century, *fondle* simply meant *to indulge*, and it was not rooted in physical touching – back then, you could fondle someone with your mind. Even earlier, *fondle* developed from the adjective *fond*, which in the sixteenth century became an adjective meaning *tenderly affectionate*. However, the earliest sense of *fond*, going back to the fourteenth century, was *foolish*: at that time, a fond lover was foolish lover. Around the same time that *fondle* was developing its current sense, the word *fam* emerged, meaning *to grope someone's genitals*. The verb *fam* probably derived from noun *famble*, meaning *hand*, which surely developed somehow from the word *fumble*. (*Famble* also meant *to stammer*, the connection being that a person who stammers seems to be "groping" for words.)

Groping, fondling and famming all have pejorative connotations, but there are plenty of words that imply a more positive form of physical intimacy. *Cuddle*, for instance, emerged in the early sixteenth century to denote affectionate snuggling. Most dictionaries say that *cuddle* is probably "of nursery or baby-talk origin," which – along with the phrase "of imitative origin" – is what etymologists often say when they have no clue as to where a word came from. In the mid nineteenth century, the synonymous *canoodle* emerged, perhaps as a playful elaboration of *cuddle*. Both *cuddle* and *canoodle* end with *le*, which is a suffix often used to form frequentatives, that is, to form a version of a word that implies a repeated action. For example, something crackles when it cracks repeatedly in a short span of time. This *le* suffix is also found on *snuggle*, which arose in the late seventeenth century as a frequentative of *snug*, meaning *to nestle*. Earlier on, in the late sixteenth century, *snug* had emerged as a nautical adjective meaning *trim* or *battened down*. A snug ship was one on which no loose ropes or tools were sliding about. In the mid-twentieth century, *snog* – meaning *to kiss and caress amorously* – was formed from *snuggle*, resulting in a new word that happens to closely resemble the old word *snug*.

Like *snuggle*, the word *caress* also appeared in the late seventeenth century, having developed from the Latin *carus*, meaning *dear*. The same Latin source also gave rise to the English words *cherish* and *charity*, and the Latin word *caritas*, the latter being a theological term denoting a Christian's love for his or her fellow humans. Earlier on, the Latin *carus* evolved from the Indo-European *ka*, meaning *to desire*, which in Sanskrit evolved into *kama*, meaning *love*, which is represented in the title of an ancient Indian treatise on love and sex known as *The Kama Sutra*. (The *sutra* part of the title means *rule*.) One of the suffixed forms of the Indo-European *ka* was *karo*, which developed through the Germanic branch into the Old English *hore*, which became the Modern English *whore*. Thus, caresses, whores, charity and *The Kama Sutra* are all etymologically linked.

One other word that pertains to foreplay is *spoon*. Since the late nineteenth century, *spoon* has been used to mean *to snuggle up beside someone*, on the analogy that spoons in a cutlery drawer nestle into one another. Further back, however, in the early nineteenth century, *spoon* meant *to woo in an overly sentimental manner*, a usage that probably developed from the late eighteenth century use of *spoon* to denote a simpleton. This sense might have arisen from the notion that the bowl of a spoon, like a simpleton, is shallow and only holds a small amount; an analogous term is *pea-brain*, which also implies a tiny cranial capacity.

Chapter Fourteen

THE INS AND OUTS OF THE IN-AND-OUT

Copulation Words

*M*ANY WORDS THAT DENOTE sexual activity are intentionally vague in their reference. For example, idioms such as *go to bed* and *sleep with* imply sexual activity without clearly articulating the precise nature of that activity – they don't reveal who put what where. Indeed, the euphemism *sleep with* is so undefined that what it really means is the opposite of what it means: if a friend tells you she slept with her husband's brother last night, you can be sure that the night did not pass in slumber. Such euphemisms are long-standing: *sleep with* has been used to imply sexual activity since the tenth century, while the verb *bed* has been used in that manner since at least the fourteenth century. In the sixteenth century, the rhyming phrase *wed and* *bed* became popular, as in Shakespeare's *The Taming of the Shrew*, where Gremio wishes that some suitor for the cranky Kate would "wed her, and bed her, and ridde the house of her."

The sixteenth century also employed euphemisms such as *amorous rites, amorous sport* and *dalliance* to vaguely allude to sexual relations. The latter term, *dalliance*, was formed from *dally*, which originally meant *to chat*. The word *conversation*, too, was used in the sixteenth century to denote sexual intimacy, but here the sexual sense predated the chatting sense: *conversation* did not come to mean *discourse* or *talking* until the late sixteenth century. After the chatting sense of *conversation* developed, the word had to be modified by an adjective in order to specify its sexual sense. Thus *conjugal conversation* emerged in the seventeenth century, and *criminal conversation* in the nineteenth century. In contrast, the word *intercourse* meant *commerce* or even *fellowship*, and only came to denote sexual activity in the late eighteenth century. The early *fellowship* sense of *intercourse* is probably where Intercourse, Pennsylvania acquired its name, the town being a social hub for the Amish who live in the vicinity. A similar shift in meaning occurred with the idiom *make love*: when that term originated in the late sixteenth century, it meant *to woo*, as when Hamlet refers to the "honeying and making love" that his mother and Claudius enjoyed after the death of Hamlet's father. *Make love* held on to that meaning up until the mid twentieth century, when it came to mean *to*

Sadism: the desire to inflict pain on a sexual partner, named after the Marquis de Sade, who wrote about his own cruel sexual exploits.

have sex. As a result of this shift in sense, many eighteenth and nineteenth-century novels contain passages that now seem highly sexual, though that is not how they were intended. For example, in Charlotte Smith's 1793 novel *The Old Manor House*, we learn that the General has designs on Isabella:

> "I believe she will consent, though she has a hundred times ridiculed the General; and when he has been making love to her – "
>
> "Making love to her!" said Orlando; "has he long made love to her?"
>
> "I think he has," replied Selina. "I know very little how people make love; but I am sure if that was not making love, I cannot guess what is."

Much more specific than euphemisms like *make love* and *sleep with* are words that denote the actual act of copulation, the best known of which is *fuck*. The word *fuck* is at the heart of one of the most well-known and totally erroneous folk etymologies. Ostensibly it arose as an abbreviation for *For Unlawful Carnal Knowledge*, which was jotted down beside the names of fornicators in the old days, a historical period that occurred, if we can trust essays written by first-year university students, sometime between "the dawn of time" and "the coming of the pilgrims." In fact, however, the origin of *fuck* is much more mundane. It likely derives from a now-lost Scandinavian source, as suggested by the fact that the Norwegian *fukka* means *to copulate*, as does the Swedish *focka*. The first recorded instance of *fuck* is from the early sixteenth century, in a bawdy poem by William Dunbar called "In Secreit Place This Hyndir Nycht," previously referred to in the chapter devoted to terms of endearment. In that poem, the male protagonist proclaims that he loves his crowdie-mowdie but in fact what he really wants is to get into her pants: "his feiris he wald haif fukkit," meaning "his companion he would have fucked." Other sixteenth-century instances of the word are equally unabashed. David Lindsay, the tutor of the future King James V of Scotland, used the word in a poem chastising his royal student for his sexual licentiousness:

> Lyke ane boisteous Bull, ye rin and ryde
> Royatouslie lyke ane rude Rubeatour,
> Ay fukkand lyke ane furious Fornicatour.

In other words, "You're like a boisterous bull – you run and ride riotously like a rude scoundrel and fuck like a furious fornicator." Lindsay also used the word in a play where he criticized the church, or at least the bishops who "may fuck thair fill and be unmaryit." That is, they get to have all the sex they want, without the responsibility of being married.

Other centuries-old usages of the word *fuck* are striking because they sound so contemporary. For example, in 1763, John Wilkes, a member of the British Parliament, wrote a satire called "An Essay on Woman" which asserted that "life can little more supply / Than just a few good fucks, and then we die." This bawdy rhyme – which anticipated the late-twentieth century idiom, *Life's a bitch, and then you die* – was not the only offensive passage in the poem, and so Wilkes was eventually fined five-hundred pounds and sentenced to one year in jail for writing the piece. The phrase *flying fuck* – usually heard as part of *I don't give a flying fuck* – might also sound like a recent coinage, but in fact it's over a hundred and fifty years old. It first appeared in a poem that was published in a volume of erotic etchings by Thomas Rowlandson, including one that depicted a couple having sex on a galloping horse:

> Well mounted on a mettled steed,
> Famed for his strength as well as speed,
> Corrinna and her favorite buck
> Are pleas'd to have a flying fuck.
> While o'er the downs the courser strains,
> With fiery eye and loosened reins,
> Around his neck her arms she flings,
> Behind her buttocks move like springs.
> While Jack keeps time to every motion,
> And pours in love's delicious potion.

The modern counterpart to a flying-fuck, or sex on horseback, is the *mile-high club*, a term first recorded in 1972 and denoting individuals who have had sex in an aircraft.

One of the most amazing things about *fuck* is the number of grammatical uses to which it has been put, and the number of idioms which it has spawned. The word can be used as a verb, as in *She fucks like a mink* (that particular idiom dates back to about 1920). It can be a noun, as in *That was a great fuck*, a grammatical usage that emerged in the late seventeenth century. It can be an adjective, as in *You fucking bitch*, a phrase that first appeared in print in the mid nineteenth century. It can be an interjection as in *Holy fuck!* or just *Fuck!*, the latter of which is first recorded in 1929. It can be an adverb, as in *That's fucking excellent*, a grammatical usage that arose in the 1940s. Finally, it can be something called an infix, as in *abso-fucking-lutely*, a word that dates back to the 1920s. (Moreover, the act of fucking is itself a kind of conjunction.)

Idioms incorporating *fuck* include the exclamations *Fuck you!* first recorded in 1895, and *Fuck off!* which arose in the 1940s, though as early as 1929 the verb phrase *fuck off* was being used to mean *to run away*, as in "They fucked off once the cops arrived." The phrase *fuck all*, meaning *nothing* or *diddly squat*, appeared in print in 1918, while *mother-fucker* emerged as an insult in the 1920s, though that incest taboo was articulated much earlier, most notably in *Oedipus Rex*, a Greek tragedy written in the fifth century BC by Sophocles. Also in the 1920s, the phrase *fuck around* emerged, meaning both *to be promiscuous* and also *to waste time*. The idiom *fucked up*, meaning *ruined*, dates back to the 1930s, though *fucked* itself had been used with that sense since the late eighteenth century.

Euphemisms for *fuck* have also arisen. In 1948, for example, the publisher of Norman Mailer's *The Naked and the Dead* convinced the author to change his use of *fuck* to *fug*, a decision which – according to literary lore – prompted Dorothy Parker to say to Mailer, upon meeting him, "So you're the young man who can't spell *fuck*." Nowadays, many people also consider *Fudge!* to be a euphemized form of *Fuck!* but in fact that use of *fudge* probably arose from the noun *fudge*, which in the eighteenth century meant *nonsense*. Earlier on, *fudge* probably developed from the verb *fadge*, meaning *to patch together*.

Fuck is also closely associated with an obscene gesture, involving a raised middle finger, usually taken to mean *Fuck off!* or *Fuck you!* The name of this gesture – *the Finger* – is not recorded in English until 1961, but the gesture itself is far older. The ancient Romans referred to it as the *digitus impudicus*, meaning *the shameful finger*, and it's alluded to even earlier in Aristophanes' comedy, *The Clouds*, written around 420 BC In that play, Socrates is teaching Strepsiades about poetic meters, one of which is called the dactyl, because it has three beats just as a human finger – or in Greek, a human *dactylos* – has three bones. Strepsiades tells Socrates that he is already familiar with the dactyl, and then demonstrates by giving him the finger – to which Socrates responds, "You are as low-minded as you are stupid." In origin, the raised middle finger represents the penis, nestled between two partially bent fingers that signify testicles.

Even older than the word *fuck*, at least in written records, is *wifthing*, an Old English compound literally meaning *woman-thing* and signifying an act of copulation. On the surface, *wifthing* might seem to parallel recent constructions such as *girl thing*, often employed in sentences such as "It's a girl thing – you wouldn't understand." However, whereas the modern *girl thing* is essentially an assertion that the thing in question belongs exclusively, and proudly, to the realm of women, the Old English *wifthing* probably arose from the notion that copulation is a thing that a man does to – or, at best, with – a woman.

Like *wifthing*, the Old English *gemana* also denoted sexual intercourse, a sense it continued to possess even when it evolved into the Middle English *mone*, unrelated to the Modern English *moan* that denotes a groaning vocalization. A fourteenth-century translation of Ranulf Higden's *Polychronicon*, for example, notes that Mary conceived Jesus "withoute mannys mone," that is, without human sexual intercourse. In origin, the Old English *gemana* evolved from the Indo-European *mei*, meaning *to change*, which eventually evolved into a cluster of words meaning *to exchange goods*. Subsequently, these derivatives came to denote the community in which the goods are exchanged; in fact, the word *community* is one of the Latin-based words that evolved from the Indo-European *mei*, along with *communicate*, *communism* and *common*. Something is *common* when it is shared and exchanged freely in a community. The Old English *gemana*, meaning *sexual intercourse*, and the Modern English *common*, meaning *shared by everyone*, are therefore related to one another; their divergent senses begin to meet again in their cousin *commune*, a word that popularly denotes a group of people living together with a laissez-faire attitude toward

Botulinonia: a sex act involving a sausage.

sexual relationships. One other Old English word pertaining to copulation was *strienan*, which was sometimes used to mean *to beget offspring*. The primary sense of this verb, however, was *to acquire*, and thus the word is no doubt related to the Old English *streon*, a noun meaning *acquisition* or *treasure*. A modern descendent of this Old English word is the noun *strain*, a variety or breed of something, as in "A new strain of flu seems to be going around."

In Middle English, dozens of words and phrases signifying copulation appeared, one of the most familiar being *fornication*, which denotes sexual intercourse between an unmarried man and woman. The first recorded instance of *fornication* is from the beginning of the fourteenth century, and yet the verb form – *fornicate* – is not recorded until the mid sixteenth century, 250 years later. This seems unusual in comparison with a word such as *obligation*, which appeared at the same time as *fornication*, and which acquired its verb form *oblige* almost instantly. On the other hand, the appearance of *fornicate* is downright prompt in comparison with *resurrection*, which also appeared at the beginning of the fourteenth century but which didn't acquire the verb form *resurrect* until 1772 – almost half a millennium after the noun. A contemporary analogue would be words such as *sanction, coronation* and *elocution*: all three are familiar nouns, and yet their expected verb forms – *to sanctate, to coronate* and *to elocute* – are either non-existent or at best extremely rare. Instead of using such forms, anglophones either use a synonym ("I will crown you at the coronation"), or use the noun form as a verb ("I do not sanction this sanction"), or use an equivalent phrase ("I speak well because of my training in elocution"). Likewise, with *fornication,* moralists and preachers were happy, for centuries, to use phrases such as "He falls into fornication" rather than "He fornicates." Indeed, the former construction, where the abstract noun is used with a pejorative verb, results in a more weighty and serious-sounding sentence, one better-suited to prick the conscience of its reader or listener. In origin, *fornication* derives from the Latin *fornix,* meaning *vaulted chamber.* The association with sexual intercourse arose thanks to the fact that Roman brothels tended to be located in cellars with vaulted ceilings. The original meaning of the Latin *fornix* is better preserved in the medical term *fornix,* which denotes a tract of tissue that arches, like a vault, over the *corpus callosum* of the human brain.

The word *copulation* also appeared in Middle English, having been derived from the Latin *copulare*, meaning *to link*. That Latin source also evolved into the verb *couple*, which since the fourteenth century has been used to denote sexual intercourse among animals, and sometimes among humans. Strangely, while the *Oxford English Dictionary* includes *copulate* and *copulatory* among its half-million headwords, it doesn't include *copulator*, even though that word appears in dozens of scholarly articles posted on the Internet by animal scientists.

Unlike *fornication* and *copulation*, many other Middle English words denoting sexual intercourse have been forgotten, such as *putage*, which signified fornication as it pertained to the woman. A man could not commit putage. Other words, such as *swink* and *swive*, have also been forgotten, except to those who have read Chaucer's *Canterbury Tales* where he uses them unabashedly. In *The Reeve's Tale*, for example, a university student gets up in the middle of the night and makes his way into the bed of Malyne, the daughter of the miller who has put him up for the night. By dawn, the student is exhausted, for he and Malyne have "swonken al the longe nyght," the word *swonken* being the past participle of *swink*. The word *swive* is used only a few lines later, when the student creeps back to bed to tell his friend what he has been up to: "I have thries in this shorte nyght / Swyved the milleres doghter bolt upright." In other words, "I have three times, in one short night, fucked the miller's daughter standing up." What the student doesn't realize is that in the darkness he has returned to the wrong bed, and has just whispered his boast into the ear of the miller, who is not pleased to hear about his daughter's nocturnal swiving. That word was also used in the Middle English phrase *smal-swivinge men*, meaning *men who rarely have sex*. In origin, *swive* derives from the Old English *swifan*, meaning *to move in a circle*, which is also the source of the Modern English *swivel*. As for *swink*, its predecessor was the Old English *swincan*, meaning *to toil*, implying that sex is hard work.

Several other Middle English words denoting copulation – *golehead* and *jape,* for example – have origins pertaining to play, rather than work. The *gole* of *golehead* derived from an Old English source meaning *merry*, while *jape* originally seems to have meant *jest* or *tomfoolery*. Earlier on, *jape* might have evolved from the Old French *japer*, meaning *to howl*. The Middle English idiom *to play under cloth* also denoted copulation, or at least the erotic play that happens under the bedclothes. Somewhat similar is *to grope under gore*, the word *gore* being a Middle English term denoting the lower part of a woman's skirt. The latter phrase is used in a wistful poem from the early fourteenth century known as "Elde Makith Me" – that is, "Age Makes Me." In this poem the speaker describes the baleful changes that old age has inflicted upon him:

> Ihc ne mai no more
> Grope vnder gore,
> Thogh mi wil wold yete,
> Y-yoket Ich am of yore
> With last and luther lore,
> And sunne me hath bi-set.

Rendered into Modern English, this stanza might read as follows:

> I may no more
> Grope under skirts,
> Though my will would yet,
> I have been yoked for some time
> With a final and withering loss,
> And the sun has set for me.

Other Middle English synonyms for copulation – such as *ride* and *tread* – were just as "action-oriented" as *grope under gore*. In Chaucer's *The Nun's Priest's Tale*, for example, Chaunticleer – a talking rooster – tells his wife that "I may nat on yow ryde, / For that oure perche is maad so narwe, allas." In other words, "I can't mount you because our roost is made so narrow, alas." Once they get off their roost, however, they have better luck, and Chaunticleer is able to tread her repeatedly before morning: "He fethered Pertelote twenty tyme / And trad as ofte er it was pryme." The word *tread* continued to signify copulation, especially between birds, into the early twentieth century, and *ride* has remained a familiar synonym for *fuck* to the present-day. More aggressive words for copulation also existed in Middle English, ranging from *pilt* (meaning *to thrust*), to *sting* (meaning *to stab*), to *rage* (meaning *to be furious*). The latter term was used in a

Masochism: the desire to experience pain during sex, named after Leopold von Sacher-Masoch, an Austrian novelist.

fifteenth-century treatise on the Ten Commandments, which noted that the seventh commandment, the one pertaining to adultery, "forbedith alle unlawful cussynges and clippinges and ragynges." That is, it forbids all unlawful kissings and huggings and copulatings.

The largest cluster of Middle English words pertaining to sexual intercourse are those that signify some sort of joining together. These include the now-obsolete verbs *felter* and *sam*, both of which essentially meant *to bring together*, as well as the still-current verbs *occupy* and *meddle*. The latter term is perhaps best known in its noun form *medley*, meaning *a mixture*. The word *occupy* first acquired its sexual sense in the mid fifteenth century, and by the end of the sixteenth century it had come to be so tarnished by this bawdy use that it was considered a dirty word. For example, in *Henry IV Part 2*, Doll Tearsheet is outraged when Pistol is referred to as a captain, and proceeds to decry the abuse of words: "A captain! Gods light, these villaines wil make the word as odious as the word *occupy*, which was an excellent good worde before it was ill sorted." Doll Tearsheet's ire recalls that of my high-school English teacher, who – in the late 1970s – fumed about no longer being able to use the word *gay*, which was "a perfectly fine word until it was taken over by the homosexuals." As for the word *meddle*, its sexual sense can be seen in a fifteenth-century autobiography known as *The Booke of Margery Kempe*. Kempe relates how she and her husband ceased to have sex after her spiritual visions convinced her that doing so was sinful. After eight weeks of celibacy, her horny husband put this question to her:

> Margery, if her come a man wyth a swerd and wold
> smyte of myn hed les than I schulde comown kendly
> wyth yow...wold ye suffyr myn hed to be smet of er
> ellys suffyr me to medele wyth yow agen?

In other words,

> Margery, if a man came here with a sword and
> threatened to cut off my head if I didn't have natural
> intercourse with you...would you allow my head to be
> cut off or else allow me to copulate with you again?

To this question, Margery replies, "I had levar see yow be slayn than we schuld turne agen to owyr unclennesse," prompting her husband to say, "Ye arn no good wyfe."

Although Margery's decision to forego sex with her husband was prompted by her desire to be more pure, her parish priest would have probably considered her celibacy to be sinful, or at least misguided. Marital sex was considered not just a privilege but an obligation that husbands and wives owed one another, as is reflected in the Middle English use of the word *debt* to denote sexual intercourse. For example, in Chaucer's *Parson's Tale* the Parson says "She hath merite of chastitee, that yeldeth to hire housbonde the dette of hir body." Somewhat similar is the Middle English noun *manred*, which derived from the Old English *mannraeden*, meaning *man-pledge*; usually *manred* denoted the homage that vassals owed their lord, but it was also employed to signify the sexual relations that spouses owed one another. Even today, a spouse's willful refusal of sex, accompanied by a failure to perform other mutual responsibilities of a marital relationship, can be considered grounds for a divorce.

Finally, two other words that denoted sexual intercourse in Middle English continue to be used in that way today – namely, *it* and *deed*. These two words are among the most non-specific in the language: the word *it* can obviously refer to any thing, and *deed* can denote almost any human action. The fact that such all-encompassing words have for centuries been synonymous with the sex act is indicative of its primary role in human experience. For example, in a fifteenth-century translation of Christine de Pizan's *Epistle of Othea to Hector*, Othea tells a tale of a man whose "stepmodir lovyd hym so hoote that sche required it of hym." More than two hundred years later, Shakespeare has King Lear decry the beastly sexuality of humankind when he says, "the fitchew nor the soyled horse goes to it / With a more riotous appetite." Likewise, in an early-seventeenth-century comedy known as *The Birth of Merlin*, the clown tells the Prince about his promiscuous sister: "Her name is Joan Go-to-it. I am her elder, but she has been at it before me; 'tis a womans fault." And nowadays, in high schools across North America, the question "Did you do it with her?" is uttered far more often than "Are you joining the glee club?"

As for *deed*, its sexual sense is clear in Middle English idioms such as *fleshly deed*, and in early-seventeenth-century idioms such as *do the deed of darkness*, which is used, for example, in Shakespeare's *Pericles*, where Lysimachus and a bawd discuss a reluctant prostitute. Sometimes the last part of the phrase *do the deed* was dropped, and the verb *do* itself denoted the sex act. This usage is apparent in Shakespeare's *Titus Andronicus*, where

Chiron and Demetrius rail against Aaron for having impregnated their mother with an illegitimate child: "Thou hast undone our mother!" Chiron cries, to which Aaron dryly replies, "Villain, I have done thy mother."

Shakespeare employs many of the other synonyms for sexual intercourse that emerged in Early Modern English. Two of those words – *cover* and *tup* – originally denoted the copulation of animals, and were only later extended to humans. With *cover*, the animals in question were horses, while *tup* referred to sheep. For example, in *Othello*, Iago taunts Brabantio, Desdemona's father, by telling him that Othello and Desdemona are having sex: "Even now, now, very now, an old black ram / Is tupping your white ewe." A few lines later, he adds that Brabantio will have his "daughter covered with a Barbary horse," and for good measure he concludes by saying that Desdemona and Othello are "making the beast with two backs," an idiom that Shakespeare invented. Elsewhere, Shakespeare alludes to the erotic coupling of Venus and Adonis by using the verb *mount*, a word which is now used almost exclusively in the barnyard rather than the bedroom.

Shakespeare might also have used the words *wap* and *niggle* to denote copulation, but he didn't. Both those words had developed sexual senses by the mid sixteenth century, and were in use throughout his lifetime. *Wap*, for example, was first used in a 1567 treatise by Thomas Harman that described the behaviour of tramps and vagabonds: "He tooke his jockam in his famble, and a-wapping he went," meaning "He took his cock in his hand, and a-fucking he went." In the same treatise, Harman also defined the cant word *niggle*: "To nygle, to haue to do with a woman carnally." The two words appear side by side in Thomas

Decker's 1611 comedy *The Roaring Girl*, where Trapdoore tries an unsuccessful pickup line on Moll Cutpurse: "Wee'l couch a hogshead vnder the Ruffemans, and there you shall wap with me, and I'le niggle with you." (*Couch a hogshead* was a slang idiom, current from the early sixteenth to the early nineteenth century, that meant both *to sleep* and *to sleep with*.) The word *wap* probably developed its copulation sense as an extension of its earlier sense of *to throw quickly*, perhaps in reference to ejaculation. As for *niggle*, its ulterior history is unknown, but in terms of its later development, it probably evolved into the Modern English *niggling* that means *annoying*, as in *a niggling doubt*. The connection might lie in the eighteenth-century use of *niggle* to describe the kind of fidgety behaviour that results from sexual frustration – that is, from feeling hot and bothered. The word shifted, in short, from denoting sexual intercourse to sexual frustration to general annoyance.

Other Early Modern English words for copulation include the verbs *roger, quiff, screw, hump* and *shag*. The first of these, *roger*, emerged in the early eighteenth century, and probably developed from the earlier use of *roger* as a synonym for *penis*. In turn, this anatomical use of *roger* developed from the given name *Roger*; that is, the male name was extended to the male member. The verb *quiff* also emerged in the early eighteenth century, but unlike *roger* it became obsolete before that century was over. Interestingly, a slang word very similar to *quiff* arose in the 1990s: *queef*, which denotes vaginal flatulence – that is, the sound of air escaping from the vagina during or after intercourse. *Screw* developed its sexual sense around the same time that *roger* and *quiff* emerged, and is yet another example of a word, like the thirteenth-century *sting*, or the eighteenth-century *bang*, or the twentieth-century *bonk*, that equates sexual intercourse with aggressive penetration or striking.

In contrast, the verb *hump* came to mean *to copulate* in the late eighteenth century not from the notion of penetration, but from the hump-like shape formed by the conjoined bodies in sexual intercourse, especially in the so-called *doggy-style*, where the man crouches over the kneeling woman. Curiously, the earliest recorded instance of this sense of *hump* is in Francis Grose's *Dictionary of the Vulgar Tongue*, where he writes that it was "once a fashionable word for copulation." From Grose's comment we can infer that the sexual sense of *hump* must have been current in spoken English well before he recorded it in 1785, and that the word was, by then, almost obsolete. This is confirmed by the fact that no other instances of *hump*, with its sexual sense, occur until 1931. During that 150 year period, *hump* might have become truly obsolete, and reappeared only because it happened to be reinvented by someone who, once again, perceived a resemblance between a copulating couple and a hump. Alternatively, *hump* might not have died out, but instead simply descended into the lowest registers of spoken English, hidden away like the Loch Ness monster, only to resurface into written English in the twentieth century. Either way, it's ironic that a sentence claiming that a word is passé is also our earliest record of that word. Clearly, the written record of a word is often just the tip of a huge and vanished oral history.

The verb *shag* would probably be unknown to most North Americans were it not for its liberal use in 1997's *Austin Powers: International Man of Mystery*. The 1999 sequel to that film brought the word into even greater prominence, thanks to its subtitle, *The Spy Who Shagged Me*. Like so many eighteenth-century cant words, the origin of *shag* is uncertain, but it may be connected to an older *shag*, dating back to the fourteenth century, that meant *to shake*. The term *shag carpet* – which sounds like the name of a rug specially designed for copulation – has no known connection to the verb *shag*.

Most of the copulation words so far mentioned, such as *quiff*, *niggle*, *wap* and *shag*, sound quintessentially British. Put any two of them together, and you end up with what sounds like the name of a village outside London: Quiffniggle or Shagwap or Niggleshag-on-Avon. Early Middle English did, however, derive several synonyms for *copulation* from foreign sources, including the noun *scortation* and the verb *subagitate*. The first of these appeared in the mid sixteenth century, having been formed from

> Let copulation thrive!
> *William Shakespeare*

the Latin *scortum*, meaning *harlot*. The second word was invented in the early seventeenth century, from the Latin prefix *sub*, meaning *under*, and *agitare*, meaning *to excite*. Although the resulting word looks as if it might mean *to under-excite*, a better rendering is *to excite under*, under the skirt or below the belt.

The mid nineteenth century contributed a cluster of idioms that denoted sexual intercourse, including *to do a bit of beef*, *to do a bit of cock-fighting*, *to do a bit of front door work*, *to do a bit of skirt* and *to do a bit of giblet pie*. The operative phrase, obviously, was *to do a bit of*, and it seems likely that almost any word could be tacked on to the end and it would still convey the notion of copulation, at least to a nineteenth-century gentleman.

For instance, over the course of the last minute, I've invented *to do a bit of pudding,* or *to do a bit of banking* or *to do a bit of spreading the Empire.* Another idiom invented in the late nineteenth century was *Wham, bam, thank you, ma'am,* a phrase denoting a quick and casual act of copulation, a meaning which is reinforced by the insistent rhythm and simplistic rhymes of the phrase. The 1920s saw the appearance of *nooky,* which, as suggested in the Introduction to this book, might have been inspired by the notion that sexual intercourse often occurs in nooks and crannies. This is reflected in Shakespeare's *The Winter's Tale* where a shepherd, upon finding an abandoned baby, says "This has been some stair-work, some trunk-work, some behind-door-work."

The verb *boff* came to denote sexual intercourse in the 1930s, a word that might have developed from the verb *buffet,* meaning *to strike,* or from the phrase *in the buff,* meaning *naked,* which as noted earlier derives from *buffalo.* The 1940s contributed two idioms, *get to third-base* and *a roll in the hay,* the first of which construes the sex act as a sporting event, much as the word *game* was used in Early Modern English to denote copulation. For example, in Shakespeare's *Troilus and Cressida,* Ulysses decries Cressida's wanton gestures as "sluttish spoils of opportunity / And daughters of the game." On the other hand, *a roll in the hay* connotes spontaneous or on-the-spot intercourse because the phrase evokes the unconstrained sexuality that has long been associated with idealized depictions of rustic or pastoral communities, places that are supposedly closer to nature.

In the 1950s, the term *ball* came to denote copulation, a usage that some etymologists have linked to the *ball* that means *testicle*, but which more likely parallels *hump* in evoking the image of a "ball" or mass of flesh formed by a pair of intertwined lovers. The seventeenth-century poet, Andrew Marvell, uses the word in this way in his erotically-charged poem, "To His Coy Mistress":

> Let us roll all our strength, and all
> Our sweetness, up into one ball:
> And tear our pleasures with rough strife,
> Through the iron gates of life.

The *ball* in idioms such as "We're having a ball!" is unrelated to the copulation *ball*. That idiom derives from the *ball* that means formal dance, which in turn derives from the French *bal*, meaning *dance*, from whence *ballet* derives. English also adopted *schtup* as a copulation word in the 1950s. In Yiddish, *schtup* literally means *to shove*, having been derived from the German *stupsen*, meaning *to push*. In the 1970s, the verb *bonk* came to denote sexual intercourse, an extension of its earlier sense of *to hit*. The word appeared in the 1930s, probably as a conflation of *bang* and *conk*. More recently, *bonk* has shifted in pronunciation and spelling to *boink*, perhaps because the *oink* sound – which evokes the squealing of pigs – seems inherently more humorous. The 1980s saw the emergence of *hide the salami*, but the equivalent *hide the wienie* was current as early as the 1910s.

Another sausage-related idiom is *ride the baloney pony*, which emerged in the 1990s. That term, however, is somewhat more specific in that it signifies an act of sexual intercourse in which the woman straddles the man, as did the eighteenth-century idiom *to ride St. George*. The latter idiom inverts the usual iconography, since St. George – the patron saint of England – is almost always depicted on horseback. St. George's association with sexual intercourse might also have been facilitated by the fact that he slew a dragon, a beast that was also known by the phallic-sounding name "the worm." Sexologists refer to this intercourse position simply as *female superior*, while most sex manuals aimed at the general public use the phrase *woman on top*. The obvious counterparts are, of course, *male superior* and *man on top*, but the term *missionary position* is also common. This name derives from the popular belief that Christian missionaries in Africa insisted that the indigenous people cease copulating from behind and instead engage only in the male superior position. Although the story itself might be apocryphal, it does reflect attitudes toward sexual positions that date back centuries. Medieval theologians, for example, considered the only proper position to be male superior because it reproduced the supposedly natural hierarchy of the sexes. Likewise, *retrocopulation* – that is, copulating from behind – was considered sinful because it was "beastly," an attitude that can still be seen in the term *doggie style*.

As late as 1969, six U.S. states still considered it grounds for divorce if a man had sex with his wife in any position other than the missionary position. Some individuals, however, have no choice when it comes to intercourse positions, due to physiological abnormalities. An individual who can copulate only while lying face-up is *supinovalent* while someone who can do so only while standing up is *stasivalent*. In the late eighteenth century, an act of sexual intercourse in which the couple stood was known by the slang name *three-penny upright*, suggesting a cheap and hurried act of prostitution. In the nineteenth century, the same thing was called a *knee-trembler* or a *perpendicular*. In contrast, the slang term *horizontals* – which was current from through the 1920s and 1930s – implies a prone position, as does the *horizontal bop*, from the 1980s, and even the much older *getting laid*, which dates back to the mid seventeenth century.

~~~

Copulation need not involve the vagina, nor even the penis. As mentioned previously, the word *copulation* simply means *a coupling*. Similarly, the word *intercourse* literally means *a running between*, which again implies the idea of connecting or coupling two things together. From this perspective, two intertwined tongues are a form of copulation, as is a digit inserted into any number of orifices. Likewise, if a man thrusts his penis into an armpit (his partner's, not his own), it is a form of intercourse, specifically axillary intercourse, a term that derives from the Latin *axilla*, meaning *armpit*. (The Indo-European sources of *axilla* was *aks*, which also developed into the Latin name for a bird's wing, *ala*; this Latin word also came to be used metaphorically to denote the *wing* of a building, and eventually was transferred to the walkway that ran down the wing of a building, which gave rise to the word *aisle*.)

On the other hand, if a man rubs his penis between the thighs of an individual, it is technically known as femoral intercourse, though slang equivalents include *dry fuck* (from the 1930s), *college fuck* (from the 1950s) and *dry hump* (from the 1960s).

When it's the cleavage of breasts that provides the friction for the penis, it's called *mammary intercourse* or *mastophallation*, though *tit fuck* (from the 1980s) and *French fuck* (from the 1930s) are the familiar slang terms, along with the humorous *trip down mammary lane*. Even earlier than *French fuck* is an unabashed description of that sex act in a letter James Joyce wrote to his wife, Nora, during a two-month period in 1909 when circumstances forced them to live in different cities:

> The smallest things give me a great cockstand – a whorish movement of your mouth, a little brown stain on the seat of your white drawers, a sudden dirty word spluttered out by your wet lips, a sudden immodest noise made by your behind and then a bad smell slowly curling up out of your backside. At such moments I feel mad to do it in some filthy way, to feel your hot lecherous lips sucking away at me, to fuck between your two rosy-tipped bubbies, to come on your face and squirt it over your hot cheeks and eyes, to stick it between the cheeks of your rump and bugger you.

We might suppose that Nora was shocked and offended when she opened the envelope containing this lupanarian letter. But the fact that she preserved it, instead of tossing it into the fireplace, would suggest otherwise. She probably, in fact, sent her husband an erotic missive in return, though if she did it hasn't survived. Perhaps Joyce wore it to bits, by making it his constant bedtime reading.

Chapter Fifteen

GO DOWN MOSES

Oral Sex Words

*I*F THE NUMBER OF words is anything to judge by, then oral intercourse is a more popular activity than axillary, femoral and mammary copulation combined. The word *oral* derives from the Latin *os*, meaning *mouth*. The word *os* also developed into the Latin *ostium*, meaning *door*, on the analogy that a door is, like the mouth, a kind of opening. *Ostium* then evolved into the Old French *huisier*, also meaning *door*, which eventually became the English *usher*, originally the name of a door-keeper, and now someone who leads you from the door to your seat.

One of the earliest words to denote oral copulation was *gamahuche*, which appears to have been adopted from French in the 1860s. In French, the word dates back to at least 1783, where it appears in an erotic work called *Le Libertin de Qualité*. It's unclear where the French acquired the word, but one possibility is that it comes from the medieval Latin *gamma ut*, which was a musical term. In the eleventh century, Guido D'Arezzo invented a six-note scale for reading music, with the notes being named *ut, re, mi, fa, sol, la*. (Later on, *ut* was replaced by the now-familiar *do*.) The note one tone lower than *ut* came to be known as *gamma-ut*, the word *gamma* denoting the third letter of the Greek alphabet; *gamma-ut* therefore represented a note below the range of the usual hexachord scale, a note that was "down there," so to speak. Thanks to this notion, the noun *gamma-ut* might have developed a verb form – *gamahucher* – denoting a sex act that takes place at an anatomically "low" level. (The idiom *to go down on someone*, which since the early twentieth century has denoted both fellatio and cunnilingus, also embodies that "low down" notion.) It's even possible that the origin of the names of the six notes in Arezzo's scale might have facilitated the transformation of the musical *gamma-ut* into the sexual *gamahucher*. Arezzo created those names by taking the first syllable from the first word in the lines from a Latin hymn to Saint John:

UT queant laxis
REsonare fibris
MIra gestorum
FAmuli tuorum,
SOLve polluti
LAbii reatum.

These lines might be rendered into English as follows: "So that we servants can resound the wonders of your deeds with loosened vocal chords, purge the guilt from our polluted lip." The reference to the polluted lip – *polluti labii* – might have prompted some bawdy-minded wag to associate the hymn with fellatio.

Gamahucher acquired a synonym in the 1880s, when *irrumation* was invented. The word was derived from the Latin *irrumare*, meaning *to suck*, which in turn was formed from *ruma*, meaning *teat*. Around the same time, the word *fellatio* entered the English language, which soon prompted the paired-terms *fellator* and *fellatrix*, which refer respectively to a male and female performer of fellatio. Strangely, the Roman author Martial calls the raven a fellator in one of his poems:

Corve salutator, quare fellator baberis,
In caput intravit mentula nulla tamen?

which might be rendered thus:

O greetings raven, why are you considered a sucker,
Even though no penis has ever entered your mouth?

Martial was probably referring to the ancient belief that ravens ejaculated semen from their beak, rather than from their penis. In origin, *fellatio* derives from the Latin *fellare*, meaning *to suck*, which in turn evolved from the Indo-European *dhelo*, which was one of the suffixed forms of the Indo-European base, *dhei*, also meaning *to suck*. Another one of its suffixed forms was *dhemna*, which evolved into the word *female*, denoting the sex that gives suck to infants, and still another suffixed form developed into the word *fetus*. Even more surprising is that *felicity* ultimately derives from the same Indo-European root: the immediate source of *felicity* was the Latin *felix*, meaning *happy*, which evolved from the aforementioned Indo-European source thanks to the notion that an infant sucking at its mother's breast is happy. One other possible relative is *felon*, which might have evolved from the Latin *fellare* as a term of abuse – in other words, etymologically, a *felon* might be a *cocksucker*.

> The function of muscle is to pull and not to push, except in the case of the genitals and the tongue.
>
> *Leonardo Da Vinci*

Most historical dictionaries of slang indicate that the earliest recorded use of the verb *suck* to denote the act of giving fellatio is from 1928. However, this date seems unrealistic, given that *cocksucker* was in use from the late nineteenth century. Moreover, for centuries before, *suck* had been used in literary contexts that at least implied fellatio. For example, in the homoerotic poem "The Tears of an Affectionate Shepheard Sicke for Love," written in 1594 by Richard Barnfield, the Shepherd-Poet creates an extended metaphor in which a sought-after young man is depicted as a bee that will suck the "honey-berries" from the Shepherd's sweet "flower":

> O would to God (so I might have my fee)
> My lips were honey, and thy mouth a Bee.
> Then shouldst thou sucke my sweete and my faire flower
> That now is ripe, and full of honey-berries.
> Then would I leade thee to my pleasant Bower
> Fild full of Grapes, of Mulberries, and Cherries;
> Then shouldst thou be my Waspe or else my Bee,
> I would thy hive, and thou my honey bee.

A bit later in the poem, *suck* reappears, again with the implication of fellatio: "Thou sukst the flowre till all the sweet be gone."

Somewhat less poetic than Barnfield's erotic poem are most of the slang synonyms for fellatio that appeared in the twentieth century, such as *blow job* and *give head* from the early 1940s, *deep throat* from 1970s, and *skull fuck* from the 1990s. More specific forms of fellatio also acquired names: fellating an uncircumcised penis, for example, came to be known in the 1990s as *curing the blind*. Sometimes, too, words were borrowed from other contexts. The words *eat, nosh* and *plate* all have culinary associations, and all came to be used as synonyms for *fellate*. Of these three, *eat* is the oldest, dating back to the 1920s, while *nosh* and *plate* appeared in the early 1960s. In origin, *nosh* derives via Yiddish from the German *naschen*, meaning *to eat on the sly* – that is, *to nibble* or *to snack*. The origin of *plate* is more circuitous: it derived from the phrase *plate of ham*, which in turn arose as rhyming slang for *gam*, which in turn emerged as a clipped form of the previously mentioned *gamahuche*.

≈

In comparison with fellatio, orolabial stimulation – the act of licking the vagina – is not well represented in the English language. There is, of course, the word *cunnilingus* itself, but it was not adopted from Latin until the 1880s, where it had been formed from *cunnus*, meaning *female pudendum*, and *lingere*, meaning *to lick*. Even further back, *lingere* derives from the same source as *lingua*, the Latin word for *tongue*, which means that it's related to many of the tongue words discussed in the Introduction to this book, such as *linguistics*, *language* and *linguine*. All other terms pertaining to cunnilingus are slang, and in written English only a few of them can be traced back more than forty years: the nouns *cunt-sucker* and *cunt-lapper* are first recorded in the 1868 and 1916 respectively, *to eat fur pie* in 1932, and *muff dive* in 1942. More recent is the small cluster of cunnilingus idioms that appeared in the 1960s: *eat out*, *eat at the Y*, *box lunch*, *pearl dive*, *talk to the canoe driver* and *yodel up the valley*. Perhaps the term *69* – signifying mutual and simultaneous oral sex – might also be included as a cunnilingus term. If so, then it's among the oldest, dating back to the 1880s, where the juxtaposition of the digit 6 and the digit 9 – the latter being an inverted version of the former – represented the posture required for mutual cunnilingus and fellatio.

The *lingus* of *cunnilingus* is also present in the word *anilingus*, denoting the licking of a partner's anus. The word is rare enough that lexicographers cannot agree upon its spelling: some dictionaries have *analingus* and others have *analinctus*. (Most don't include it at all.) Slang equivalents include *rimming*, probably inspired by the notion that the anus is the rim of the rectum, as well as *e-coli pie*, *rimadonna* and *39*. (With regard to the latter term, the double-arc of the digit 3 perhaps represents the shape of the buttocks.) At least one anilingus term is highly specific in its reference: the word *felch* denotes the act of sucking one's own semen out of another

Fetish: an object, such as a shoe or pantyhose, that becomes a source of sexual excitement. The word derives from the Latin *factitius* meaning made artificially.

person's rectum. The origin of the word is uncertain: it can be traced back to the late 1960s, where it might have arisen in imitation of the sound produced by that sex act. Alternatively, it might be eponymous, that is, inspired by the last name of someone who specialized in that act. An on-line phone directory for the U.S. lists over thirteen hundred people with the name *Felch*, and almost two hundred with the name *Felcher*. Any one of them, or their predecessors, might be the namesake of felching. (Oddly, in Canada, there are only four phone listings for *Felch*, and none at all for *Felcher*.)

Chapter Sixteen

BRINGING UP THE REAR

Anal Sex Words

ALTHOUGH SOME OF THE aforementioned sex acts, like femoral intercourse or felching, might be considered unusual, they have not been demonized like anal intercourse. For many centuries, individuals who engaged in anal sex were severely punished. Even at present, ten U.S. states still have laws prohibiting anal sex, regardless of whether the individuals involved are same-sex or opposite-sex, and four more states have laws prohibiting anal sex between men. In South Carolina, the relevant statute reads as follows:

> Whoever shall commit the abominable crime of
> buggery, whether with mankind or with beast, shall, on
> conviction, be guilty of felony and shall be imprisoned
> in the Penitentiary for five years or shall pay a fine
> of not less than five hundred dollars, or both, at the
> discretion of the court.

In Canada, anal intercourse is illegal if one or more of the participants is younger than eighteen, but other forms of sex, including vaginal intercourse, are permitted even if one of the participants is as young as fourteen. This negative attitude toward anal intercourse is reflected in some of the early words that were used to denote it. In Middle English, for example, *misuse* was employed to describe the act of anal intercourse, though it's true that this verb was also used to denote other forms of supposedly deviant behaviour. The word is used in John Wycliffe's 1382 translation of the Bible, in the Book of Judges where a band of men come to a house, pound on the door, and demand that the owner "bryng out the man that is gon in to thi hous that wee mys-usyn hym." Other Middle English words that allude to anal sex include *foulness* and *the sin of horribility*, though both of these could also denote bestiality. Elsewhere, in the Book of Jude, Wycliffe translates the Greek *sarkos heteras*, which denotes the thing that the wicked citizens of Sodom and Gomorrah hankered after, as *other flesh*. Later on, in 1526, William Tindale translated the same Greek passage as *strange flesh*, a phrase that the King James Bible retained in 1611, and which therefore continued to be a familiar euphemism for anal intercourse for centuries to come.

Because the citizens of Sodom had a yen for strange flesh, the name of their city also came to denote anal intercourse, a usage that dates back to the late thirteenth century. Here, too, as with most of the previous phrases, *sodomy* could denote a wider variety of supposed sins than just anal sex, but that particular act tended to dominate the sense of the word. In the early nineteenth century, *sodomy* gave rise to the shortened form *sod*, which became a nasty term of abuse for a man, though by the 1930s the word had softened, and was often being used in chipper phrases such as *lucky sod*. As for Sodom's sister city, Gomorrah, there was an attempt, in the sixteenth century, to turn its name into a synonym for *sodomite*; however, *gomorrhean* did not survive the seventeenth century. Marcel Proust, in the early twentieth century, did attempt in *Remembrance of Things Past* to use *Sodom* to denote male homosexuality, and *Gomorrah* to denote female homosexuality, but that distinction never really took hold. Similarly, sexologists have recently attempted to distinguish anal intercourse with a male partner and anal intercourse with a female partner by creating the terms *androsodomy* and *anomeatia*, but that pair of words has never entered common parlance.

Like *sodomy*, the word *buggery*, which also denotes anal intercourse, was inspired by a group of people – not just a city, but an entire nation. That nation is Bulgaria, whose citizens were once considered by Roman Catholics to be heretics, because they belonged to the Eastern Orthodox Church. As a result, the Latin word *bulgarus* came to mean *heretic*, a sense it maintained as it evolved into the Old French *bougre*, which in turn was adopted into English in the mid fourteenth century as the agent noun *bugger* and as the abstract noun *buggery*. Over time, the *heresy* notion of *buggery* came to be supplanted by the *anal sex* notion, thanks to the fact that heresy and sodomy were both considered heinous crimes. The word *buggery* continues to be used with its *anal sex* sense in legal contexts, but *bugger* – like the previously mentioned *sod* – has lost much of its pejorative force. For example, I recall my grandfather affectionately referring to me as a little bugger, and in fact he probably would have been shocked to realize that he was calling me a sodomite.

Unlike *sodomy* and *buggery* which have negative, if not criminal, connotations, the phrases *anal sex* and *anal intercourse* emerged as non-judgemental equivalents for those older terms. Neither of those latter two phrases appears in the *Oxford English Dictionary*, though psychoanalytic terms such as *anal sadism* and *anal retentive* are included. The absence of *anal sex* and *anal intercourse* from that dictionary might be due to editorial prudery, but more likely it has resulted from the fact that both terms are of fairly recent coinage. For instance, in the *New York Times*, the phrase *anal intercourse* first appeared on December 10, 1972, while *anal sex* was not printed in its pages until February 18, 1974. (In contrast, *sodomy* and *buggery* have appeared in that newspaper's court reports since the 1850s.) For ten years after 1974, *anal sex* and *anal intercourse* appeared sporadically in the *New York Times*, usually in news items pertaining to legal challenges of sodomy laws. Then, in 1984, the onset of the AIDS crisis prompted the appearance of those terms in hundreds of articles, thanks to the correlation of the disease with that form of sexual activity. For some people, that correlation was so powerful that graffiti began to appear on the walls of public bathrooms, proposing a mean-spirited alternative origin for the AIDS acronym: Anal Intercourse – Don't Start.

Slang equivalents for anal sex have proliferated since the late eighteenth century. For example, in his 1785 *Dictionary of the Vulgar Tongue*, Francis Grose records the phrase *to navigate the windward passage*. A hundred years later, the 1880s saw the appearance of *back-door work* and *backscuttle*. With regard to the latter word, it was probably not formed from the *scuttle* that means *to scurry away*, but rather from the unrelated naval *scuttle* that means *to bore a hole*, originally used in reference to the intentional sinking of one's own ship. Somewhat similar is *ream*, which came to signify anal intercourse in the 1940s, but which had originally, in the early nineteenth century, denoted the process of increasing the diameter of a hole. More common than any of these terms, perhaps, are *bum-fuck*, *ass-fuck* and *butt-fuck*, from the 1860s, 1940s and 1960s respectively.

One other term that now denotes anal intercourse is *Greek love*, which first appeared in the 1930s, and has more recently been shortened to just *Greek*. For example, pick up the your local newspaper, glance at the Business Personals, and you will probably spot an ad for an escort – male or female – who lists "Greek" as a specialty. This sense of *Greek love* is a far cry from the ancient homosocial tradition that inspired the term. That tradition originated in Greece about 600 BC and lasted for about a thousand years, during which time upper-class men engaged in what was then called *paiderastia*, a close mentorship between a male adult and a male adolescent. Typically, the young man, at about age twenty, would select an adolescent of about twelve, whom he would befriend, love and train in the fine or military arts. The relationship would last about ten years, at which point the older male would find a woman to marry, and the younger male would become a mentor to an apprentice of his own. While such relationships could encompass sex, they often did not. The real thrust of the friendship was the emotional and intellectual bond between the two individuals, and the guided maturation of the younger male. This goal is reflected in the origin of the word *paiderastia*, which was created by combining the Greek *paidos* – the genitive form of *pais*, meaning *child* – with *erastia*, meaning *love*. The word, therefore, literally means *love of a child*. When English adopted *paiderastia* as *pederasty* in the early seventeenth century, it narrowed and debased the meaning of the word. It came to denote what the *Oxford English Dictionary* calls "an unnatural connexion," a synonym, in other words, for *sodomy*. This sense can be seen in Samuel Purchas' *Pilgrimage*, published in 1613, where he refers to "pederasts who buy boyes at an hundred or two hundred duckats, and mew them up for their filthie lust." It was also this debased conception of the ancient Greek tradition of *paiderastia* that people had in mind when the term *Greek love* was invented.

Chapter Seventeen

KNOWING DOROTHY

Sexual Orientation Words

*A*S MENTIONED ABOVE, THE word *sodomy* originally denoted a range of sexual acts that were considered deviant. Over time, however, the word came to be associated more specifically with anal sex, and eventually it narrowed even further and came to denote – at least in popular usage – anal sex between two men. Likewise, the word *sodomite* narrowed from *a person who engages in deviant sex* to *a person who engages in anal sex* and then to *a man who engages in anal sex with another man.* Over the centuries, numerous synonyms for this narrow sense of *sodomite* have been invented, ranging from *deler* to *ingle* to *pathic.* It's not entirely accurate, though, to say that these words were synonymous with *male homosexual.* Properly speaking, homosexuality (like heterosexuality) is an orientation, something that exists in the mind or the heart, whereas sodomy originally denoted an act, something that is done with the body. To put it another way, it's possible to be homosexual, or heterosexual, and never have sex; it's even possible to be homosexual and to engage only in heterosexual sex, due to an overwhelming social pressure to conform to a certain rigid standard. This bears upon my discussion because it means that many of the words that I'm about to discuss – like *catamite* – should really be described as synonyms for *sodomite*. Yet in actual use, they often overlap with words that are commonly understood to be synonyms for *homosexual male*, such as *faggot*. For simplicity's sake, I'll employ the term *homosexual male* when discussing the next cluster of words, bearing in mind that the word *homosexual*, and even the notion of homosexuality as an orientation rather than an act, was – according to French theorist Michel Foucault – unknown up until at least the late nineteenth century.

Shim: a term coined in the 1970s to denote a transexual, formed by combining she and him.

One of the earliest words used to denote a homosexual male was the Old English *baedling*. A writer from the eleventh century, for example, used the plural form of that word – *baedlingas* – to translate the Latin word *effeminati*, meaning *effeminate men*. Earlier on, *baedling* developed from the Old English *baeddel*, which meant *hermaphrodite*. Because the word *baedling* had negative connotations, it developed around the thirteenth century into the familiar adjective *bad*, which then inspired the comparative and superlative forms *badder* and *baddest*. Those forms persisted until the eighteenth century, when they were finally supplanted by *worse* and *worst*. The evolution of *baedling* into *bad* is paralleled by the recent slang use, mostly by adolescents, of the word *gay* to describe something that seems stupid or disdainful. For instance, I once had a student tell me, "*Wuthering Heights* is so gay!"

In Middle English another word used to denote homosexual males was *ferblet*, which probably developed from the word *blete*, meaning *soft*. This origin is made more probable by the fact that the notion of softness is at the root of other words that have been used to denote effeminate or homosexual men. The Vulgate Bible, for example, uses the Latin word *molles*, meaning *soft ones*, where later translations have rendered the same word as *catamite* or *homosexual*. Likewise, the word *soft* itself was turned in the mid sixteenth century into *softling*, which was used as a synonym for *sodomite*. The word *dealer*, too, was used in Middle English to signify a homosexual man, especially in the phrase *dealer with males*. A fifteenth-century translator of Paul's Epistles, for example, wrote that "neyther fornicatourys...nor delares with malys...schal hafe the kyngdam of god."

In Early Modern English, the word *bardash* emerged in the mid sixteenth century as a new name for a male homosexual. This word is somewhat unusual in that it derived not from an Indo-European language, but from a Semitic one, specifically Arabic, where *bardaj* means *slave*. The word *bardash* became obsolete in the early eighteenth century, but was then re-adopted from French a hundred years later as *berdache*, after being bestowed on male members of Native American tribes who assumed the role and dress of women. Unlike the *ferblets* and *softlings*, these Native American individuals were highly respected within their culture, and were thought to have two spirits, allowing them to see an issue from both a male and female perspective. In fact, in the early 1990s, this indigenous tradition inspired the phrase *two-spirited*, a term encompassing both homosexual and bisexual orientations. Later on in the sixteenth century, the word *androgyne* emerged as a synonym for *sodomite*, having been formed from the Greek *andros*, meaning *man* (as in *android*), and *gyne*, meaning *woman* (as in *gynecology*). The pejorative force of the word can be gauged from a 1587 translation of a sermon by Theodore Beza which refers to "vile and stinking androgynes, that is to say, these men-women, with their curled locks." This sense of *androgyne* became obsolete by the eighteenth century, but the word itself persisted in scientific contexts, and is now most familiar as the adjective *androgynous*, which does not denote homosexuality but rather gender ambiguity.

Between 1591 and 1603, a mere twelve-year period, ten new epithets for homosexual men appeared. The first was *ingle*, which seems originally to have denoted a boy who was kept by a man for sexual purposes; the modern equivalent, since the 1940s, would be *chicken*, with the older man being the *chicken-hawk*. The origin of *ingle* is uncertain, but it might be connected to another *ingle*, Scottish in origin, that meant *fire*. The fire *ingle* might have been extended to the homosexual *ingle* because the young man in such relationships was seen as the "flame" of the other man. It might also be tempting to propose an alternative connection between the two *ingle*s: namely, that homosexual men in England were burned for their supposed crime, and therefore the *ingle* that meant *fire* was transferred to them. However, even though homosexuality was a crime in sixteenth-century England, few men were ever charged, and those that were charged were fined, not burned at the stake (unless they also happened to be accused of heresy, which was indeed punishable by burning to death). It was not until the 1730s that the English state began to vigorously prosecute homosexuals. On the continent, things were different: there, homosexuals had been persecuted and prosecuted since the thirteenth century.

One other fact about *ingle* is that it spawned the synonymous *ningle* through a process called metanalysis, whereby a letter shifts from one word to a nearby word. This happened, for example, with the word *nickname*: the original form of that word was *eke-name*, meaning *also-name*. However, since that term was often preceded by the word *an*, the *n* slid over from the indefinite article to the noun it modified. Thus *an eke-name* became *a neke-name*, and later *a nickname*. Likewise, the phrase *an ingle* was eventually misconstrued as *a ningle*, with the new form persisting for a century and a half.

Also in 1591, the name *Ganymede* came to denote male homosexuals, specifically the passive partner during anal intercourse. Ganymede was the beautiful young man who, in Greek mythology, was abducted by the god Zeus and made into his lover and cupbearer. The relationship between the god and the boy prompted the astronomer Simon Mayer to give the name *Ganymede* to one of Jupiter's moons in 1614, *Jupiter* being the Roman name for Zeus. *Ganymede* is represented in English in another word as well. In Latin, the Greek form of the name *Ganymedes* was corrupted to *Catamitus*, which in 1593 entered English as *catamite*, which also originally denoted the passive partner in same-sex anal intercourse.

In 1594, the word *hermaphrodite* also came to denote male homosexuals, as is evident in a 1594 passage about the

Assyrian king Sardanapalus, "a monstrous Hermaphrodite who was neither true man, nor true woman, being in sexe a man, and in heart a woman." The word *hermaphrodite* derives from *Hermaphroditos*, which was the Greek name of the son of Hermes and Aphrodite. (Likewise, in the late seventeenth century, the term *Will-Jill*, formed from a typical man's name and woman's name, was used to denote homosexual men.) According to Greek mythology, the nymph Salmacis loved Hermaphroditos so much that she prayed never to be separated from him; the overly-literal gods responded by merging the two of them into one, part male and part female.

The *homosexual* sense of *hermaphrodite* died out in the eighteenth century, but the word continues to be used to denote individuals who are born with ambiguous sex organs, though it too is being supplanted by the term *intersexual*. Several words are related to either the first half or the second half of *hermaphrodite*. For example, in the early eighteenth century, natural scientists borrowed the name of Aphrodite – the goddess of love – and created the word *aphrodisiac*, denoting a food that really or supposedly increases sexual desire, such as oysters or chocolate. The name *Hermes* is represented in the word *hermeneutics*, denoting the art of interpreting texts, so named because Hermes was associated with eloquence and messages. Through a more indirect route, his name is also present in the word *hermetic*, meaning *airtight*. In the Middle Ages, a long-dead Egyptian priest came to be known as Hermes Trismegistus, meaning *Hermes thrice-greatest*, because he was thought to be even more skilled than Hermes the god. One of the skills attributed to this Egyptian priest was the magical ability to make perfectly airtight vessels, and thus his medieval nickname came to denote such hermetically sealed containers.

Another synonym for *sodomite* that appeared at the end of the sixteenth century arose from a sex act which, according to the historian Suetonius, was invented by the Roman Emperor Tiberius. In this sex act, a circle of men engaged in simultaneous anal intercourse, each man penetrating the man in front of him. The resulting formation resembled a bracelet, or in Latin a *spinther*, and thus the male participants came to be known as *spintriae*. This Latin word was adopted in 1598 as *spintry*. In the 1940s, the term *daisy chain* arose to denote the same sex act. Incidentally, the similar-looking *spinster*, which in the early seventeenth century came to denote an unmarried older woman, is not related to *spintry*; instead, *spinster* derives from *spin*, the notion being that unmarried women keep themselves busy, and support themselves, by spinning wool.

In 1599, English adopted the Italian word *nimfadoro* to denote homosexual men, a word that must somehow be related to *nymph*, a name given to semi-divine maidens that inhabit forests and oceans. The Italian *nimfarsi*, meaning *to dress-up like a nymph*, was current around the same time. Two or three years after *nimfardo* appeared, Shakespeare invented another synonym for *sodomite* – *male varlet* – in *Troilus and Cressida*:

Thersites:	Prythee, be silent, boy; I profit not by thy talke: thou art thought to be Achilles' male varlet.
Patroclus:	Male varlet, you rogue! what's that?
Thersites:	Why, his masculine whore.

Though *varlet* is now an archaic word, one of its variants is still familiar: *valet*.

In 1603, two more words denoting homosexual men appeared, *pathic* and *sellary*. The first of these derived from the synonymous Latin word *pathicus*, which in turn evolved from the Greek *pathikos*, meaning *suffering*. This origin is reflected in the English derivative, since a pathic was, specifically, the passive participant in same-sex anal intercourse. In fact, the word *passive* is closely related to *pathic*, as are other words that imply suffering, such as *pathetic*, *sympathy* and *pathology* (literally meaning *the science of suffering*). Even the word *passion* derives from the same source. When it emerged in the twelfth century, *passion* meant *suffering*, as is still apparent in references to the Passion of Christ, that is, the suffering he underwent while being crucified. By the thirteenth century, *passion* was being used more metaphorically to denote any feeling that overwhelmed one's heart, and by the late sixteenth century it had come to be associated with love in particular. In 1758, Horace Walpole alluded to an imaginary device he called a *passionometer*, a kind of emotional barometer that would measure the level of one's passion. In the late twentieth century, sexologists invented such a device, the *penile plethysmograph*, which measures changes to the volume of a penis as an indication of sexual arousal. As for the word *sellary*, that synonym for *sodomite* appeared, like *pathic*, in 1603, and derived from the Latin *sella*, meaning *couch*, presumably because that is where such sexual liaisons often occurred.

In the eighteenth century another cluster of names for homosexual men appeared, starting with *suiterer* around 1720. Unlike words such as *catamite*, *ingle* and *pathic*, which tend to denote the passive partner in a homosexual relationship, the word *suiterer* referred to the active partner, the one who pursued the other. This sense of the word is reflected in the Latin word from which *suiterer* derives: *sequi*, meaning *to follow*. The unusual doubling of the *er* at the end of *suiterer* occurred because the older noun *suitor*, meaning *wooer*, developed a verb sense. For example, in 1672, a character in Thomas Shadwell's comedy, *The Miser*, says "How did you go to work to suitor my Mother?" Once this verb sense of *suitor* was established, it was an easy leap for people to create a noun out of it by adding the *er* suffix, with the result being *suitorer*, later respelt *suiterer*. The same thing happened with the word *caterer*: a person who provided dainty food, or cates, became known as a *cater*. This agent noun then came to be used as a verb – *to cater* – which meant that a new agent noun had to be formed, with the result being *caterer*.

Around the middle of the eighteenth century, the term *molly* came to be used as a synonym for *sodomite*, a pejorative use of the woman's name *Molly*. Later on, in the late nineteenth century, it inspired the verb *mollycoddle*, meaning *to coddle or indulge oneself in an effeminate manner*. The name *Molly* was only the first of several to be transferred from women to homosexual men: *Madge* followed in the late eighteenth century, *Nancy* and *Ethel* in the early twentieth century, and *Nelly* in the mid twentieth century. The late eighteenth century also saw the appearance of two more slang synonyms for *sodomite*: *backgammon player* and *fribble*. The first of these was simply a pun on the game called *backgammon* and various slang names for the buttocks or anus, such as *backside* or *backdoor*. As for *fribble*, it probably arose as a variant of *frivolous*, the notion again being that homosexual men were more frivolous and mollycoddling than other men. The word is strikingly similar to the previously mentioned *ferblet*, but a direct connection is unlikely because *ferblet* seems to have died out in the fourteenth century.

In the nineteenth century, the first word to appear that denoted male homosexuals was *poof*, a variant of the much older word *puff*, meaning *a breath of air*, a usage that was probably inspired by the foolish notion that there is something insubstantial and "light" about gay men. This notion is also apparent in the use of *fairy*, which came to denote gay men near the end of the nineteenth century. Around the same time, *sissy*, a diminutive form of *sister*, developed its pejorative *effeminate man* sense. Shortly after, *gunsel* appeared as the name of a boy who accompanied and had sex with a hobo; the hobo, in such a relationship, was called a *jocker*. The word *gunsel* derives via Yiddish from the German *Gänslein*, meaning *little goose*; the word *jocker* probably evolved from the much older *jock*, meaning *penis*.

The word *homosexual* itself also appeared at the end of the nineteenth century, in an 1892 translation of a German work called *Psychopathia Sexualis*, which also introduced the word *heterosexual* to the English language. The latter word is derived in part from the Greek *heteros*, meaning *other*, and the former from *homos*, meaning *same*. (The Latin *homo* – as in *homo sapien*, meaning *thinking man* – is not related to the Greek *homos*.) The term *homosexual* won out over the synonymous *uranist*, which was invented by neurologists in 1895. The word derives from the Greek *ouranos*, meaning *heavenly*, the connection being that in Plato's *Symposium*, Pausanius suggests that there are two Aphrodites, that is, two goddesses of love. One is the "common" Aphrodite who oversees love between men and women, and the other is the "heavenly" Aphrodite who oversees love between men. The latter love, Pausanius implies, is more heavenly because it is more intellectual and spiritual. Writing in 1898, Oscar Wilde used a form of *uranist* in one of his personal letters: "To have altered my life," he wrote, "would have been to have admitted that Uranian love is ignoble."

The word *faggot* came to denote gay men around 1914, with the shortened form *fag* appearing around 1923. A popular but improbable etymology derives the homosexual sense of *faggot* from the fact that *faggot*, since the fourteenth century, has denoted a bundle of sticks gathered together for burning. Supposedly this *burning sticks* sense of *faggot* was transferred to homosexual men because they were also used to fuel fires. However, as noted earlier, homosexuals were not burned at the stake in England, and if they had been, it would have occurred in the sixteenth century or earlier, hundreds of years before *faggot* came to mean *male homosexual*. A better explanation for the *homosexual* sense of *faggot* pertains to the word's use, since the late sixteenth century, as a synonym for *old woman*. James Joyce employed the word with that sense in *Ulysses*, where Mrs. Riordan is called "that old faggot." The *old woman* sense of *faggot* was probably transferred to gay men in the same way that women's names were bestowed upon them. As to the question of why old women came to be called *faggots*, the answer is probably that it was a shortened form of *faggot-gatherers*, a name bestowed in the early nineteenth century on people who eked out a living by gathering and selling firewood. Such people tended to be elderly widows, since they had few other career options. Jean-François Millet's 1854 painting, *The Faggot Gatherers Returning from the Forest*, depicts several elderly women almost hidden beneath their huge bundles of sticks.

In the 1920s, the word *queen* came to be used as a pejorative term for a male homosexual. The word was probably inspired by the fact that *quean* had been used since the sixteenth century to denote a loose woman, a strumpet or harlot. Earlier on, dating back to the eleventh century, *quean* had lacked a pejorative sense, and simply meant *woman*. The two words – *queen*, meaning *female monarch*, and *quean*, meaning *woman* or *strumpet* – derive from the same Indo-European source, but in English they were usually distinguished in spelling, and sometimes in pronunciation. For example, at the end of the fourteenth century, in *Piers Plowman*, Piers says that in a charnel house or tomb it is difficult to tell a "queyne fro a queene." In other words, after death, you can't tell a whore from a monarch.

> Although they are only breath, words which I command are immortal.
>
> *Sappho*

In the 1940s, the term *drag queen* emerged, denoting a gay transvestite. Earlier on, dating back to the 1870s, the word *drag* denoted women's clothing worn on stage by a male actor, a word that inspired the familiar idiom *in drag*. This sartorial sense of *drag* might have arisen from the fact that such costumes could not be worn in public, and thus had to be dragged about in trunks from theatre to theatre. The word *camp*, while not synonymous with *in drag*, also implies a flamboyant theatricality, and has been associated with gay culture since the 1930s. In origin, this usage of *camp* might derive from the French *camper*, which in its reflexive form of *se camper* can mean *to pose for an audience*.

Other names for gay men that emerged in the twentieth century include *pansy* in 1929, *tart* in 1935, *bum-boy* in 1937, *swish* and *minty* in 1941, and the adjective *bent* in the 1950s. (The counterpart to *bent* was *straight*, which came to mean *heterosexual* in the early 1940s.) More important, perhaps, are those terms that emerged as terms of abuse, but which have been reclaimed in the twentieth century by the gay community itself. One such word is *gay*, which has undergone a rollercoaster of semantic shifting. When it arose in the early fourteenth century, it meant *mirthful*, but by the seventeenth century it had developed a rival sense of *loose* or *dissolute*, as in *gay Lothario*, an idiom that dates back to Nicholas Rowe's 1703 tragedy *The Fair Penitent*. That dissolute sense is also the one intended by Henry Fielding in his 1730 comedy, *The Temple Beau*, where Lady Lucy Pedant tells Bellaria:

> I am heartily sorry for Your Misfortune; because I know nothing so inconvenient, As being married to a very gay Man. Mr. Wilding May be a diverting Lover, but he is not fit for a Husband.

Next, in the early nineteenth century, the word *gay* came to describe a fallen woman or prostitute, as in this passage from the July 19, 1868 issue of the London *Sunday Times*: "As soon as ever a woman has ostensibly lost her reputation, we, with a grim inappositeness, call her *gay*." By the early twentieth century, the word was being applied to homosexual men, with the first recorded instance being in a 1935 dictionary called *Underworld and Prison Slang*, which defined *geycat* as "a homosexual boy." By the early 1970s, *gay* was being reclaimed by the homosexual community, who embraced it as a badge of proud self-identification, thus stripping it of its pejorative force. The term *gay pride* appeared around this time. In the *New York Times*, that phrase first appeared on June 28, 1971, in an article about a homosexual rally that was held as part of the "second birthday celebration of the Gay Liberation Movement." This reclamation of the word *gay* met with some resistance from the public at large. For example, in the September 27, 1981 issue of the *New York Times*, language columnist William Safire wrote, "I resist the word *gay* because homosexual-right groups insist upon it; I don't say *queer*, because that is a slur, but *homosexual* is neutral and accurate."

Safire's comment indicates that by 1981, the gay community had not yet reclaimed the word *queer*, a word that had been applied to homosexual men since the 1920s. The pejorative status of *queer* soon changed, however. In a column that appeared in the January 16, 1994 issue of the *New York Times*, Safire commented that "the word queer – like *queen* and *fairy*, long used as a derogation – is being stolen by homosexuals for their own use." In the same year, a book entitled *Queering the Renaissance* appeared, the first of many books to use the word *queering* to denote the act of re-interpreting literary texts and cultural artifacts from a gay or lesbian perspective. Subsequent books included *Queering the Middle Ages, Queering the Canon, Queering Elementary Education, Queering the Moderns, Queering Christ* and *Queering Femininity*, all of which suggest how successfully the gay community has been in "stealing back," as William Safire says, the word *queer*.

∿

In contrast with the many synonyms for *male homosexual*, the number of words that have denoted female homosexuals is paltry. In one sense, that number has even shrunk since the beginning of the twentieth century. The word *gay* originally denoted a homosexual person of either sex, but over the last forty years or so, *gay* has come to be seen as a male term, with *lesbian* as its female counterpart. Admittedly, some overlap remains, as evidenced by the fact that a lesbian might still refer to herself as a gay parent, but the prevalence of the phrase *gay and lesbian*, which obviously distinguishes the two groups, suggests the gradual slide of *gay* towards male, rather than female, homosexuality. It's interesting, too, to note that the male/female sequence that traditionally characterizes most gendered pairs – such as *Mr. and Mrs.* not *Mrs. and Mr.* – is reproduced even with *gay and lesbian*. On the Internet, that sequence outnumbers *lesbian and gay* two to one.

In the fifth-century Vulgate Bible the first thing Adam calls Eve is *virago*, a word derived from the Latin *vir*, meaning *man*, and which was bestowed on Eve because she was created from a man's rib. Later on, in the fourteenth century, *virago* came to denote a masculine woman, a sense that has sometimes caused it to be used as a euphemism for *lesbian*. Similar is the word *amazon*, which appeared in the late fourteenth century as another name for a masculine woman. The word was adopted from the ancient Greeks, who had used it to denote a tribe of warrior women who supposedly existed in Scythia. The Greeks believed that their word *amazon* had been formed from the negating prefix *a*, and the word *mazos*, meaning *breast*, since the Amazons were reputed to burn off their right breast so that they could draw their bows without hindrance. In fact, however, this is probably a folk etymology, and in reality the word *amazon* likely derives from an Indo-Iranian source. Today, both *amazon* and *virago* have been incorporated into the names of various organizations or projects pertaining to lesbians. On the Internet, for example, www.amazon.org (not to be confused with www.amazon.com) is the web site of Amazon Online, founded in 1995 to support women, especially lesbians and bisexual women, in the San Francisco Bay Area.

The first word in English that explicitly denoted a woman who has sex with another woman was *tribade,* which appeared at the beginning of the seventeenth century, and then vanished until it was revived in the late nineteenth century. In the 1960s, *tribadism* came to denote the act of one woman lying on another so that their clitorises rub together. This sex act recalls the origin of *tribade*, which derives from the Greek *tribein*, meaning *to rub*. In 1870, the word *lesbianism* appeared in English, followed in 1890 by *lesbian*, and still later, in the early twentieth century, by slang forms such as *lizzie* and *lez*. The Greek source of these words was *Lesbos*, the name of an island where the poet Sappho lived some 2600 years ago. The island's name, which probably evolved from a source meaning *wooded*, became associated with female homosexuality because Sappho wrote passionate verse to other women. In the late nineteenth century, Sappho's own name gave rise to *sapphism*, an outdated synonym for *lesbianism*. In the 1940s, the slang term *dyke* arose, sometimes spelt *dike*. This word is not related to the *dike* that denotes an embankment that holds water back, but instead probably arose from the last syllable of *morphadite*, a word that emerged in the early eighteenth century as a corruption of *hermaphrodite*. In the second half of the twentieth century, two more slang synonyms for *lesbian* appeared, *butch* in 1954 and *femme* in 1961, with the former denoting a "masculine" lesbian and the latter a "feminine" lesbian. Since the late 1980s, the term *lipstick lesbian* has also been used to denote a femme lesbian.

≋

The word *bisexual* appeared in English in 1824 as a synonym for *hermaphrodite*; it was not until the late nineteenth century that that word acquired its current sense, and not until 1956 that the word developed its slang form, *bi*. The psychiatric community also employed the term *amphigenic invert* to denote bisexual people, and the *amphi* part of that word – which in Greek means *both* – has also been employed in recent coinages such as *amphisexual* and *amphieroticism*. The Latin equivalent – *ambi* – has also inspired the term *ambisextrous*, formed by analogy with *ambidextrous*. None of these terms has become commonly used, nor have the equivalent *omnisexual*, *pansexual* and *Zwischenstufe*, the latter word being German for *intermediate step*. Slang terms have met with more success, such as *AC/DC* (short for *Alternating Current/Direct Current*), which came to mean *bisexual* in the 1950s, and *AM/FM* (short for *Amplitude Modulation/Frequency Modulation*), which appeared in the 1980s. In prison slang, *knick-knack* came to mean *bisexual* in the 1960s, not because of the original meaning of that word, but because its reduplicated syllables suggest "doubleness." Baseball has provided several euphemisms, including *switch-hitter* from the 1950s, *swings both ways* from the 1960s, and *bats for both sides* from the 1990s. The 1990s also provided the euphemism *bicoastal*.

꩜

Most of the preceding *homosexual* words were invented or used by heterosexuals to denote individuals whose sexual orientation they condemned. Somewhat different are the code words formerly used by members of the gay, lesbian and bisexual communities to safely identify themselves to one another. For example, in the 1940s, some men referred to their male travelling companion as their *secretary*. In the 1950s, a gay man might ask another man whether he was *musical* or whether he was a *friend of Dorothy's*; the latter idiom arose either as a reference to Dorothy Gale from *The Wizard of Oz* (which became a cult favourite in the gay community) or to author Dorothy Parker, whose husband, Alan Campbell, was homosexual. The need for such code words declined in the latter half of the twentieth century, as homosexuality became more acceptable, and gay men and women began to acknowledge their sexual orientation. In the late 1960s, that acknowledgement came to be known as *coming out.* At first, that term denoted only a personal or private acknowledgement – in other words, when a man recognized that he was gay, he had *come out* even if he had not shared that realization with anyone else. By the 1970s, however, the phrase *to come out* had come to denote the act of publicly asserting one's homosexuality or bisexuality. Around the same time, the more metaphorical phrase *to come out of the closet* emerged, though the term *closet queen*, denoting a man who conceals his homosexuality, was in use even in the late 1950s. In the 1990s, *out* came to be used as a verb denoting the act – often malicious – of revealing someone else's homosexuality. Chastity Bono, for example, was outed in 1990 by a tabloid newspaper.

Chapter Eighteen

STRUMPETS, WHORES, CHEATERS AND BASTARDS

Wanton Words

ONCE YOUR NEIGHBOURS START to wonder about your sex life – what you're doing, who you're doing, how often you're doing it, and so on – a whole new dimension is added to the mix, one that introduces notions of immorality and impropriety. For instance, for many centuries, if you had sex without being married, or if you were married but had sex too often, or if you didn't have sex too often but liked it too much when you did, you could be labelled *wanton*, a word that embodied social, moral and even religious disapproval. The word *wanton* emerged in English in the fourteenth century, and was created from the negating prefix *wan* and the verb *towen*, meaning *to pull* or *to tow*. *Wanton* therefore literally means *un-pulled*, an apt description of a person who is not drawn toward a specific goal, but instead pours out in looseness in all directions.

Wanton was not the first word in English to denote behaviour that was considered sexually immoral. Even earlier was the adjective *nesh*, which dates back to at least the eleventh century, and which ultimately derived from the Old English *hnesce*, meaning *soft* or *yielding*. This sense of *nesh* became obsolete in the fourteenth century, around the same time that the word *lewd* came to mean *wanton*. Originally, however, *lewd* meant something quite different. When it emerged in the ninth century, it denoted a member of the laity, that is, a lay person, one who did not belong to the clergy. By the thirteenth century, *lewd* had come to mean *ignorant* or *unlearned*, thanks to the fact that few occupations, other than the clergy, provided any education. The subsequent shift of *lewd* from meaning *ignorant* to meaning *wanton* occurred as the clergy came to assume that uneducated people tend to be promiscuous.

Unlike *wanton*, *nesh* and *lewd*, the word *concupiscent* is Latin in origin, deriving from the intensifying prefix *con* and the verb *cupere*, meaning *to desire*. *Cupere* is also the source of *Cupid*, the Roman name of the arrow-shooting god of love, son of Mercury and Venus. *Cupere* also evolved, via French, into the word *covet*. Latin also gave English several other wanton synonyms, including *licentious* and *lubricious*. The first of these, *licentious*, emerged in the mid sixteenth century, and derived paradoxically from the verb *licere*, meaning *to be lawful*. The word's shift from *lawful* to *immoral* was prompted by the belief – perhaps accurate – that people who have a legal right to do something tend to take advantage of that right, and thus they end up doing things that are immoral, albeit lawful. For example, according to the *jus primae noctis*, a medieval overlord had the right to sleep with the daughters of his serfs on their wedding night. Such an act would have been licentious: that is, legal but immoral. Incidentally, the *jus primae noctis* probably never really existed; it appears to have been a myth created in the seventeenth century.

As for *lubricious*, it also appeared in the sixteenth century, having been created from the Latin *lubric*, meaning *slippery*. Obviously, the word *lubricant* also derives from *lubric*, but several other words are also more distantly related. The source of them all is the Indo-European *sleubh*, meaning *to slip* or *to slide*, which not only became the Latin *lubric*, but also the English *sleeve* (something that your arms slips into) and *slovenly* (looking as if your clothes have slid out of place). The word *slippery* itself also derives from this Indo-European source, and in fact *slippery* was

> There's language in her eye, her cheeke, her lip,
> Nay, her foote speaks; her wanton spirites look out
> At every joint and motive of her body.
>
> *William Shakespeare*

also used, in the sixteenth century, to describe a wanton person. For example, in Shakespeare's *The Winter's Tale*, the insanely suspicious Leontes exclaims, "My wife is slippery," before he proceeds to banish her from his presence. Also embodying the notion of *slippery* is the word *loose*, which has been used since the fifteenth century to denote wanton behaviour; that sense of the word is still current, especially in the phrase *loose women*. In contrast, *palliardise* – which was once a synonym for *wanton* – has been obsolete since the seventeenth century. The word derived from the French *paille*, meaning *straw*, due to the long-standing belief that straw piles and haystacks are the frequent scenes of amorous trysts, an association that is still evident in the idiom *a roll in the hay*.

Nowadays, if you traipse into your apartment at three in the morning, your nosey neighbour is unlikely to refer to you as *wanton* or *lubricious*, but you might get a reputation for being promiscuous. That word appeared in English in the early seventeenth century, and derives from the Latin prefix *pro*, meaning *forth*, and the verb *miscere*, meaning *to mix*. Promiscuity is therefore a *mixing forth*, a tendency to mix and mingle indiscriminately. Other words that have developed from the Latin *miscere* include *miscellany* and *miscegenation*, the latter being a nineteenth century term that denoted the inter-breeding of blacks and whites.

≈

In addition to the foregoing adjectives, English has invented many nouns that denote wanton individuals. For the most part, these nouns are gendered: that is, promiscuous women are called different names than promiscuous men. For men, one of the oldest terms is *lecher*, still commonly heard in its clipped form of *lech*, sometimes spelt *letch*. This clipped form appeared in the 1940s, but the original word is much older. It dates back to the late twelfth century, where it was used in all kinds of contexts. John of Trevisa, for example, used it in his translation of a Latin encyclopedia of natural science: "Elephantes hateth the werk of leccherye, but oonliche to gendre ofsprynge." In other words, "Elephants hate the act of lechery, and only do it to engender offspring." In origin, the word *lechery* derives from the French verb *lechier*, meaning *to live in debauchery*. In turn, *lechier* ultimately developed, via the Germanic *likkon*, from the Indo-European *leigh*, meaning *to lick*. Semantically, debauchery and licking are linked by the fact that the tongue is employed in all kinds of sensual gratification, ranging from food to sex. The Germanic *likkon* also developed into the English *lick*, making it a close cousin of *lecher*, while a more distant relative is *lichen*, the name of an organism often found growing on rocks. Here the connection is perhaps that lichen spreads over a rocky surface by slowly "licking" its way forward, somewhat similar to how we sometimes use the word *lick* to describe the advance of flames. One other word that developed from the same Indo-European source is the Latin *lingere*, also meaning *to lick*, which – as mentioned previously – is represented in the last part of *cunnilingus*. Licking, lechery, cunnilingus and lichen are thus all etymologically linked.

Lecher acquired a synonym in the early thirteenth century when *holour* was adopted from French. In turn, the French form arose as a variant of *horier*, which had evolved from the Germanic *huorari*, meaning *whorer*, one who frequents whores. Related forms include the sixteenth century's *whoremaster* and *whoremonger*. The sixteenth century also contributed *Corinthian* and *libertine* as synonyms for *lecher*. The first of these, *Corinthian*, was inspired by the ancient notion that the citizens of Corinth were inveterate sex fiends, as evidenced by the fact that the Apostle Paul, in his first Letter to the Corinthians, bluntly tells those citizens to "flee fornication" and adds that "it is good for a man not to touch a woman." The reputation of Corinthians did not improve much with time. In 1697, John Potter wrote in his *Antiquities of Greece* that "to act the Corinthian is to commit fornication," and *Corinthian* continued to be used as a synonym for *lecher* into the nineteenth century. As for the word *libertine*, when it first appeared in the late fourteenth century, it denoted a freed slave, but by the late sixteenth century it was being used to refer to men who were too "liberal" in sharing their bodies with women. More quaint than *libertine*, perhaps, are the sixteenth-century terms *limb-lifter*, *bed-presser* and *carpet-knight*, the latter of which is a mocking description of an aristocrat whose chivalrous deeds are limited to the amorous exploits that he undertakes on the carpeted floor of his paramour's chamber. *Carpet-knight* anticipates the late-twentieth-century *rug-burn*, which denotes the abrasions caused by copulating on a carpet.

In the last half of the seventeenth century, the words *rake* and *rover* came to denote a sexually promiscuous man. The first of these, *rake*, is in fact the same word that denotes a garden implement. It was formed as a shortened version of the synonymous *rakehell*, which dates back to the mid sixteenth century. That word arose to denote a man who was so wicked, so debauched, that you would have to "rake hell"

Poodle-faker: a man who pretends to enjoy the company of women, in order to gain social advancement.

to find his equal. As for *rover*, that word denotes someone who rambles about without a fixed destination. In a sexual context, this implies a man who "plays the field," who dallies with one woman and then another. In origin, the word *rover* derives from archery: *to rove* referred to the act of shooting an arrow without a specific target in mind, in order to get a sense of the range of the bow.

In the early eighteenth century, the name *Lothario* became synonymous with *lecher*, thanks to Nicholas Rowe's tragedy, *The Fair Penitent*, where the "haughty, gallant, gay Lothario" seduces and then abandons the too-trusting Calista. *Lothario* was only the first of several men's names to be applied to promiscuous young men. *Romeo*, for example, acquired a *lecher* sense in the mid eighteenth century, a somewhat inaccurate application of the name, considering that Shakespeare's Romeo only has one girlfriend before Juliet – Rosalind, who never appears on stage – and that Romeo kills himself when he believes he has lost his beloved Juliet. *Don Juan* followed in the mid nineteenth century, a name that originally belonged to Don Juan Tenorio, a legendary Spanish lover and nobleman. Don Juan became the subject of numerous plays, poems and operas, all of which revel in his astonishing lechery. For example, in Mozart's version – the opera *Don Giovanni* – the hero's valet tells Lady Elvira that his master has had thousands of mistresses, including 640 in Italy and 1,003 in Spain. *Don Juan* was joined by *Casanova* in the late nineteenth century, the surname of Giovanni Jacopo Casanova, a notorious Italian philanderer who wrote a memoir, published in English in 1832, that recounted the sexual liaisons he had with 122 women.

Unlike most of the earlier terms such as *lecher* and *whoremonger*, the terms *Casanova* and *Don Juan* are sometimes complimentary, implying that the man in question is not simply horny, but rather in possession of a sexual skill-set that allows him to give unrivalled pleasure to women. The same is true of many of the other names for promiscuous men that arose in the nineteenth century, such as *ladykiller, playboy* and even *wolf*. There was, however, no sense of admiration attached to the word *roué* when it was invented as a name for the debauched companions of the fun-loving Philip II, Duke of Orleans. Angry Frenchmen created *roué* from *rouer*, meaning *to break on the wheel*, a form of torture that many wanted to inflict on Philip's dissolute companions after the Duke lost power in 1723. English adopted *roué* as a synonym for *lecher* at the beginning of the nineteenth century.

Unlike *roué*, the word *philanderer* emerged from a source that had positive connotations and degenerated into a disparaging term over time. The word comes from the Greek *philandros*, which in turn was derived from *philein*, meaning *to love*, and *aner*, meaning *man*. The word *philandros* therefore meant *the love of man* or, more idiomatically, *fond of a man*. A Greek woman who loved her husband would be *philandros*. When the word entered modern European languages, however, the original Greek was misconstrued, and the word shifted from denoting someone who loved men, to a man who loved someone. Thus, in the sixteenth-century Italian epic *Orlando Furioso*, a young man named Filandro falls in love with Gabrina, and in the seventeenth-century comedy *The Laws of Candy*, Philander falls in love with Erota. By the late seventeenth century, *philander* was being used generically to denote male lovers, which eventually led to the word being used as a verb, meaning *to flirt*. From this verb sense, a new and more disparaging noun was created in the mid nineteenth century, *philanderer*, which remains the familiar form.

〰〰

One of the first words to denote a promiscuous woman was *strumpet*, which dates back to at least the early fourteenth century. The origin of *strumpet* is uncertain, though some etymologists have suggested that it's related to the Latin *stuprare*, meaning *to defile*, which is also represented in word *masturbate*, as mentioned earlier. One misogynistic proverb from the early sixteenth century links *strumpet* to another name for promiscuous women: "The smellere pesyn, the mo to the pot; likewise, the fayrere womman, the more gygelot or strumpet." In other words, "the smaller the peas, the more that fit into the pot; the fairer the woman,

To lead apes in hell: a sixteenth-century expression describing the supposed fate of old maids.

the more she is a gigelot or strumpet." This word – *gigelot* – first appeared in the fourteenth century, and continued to be used as a synonym for *strumpet* up until the late nineteenth century. In origin, it probably derives from the French *giguer*, meaning *to dance*, the connection being that dancers, like actors and jugglers and tumblers, were long considered to be morally bankrupt. In French, the word *gigelot* – or rather *gigolette* – became the name of a dancing girl, which in the mid nineteenth century acquired a masculine counterpart, *gigolo*. In the 1920s, this word was adopted by English as the name of a male prostitute, one that conventionally services rich, older women.

In the early fifteenth century, the word that is presently the most common name for a promiscuous woman emerged – *slut*. The current pre-eminence of *slut* can easily be confirmed: together, the words *slut* and *sluts* appear more than ten million times on the

Internet, far more than any of the other words that also denote promiscuous women. (*Nympho* and *nymphos*, for example, appear about two million times, while *strumpet* and *strumpets* appear a paltry 25,000 times.) When *slut* first appeared, it signified a woman who was physically dirty. Cinderella, whose job was to clean the cinders from the fireplace, would be a slut in this sense of the word. By the mid fifteenth century, however, the meaning of *slut* had shifted from a physically dirty woman to a woman who was morally or sexually dirty, the sense it has retained to this day. The origin of *slut* is unclear, but it would seem to be related to the synonymous *slattern*, which appeared in the seventeenth century.

Like *slut*, the origins of several other strumpet synonyms are also unknown – *callet* and *trull* from the early sixteenth century, for example, and *trub* from the early seventeenth. Likewise, no one knows the source of the word *punk*, which appeared in the late sixteenth century. One might guess that it's somehow related to *puncture*, as if a strumpet is merely a kind of hole, but there is no documented evidence to support that speculation. The subsequent history of *punk* is, however, quite clear. After it appeared in the late sixteenth century, it continued to be used as a synonym for *strumpet* until the end of the nineteenth century. Then, in the early twentieth century, it came to denote a male prostitute, as well as a male inmate used by other prisoners for sex. In the 1910s, *punk* became the name of a young gang member, and in the 1920s it became the name of a young man who travels and sleeps with an older tramp. In the 1950s, the term generalized somewhat, as it came to signify any male homosexual. Finally, in the 1970s it was adopted as the name of an anarchist musical movement, *punk rock*, though it's likely that this use of the word was an extension of its older *gang member* sense, not its more recent *male homosexual* sense.

Other synonyms for *strumpet* that appeared in late sixteenth and early seventeenth century include *Jezebel, bona-roba, cyprian, fricatrice, jumbler* and *trollop*. The first of these, *Jezebel*, arose from the Old Testament story of Jezebel, a strong-willed woman who dominated her husband Ahab. Worse yet, moments before she was killed, Jezebel proudly applied her makeup, or – as the King James Bible puts it – "she painted her face." It was probably this last act that caused her name to become a synonym for *strumpet*. In the sixteenth century, women's use of "face painting" was often decried as immoral. *Bona-roba* was adopted from Italian, where it meant *good garment*, the kind of showy clothing typically associated with wanton women. *Cyprian* came to mean strumpet because the Cyprians – that is, the citizens of the Mediterranean island of Cyprus – were well-known for their worship of Venus. The word *fricatrice* also denoted a sexually aggressive woman, and derived from the Latin *fricare*, meaning *to rub*. *Jumbler*, as the word might suggest, denoted a woman whose legs and arms were often jumbled up with those of a man. *Trollop* derives from *troll* – not the frightful troll that lives under bridges, but the verb *troll*, meaning *to saunter about*. A trollop, in other words, trolls the streets looking for a sexual partner.

In the late eighteenth century, Francis Grose recorded numerous synonyms for *strumpet* in his *Dictionary of the Vulgar Tongue*. The term *barber's chair*, for example, was employed because it, like a promiscuous woman, is sat on by many men. *Demy-rep* was also current, a clipped form of *demi-reputation*, the prefix *demi* meaning *half*. *Biter*, according to Grose, referred to a strumpet whose vagina was so eager that it was ready to take a bite out of her own rear end. Grose also reported that the term *fusty luggs* denoted "a beastly, sluttish woman," while *blowsabella* signified a dishevelled slattern, presumably one whose clothing had come untucked from a quick roll in the hay.

The late nineteenth century contributed *flapper* as a synonym for *strumpet*, which probably arose as an elaboration of the noun *flap*, which had been used since the early seventeenth century to denote a strumpet. In turn, *flap* might have arisen from a misogynistic tendency to equate women with the "flaps" of skin that form the vulva. (A modern slang name for the vulva is, in fact, *piss-flaps*.) A similar kind of thinking lies behind the much more recent use of *slot* as a slang synonym for *woman*; both usages – *flap* and *slot* – reduce women to their mere genitals. Despite this potentially vulgar origin, the offspring of *flap* – *flapper* – became more innocent as the years passed. This is unusual: most slang words pertaining to women become more lurid over time. By the 1920s, *flapper* merely signified a rebellious young woman: one who liked jazz, danced the Charleston, dressed unconventionally, and smoked.

Notable synonyms for *strumpet* that appeared in the twentieth century include *floozie, scarlet woman, nympho* and *skank*. The first of these, *floozie*, appeared in 1911, and probably derives from *flossy*, which in the nineteenth century meant *showy*. This *showy* sense of *flossy* arose from the fact that floss was a kind of silk used to make fancy garments. Even earlier, it's possible that *floss* derived from the same source as *fleece*, denoting the fibres that are sheared from sheep and turned into wool. The use of *floss* as a name for the thread that you run between your teeth in the morning dates back to 1934. In the 1920s, the term *scarlet woman* arose to signify a woman of suspect virtue. The term probably developed from the Book of Revelation, where the wicked woman that rides upon the seven-headed beast is dressed in scarlet. Christian commentators later dubbed that woman the Whore of Babylon, but she was also called the Scarlet Lady or the Scarlet Woman. The association of scarlet with promiscuity might also have been fostered by Nathaniel Hawthorne's 1850 novel, *The Scarlet Letter*, in which a woman accused of committing adultery is made to wear a scarlet "A" on her clothing.

In the 1930s, the slang term *nympho* came to denote a woman who was considered sexually insatiable. This word was shortened from *nymphomaniac*, which first appeared in a medical book called *Hints on Insanity* in 1861. Even older, however, was the term *nymphomania*, which first appeared in 1775 as the title of a medical treatise devoted to what it called "furor uterinus." The *mania* part of *nymphomania* represents the Greek word for madness, while the *nympho* part derives from the Greek *numphe*, which could mean both *bride* and *nymph*, the latter being

> The mouth of an adulteress is a deep pit.
> *Proverbs 22:14*

a kind of nature goddess. In the 1950s, *nymph* inspired the diminutive *nymphet*, denoting a sexually desirable woman. One of the most recent synonyms for *strumpet* is *skank*, which denotes a woman who is both promiscuous and unattractive. The word appeared in the 1970s, and probably derives from the synonymous *skag*, which dates back to the 1920s. In turn, it's possible that this sense of *skag* evolved from *scag*, which had been used since at least 1915 to denote a cigarette butt. The distasteful sight of an ashtray full of discarded, crumpled, lipstick-stained cigarette butts might have prompted the word to be extended to unattractive and "used-up" women.

〰︎

Nowadays, the distinction between promiscuity and prostitution is, at least in theory, quite clear. Both activities involve sex with multiple partners, but the latter involves the exchange of money. The distinction is also important from a legal perspective: promiscuity is not a crime, but prostitution is, or at least it is subject to judicial constraints. Such was not always the case. Centuries ago, the distinction between promiscuity and prostitution was blurry, if only because the nature of transactions in pre-industrial societies differed from today. Then, a doctor might be paid with a chicken rather than a shilling, and a servant might receive no remuneration other than food and board. Likewise, in the seventeenth century a woman might board a ship and spend the next four months having sex with the crew, in exchange for shelter and meals. It's difficult to say whether such a woman would have been considered a strumpet or a whore, a trull or a bunter, a jumbler or a harlot. Moreover, considering that women were often forced into such sex-provider roles, all these terms might now seem both inadequate and unsympathetic. Still, in order to discuss such words, a generic term is needed, and so for my purposes *prostitute* is probably the best choice.

In Old English, one of the earliest prostitute words was *myltestre*, which ultimately derives from the Latin *meretrix*. The word was not simply adopted from Latin by pot-bellied scholars reading dusty classical texts in England. Instead, it was borrowed by Germanic tribesmen who encountered Roman soldiers on the continent as they patrolled the outreaches of their empire. Thanks to the interaction of the two groups, dozens of Latin words entered the Germanic predecessor of the English language. *Meretrix*, meaning *prostitute*, was one of the words, which is not surprising considering that the Roman soldiers were lonely and living far from home. When they migrated to England, the Germanic tribes – the Anglo-Saxons – brought these Latin words with them, though naturally in an altered form. For example, by the time *meretrix* appeared in written Old English, its form had been altered to *myltestre*. This Old English word no longer survives, but in the mid sixteenth century, *meretrix* was re-adopted from Latin, this time by pot-bellied scholars reading dusty classical texts in England. Eventually, in the early seventeenth century, *meretrix* gave rise to the adjective *meretricious*, meaning *distastefully showy*.

The word *whore* also emerged in Old English, where it was spelt *hore*. The *w* was added to the beginning of the word in the sixteenth century, as it was to several other words that had previously begun with an *h*, such as *whole, whood, whoard, whoop* in place of the earlier *hole, hood, hoard* and *hoop*. Over time most of these words reverted back to their original spelling, and thus *hood, hoard* and *hoop* reappeared, while *whore* and *whole* retained their modified forms. Old English probably acquired *hore* from Old Norse, and even further back the word evolved from the Indo-European *ka*, meaning *to desire*. As noted in Chapter Thirteen, devoted to kissing and fondling words, *ka* also developed into the words *caress* and *charity*. An abbreviated form of *whore* – *ho* – emerged in Black English in the 1950s, and is sometimes used not to mean *prostitute* but simply *woman*.

In Middle English, *harlot* became a synonym for *whore* in the early fifteenth century. However, when *harlot* first appeared in English, in the early thirteenth century, it meant *rascal*, and was applied to men both as a term of abuse and affection. For example, in his Prologue to *The Canterbury Tales*, Chaucer describes the Summoner as a "gentil harlot." As often happens with such words, however, their connotation degenerates over time. *Knave*, for example, originally meant *boy*, but eventually came to mean *dastardly fellow*. More unusual is the shift of *harlot* from denoting men to denoting women, a change that began to take place in the early fifteenth century, and which seems to have overtaken the original *rascal* sense of the word by the seventeenth century. This shift might have been prompted by a perceived resemblance between *harlot* and *whore*, especially considering that *whore* was still being spelt *hore*. In actual fact, though, those two words are unrelated. The immediate source of *harlot* was the French *arlot*, meaning *vagabond*, though its ulterior history is unknown.

The sixteenth century saw the appearance of the words *puzzel*, *drab* and *stale* as synonyms for *whore*, none of which survive. These words were followed, however, by the still-familiar *prostitute*, which appeared in the early seventeenth century. In origin, *prostitute* derived from the Latin *prostitutere*, which idiomatically means *to expose publicly*. In turn, this Latin word was formed from the prefix *pro*, meaning *forth*, and *statuere*, meaning *to cause to stand*. Literally, therefore, *prostitutere* means *to cause to stand forth*, which indeed is how prostitutes were and are marketed by their pimp or employer, whether on a street corner in Vancouver or behind a window in Amsterdam.

The eighteenth century contributed numerous prostitute words to the English language, many of which signified specific kinds of prostitutes. For example, a *wrinkle* was a prostitute who had given birth to many children; a *doxy* was a prostitute who lived with a beggar; a *hedge-whore* was a prostitute who worked in the open air rather than in a brothel; a *Drury-Lane vestal* was a city-based prostitute; a *courtesan* was a high-class prostitute; and a *blowen* was a highway robber's prostitute.

The word *hooker* came to mean *prostitute* in the mid nineteenth century, though earlier on, dating back to the mid sixteenth century, the word had also been used to denote a thief who would use a long hook to reach through an open window and snag valuables. This notion of *hooking* also lies behind the *prostitute* sense of the word. A hooker trolls the streets, spots an upstanding young man, and pulls him willy-nilly toward immoral behaviour – or so the word would have us think.

Balum rancum: an eighteenth-century dance, where all the women are prostitutes, and all the dancers are naked.

Unlike *hooker*, some words construe prostitutes in positive or at least euphemistic terms. For example, in the early eighteenth century, *fille de joie* was adopted from French, where it means *girl of joy* or, more idiomatically, *woman of pleasure*. Likewise, *lady of the evening* and *escort* both became euphemisms for prostitute around 1930. The latter term is still common in *escort service*, a phrase that has become so associated with prostitution that it has lost all of its original euphemistic force. Escort services often employ *call girls*, a name that arose in the 1940s, as the widespread use of telephones made it possible to hire a prostitute from a distance, instead of in an alley. *Call girl* was followed in 1968 by *working girl*, a term that reflected a grudging respect for what Rudyard Kipling referred to, in the nineteenth century, as "the oldest profession on earth." Likewise, activists working on behalf of the sex-trade industry invented the term *sex-trade worker* in the late twentieth century as a non-pejorative job title.

In 1785, Francis Grose recorded the terms *petticoat pensioner* and *fancy man* in his *Dictionary of the Vulgar Tongue*; both terms, he reported, referred to men "kept by a lady for secret services." More than a century later, the term *male prostitute* emerged – that phrase is used, for instance, in a letter that appeared in the June 6, 1913 issue of the *New York Times*. The word *gigolo* followed in the early 1920s (as previously discussed in relation to *gigelot*), and later on, in the 1930s, the word *hustler* also came to denote a male prostitute. This sense of *hustler* evolved from its earlier use to denote a female prostitute, a usage that dates back to the early 1920s. Even further back, in the 1880s, *hustler* denoted a hard worker. In the 1960s, the term *rent boy* appeared, which also refers to a male prostitute who services male clients.

〰〰

Prostitutes often work under the protection or coercion of someone else, now known as a *pimp* or *madam*. The earliest name for such individuals, however, was *bawd*, which dates back to the fourteenth century. The word appears frequently in Shakespeare's plays, as in *Measure for Measure* where Escalus scolds Pompey for his line of work:

Escalus: How would you live, Pompey? by being a bawd? What doe you thinke of the trade, Pompey? is it a lawfull trade?
Pompey: If the law would allow it, sir.

Bawd probably arose as a shortened form of the synonymous *bawdstrot*, which appeared in French in the thirteenth century. In turn, *bawdstrot* was probably formed from the French *baud*, meaning *merry*, and *troter*, meaning *to trot*. A *bawdstrot*, in other words, was a kind of "merry-runner," an amorous go-between, someone who ran about to find whores for customers. The word *bawd* originally denoted a person of either sex, but by the eighteenth century it referred only to women. Nowadays, the word is little known outside of Shakespeare, but one of its derivatives – *bawdy*, meaning *ribald* or *risqué* – is still current.

In the early fifteenth century, *bawd* acquired a rival in *mackerel*, which is also the name of a fish, best known from the exclamation *holy mackerel*, which might have arisen from the Roman Catholic practice of eating fish on Fridays. It's unclear, however, whether the *mackerel* that means *bawd* is connected to the *mackerel* that means *fish*. Later synonyms for *bawd* – such as *fishmonger* – might support the connection, but it's also tempting to derive the word from the Dutch *makelaar*, meaning *broker*, a person who negotiates deals between clients. After *mackerel*, the next synonym for *bawd* to appear was *pander*, in the early sixteenth century. This word was inspired by a character in Chaucer's *Troilus and Criseyde*: Pandarus, the uncle of Criseyde, who acts as a matchmaker in getting the two youngsters together. Although *pander* is no longer used as a synonym for *bawd*, it is still used as a verb, meaning *to cater to someone in a servile manner*. The familiar *pimp* first appeared in the early seventeenth century, and then as now it seems to have referred only to men; in origin, *pimp* might have evolved from the Middle French *pimper*, meaning *to dress elegantly*. The word *aunt* came to denote a female bawd around the same time as *pimp*, and it anticipated two other words that later developed bawd senses: *abbess*, in the mid eighteenth century, and *madam*, in the early twentieth century. All three of these words equate bawds with older and presumably trustworthy women. Finally, *ponce* is a curious word in that it emerged as a synonym for *pimp* in the mid nineteenth century, and then – in the 1930s – came to denote an effeminate man. The shift in sense might have been prompted by the fact that ponces did not have to labour for a living. Instead, they lounged about until it was time to collect money from their prostitutes, much of which was probably spent on jewellery and fancy duds.

≈

One of the earliest names for a house of prostitution was *bordel*, which dates back to the early fourteenth century. The word was adopted from French, where it meant *hut*, and in turn the French *bordel* evolved from a Germanic source meaning *board*, that is, a plank from which a hut is constructed. *Bordel* is now obsolete, but its cousin – *bordello*, which was adopted from Italian in the late sixteenth century – is still current. The word *bordel* happens to resemble the word *brothel*, but the two words are not related. Nonetheless, the accidental similarity between them caused the meaning of *brothel* to change. Originally, *brothel* meant *prostitute*, a sense that dates back to the late fifteenth century; however, because of confusion with the word *bordel*, in the late sixteenth century the word *brothel* shifted from meaning *prostitute* to meaning *a house of prostitutes*. In origin, *brothel* derives from the Old English *breothan*, meaning *to go to ruin*.

Three more synonyms for *brothel* all derived from words that originally denoted what we would now call a public sauna, open to both men and women. The first of these words, *stew*, came to mean *brothel* in the mid fourteenth century. Prior to that, *stew* signified a room heated with steam, where one might soak in a bath or simply sit and sweat. This notion of soaking in hot water also prompted *stew* to develop its familiar culinary sense. In origin, *stew* derives from an Indo-European source that also evolved into the word *stove*. Much like *stew*, the term *hot-house* became a synonym for *brothel* in the early sixteenth century. Later, in the early seventeenth century, *bagnio* did as well, a word that derives, via Italian, from the Latin *balneum*, meaning *bath*. In short, all three of these words – *stew*, *hot-house*, and *bagnio* – originally denoted public saunas, but became synonyms for brothels. The semantic shift simply reflects the fact that a hot, steamy room filled with nearly naked men and women is conducive to amorous congress, including the kind you have to pay for.

In the late sixteenth century, the word *nunnery* also came to mean *brothel*, an ironic usage, analogous to the use of the *abbess* to mean *bawd*. Around the same time, the synonymous *leaping-house* also emerged, which anticipated the eighteenth-century terms *vaulting-school* and *pushing-school*, all implying vigorous acts of sex. *The school of Venus* was another eighteenth-century name for a brothel, and so was *The Academy*. The "school" metaphor that characterizes the last four terms is notable: it would seem to persist in British erotica, which (I'm told) often features women dressed in school-girl uniforms. The early nineteenth century contributed the euphemism *disorderly house*, which was probably inspired by the phrase *house of ill-repute* from the early eighteenth century. *Disorderly house* remained the "polite" way of referring to brothels well into the twentieth century, with newspapers featuring story after story about raids on a seemingly endless stream of disorderly houses. Those same newspapers also employed the term *red-light district*, which appeared at the beginning of the twentieth century, to denote neighbourhoods where pimps and prostitutes congregated. The term arose from red lanterns that were hung outside brothels to advertise the establishment to potential johns. Similarly, barbers – who were once authorized to perform dentistry and minor surgeries – used a red-striped pole, symbolic of bloody bandages, to advertise themselves.

Nimgimmer: an eighteenth-century name for a doctor who specializes in curing venereal disease.

In the case of brothels, red was chosen probably because of its longstanding associations with passion and because of the previously-mentioned Scarlet Whore of Babylon. Incidentally, the customers who frequented red-light districts came to be known as *johns* in the early twentieth century. Since the mid eighteenth century, *John* had been used to mean *man* or *fellow*. In the 1960s, *punter* arose as a synonym for *john*.

Sometimes, when you come across a word that existed many centuries ago, you realize what a huge gulf exists between the past and the present. Such is the case with *cuckold*. That word emerged in the mid thirteenth century as a derisive name for a husband whose wife had cheated on him. *Cuckold*, in other words, was applied not to the woman who had cheated, but to the husband who had been cheated on. From our perspective, it seems ludicrous to mock a person who has been betrayed. However, back then it was felt that when a wife was unfaithful to her husband, it somehow diminished the husband himself. As a result, an intense "cuckold anxiety" gripped men from the thirteenth century to at least the eighteenth century, because a man's honour depended not only on his own actions, but upon the actions of his wife as well. To put it another way, women had the power to make their husbands into laughingstocks, which scared the heck out of men (and sometimes drove them to desperate measures such as chastity belts). Indeed, for many men, the worst thing about being cheated on was not the sense of emotional betrayal, but the social stigma that ensued. This comes

across loud and clear in an eighteenth-century comedy called
The Beaux Stratagem, where a husband rebukes his wife:

> Look, Madam, don't think that my anger proceeds
> from any concern I have for your honour, but for my
> own, and if you can contrive any way of being a whore
> without making me a cuckold, do it and welcome.

The word *cuckold* derives from the Old French *cucu*, the name
of a bird whose name in English is spelt *cuckoo*. The cuckoo's
name became associated with marital infidelity because it
sometimes lays its eggs in the nest of another bird, which will
then raise the baby cuckoos as its own. Further back, the name
of the bird arose in imitation of its cry.

Cuckold acquired a synonym in the early fifteenth century
when English adopted the word *cornuto* from Italian. In turn,
cornuto ultimately descended from the Latin *cornu*, meaning
horn, as in *cornet, unicorn, capricorn* (meaning *goat-horned*)
and *cornucopia* (meaning *horn of plenty*). The association of
horns and infidelity is ancient, and might have evolved from the
fact that a male deer, after selecting a female for mating, will
sometimes be challenged by another male. The two stags will
butt heads and "lock horns," with the winner getting the doe and
the loser getting the boot. Eventually, the horns of the defeated
stag were adopted as an emblem of sexual loss. Not surprisingly,
the word *horn* itself also came to be associated with cuckoldry.
A man whose wife was unfaithful was said to be *horned* or
hornified, and sometimes his shame would be so great that he
would go *horn-mad*. This is essentially what happens to Othello,

who says to Iago, "A horned man's a monster and a beast." Other horn-related terms were also invented in the early seventeenth century to denote cuckoldry, such as *capricornify* and *actaeon*, the latter of which was used as a verb, and which alluded to the myth of Actaeon who was transformed into a horned stag after he accidentally saw the goddess Diana naked.

Another name for a cuckold that emerged in the seventeenth century was *skimmington*. That word was often used in descriptions of a traditional punishment that was inflicted when a wife was unfaithful. She and her husband – the skimmington – were mounted backward on a horse and paraded through the streets, while their neighbours banged pots and kettles. That both the husband and the wife had to endure this punishment is made clear by Richard Brome's 1634 comedy, *The Late Lancashire Witches*, where a stage direction says, "Enter a skimmington and his wife on a horse." In origin, the word *skimmington* might allude to a utensil called a skimming ladle, employed to remove fat from culinary preparations. An illustration of a skimmington from 1639 shows a wife whacking her husband with just such a ladle. Incidentally, the clanging of pots that accompanied this parade of infidelity was known as *rough music* or *the black sanctus*, the latter term alluding to the Sanctus hymn that was sung during communion. Such clanging of pots also occurred when neighbours found out that a husband had beaten his wife, but in that case it was called a *ran-tan*.

If there was one thing worse than being a cuckold or skimmington, it was being a wittol. That word emerged in the fifteenth century to denote a specific kind of cuckold, one who knew that he was a cuckold but didn't care. The word was often used to denote a man who actually encouraged his wife to take lovers, in order to profit from them; a wife that did so was called a *wittee*. The word *wittol* developed from the earlier *wetewold*, which was probably formed by conflating the word *cuckold* with the word *wit*, meaning *to know*, as in the archaic legal idiom *to wit*. Etymologically, therefore, a wittol is a knowing cuckold. *Wittol* became obsolete in the nineteenth century, when it was replaced by the synonymous French phrase *mari complaisant*, meaning *agreeable husband*. A related term is the verb *condone*, which emerged in the mid nineteenth century with a specific legal meaning: it denoted the act of ignoring or overlooking a spouse's infidelity. Thus, if a court found that a man had condoned his wife's adultery – that is, that he had known of it but done nothing – it made him culpable in the offence. The root of the word *condone* is the Latin *donare*, meaning *to give*, also found in *pardon*.

Green sickness: a sixteenth-century name for a condition thought to afflict young women who are unwillingly celibate.

As for the woman who cuckolded her husband, she might be called any number of the strumpet words previously mentioned, but more specific terms, ones that emphasized the marital infidelity, were also at hand. For example, in the seventeenth century, she might be called a *bed-swerver* or a *jilt*. The latter term developed from *gillot*, which in the sixteenth century denoted a promiscuous woman, which in turn derived from *gill*, which in turn derived from the woman's name *Gillian*, which was an anglicized version of the Latin *Juliana*, which was the female form of *Julius*, which is also where the month *July* gets its name.

It might seem incredible, but sometimes it was the husband, not the wife, who was the adulterer. In such cases, a woman, since at least the sixteenth century, would be said to *wear the willow*, the willow tree being the traditional symbol of grief. Desdemona, for example, sings a "willow song" just moments before Othello smothers her:

Her hand on her bosom, her head on her knee,
Sing willow, willow, willow:
The fresh streams ran by her, and murmur'd her moans;
Sing willow, willow, willow.

A woman abandoned by her husband might also be called a *grass widow*, a term that arose in the early sixteenth century and which was current into the twentieth century. The word *grass* in this idiom might be an allusion to the passage "All flesh is grass," from the King James version of the Book of Isaiah. If so, then a *grass widow* is a "flesh" widow, one whose husband is not dead but who has left her to seek the flesh of another woman.

Numerous terms have also been invented to denote not just the people involved, but the act of adultery itself. The word *adultery* was, in fact, one of the earliest such terms: it was adopted in the fourteenth century from Latin, where it had ultimately been formed from the phrase *ad alterum*, meaning *toward the other*, implying a departure from one partner and a move to another. The word *adult* derives from an unrelated source. Adultery was also, in the fourteenth century, called *unsteadfastness*. Later on, in the sixteenth century, an adulterer might be called *unconstant*, or *light of love* or *secret-false*. If the adulterer was a woman, then her paramour might be said to *steal a shive from a cut loaf*, meaning that he was having sex with a woman whose virginity had already been taken by her husband. The word *infidelity* also appeared in the sixteenth century, having been derived from the Latin *fidere*, meaning *to trust*. That Latin root also appears in words such as *confident* and *affidavit*, and in names such as *Fidel* and *Fido*, the latter a name for a trustworthy dog.

In the 1930s, the term *extramarital sex* was invented as a generic term, capable of denoting any act of adultery, ranging from cheating to swinging. The latter term, *swinging*, emerged in the 1960s, to denote marriages in which a husband and wife sought out sexual relationships with other couples. Earlier on, dating back to the mid nineteenth century, such open arrangements had been referred to as *hetaerism*, which derived from the Greek *hetairos*, meaning *companion*. (Surprisingly, the Greek *hetairos* is not related to the Greek *heteros*, meaning *other*, found in *heterosexual*.) The word *cheat* was not used in reference to adultery until the 1930s. Earlier on, dating back to the seventeenth century, the noun form of that word, *cheater*, had been used to denote a card swindler, and even earlier, in the fourteenth century, *cheater* was the official name of the person who looked after the king's escheats, that is, properties that were confiscated when no heir was available to claim them. In the public's mind, such confiscation seemed unfair, and thus *cheater* eventually developed a pejorative sense.

~~~

It seems a shame to throw children into this mix of strumpets, whores, philanderers and cuckolds, but in fact that is where bastards – the offspring of an unwed couple – were traditionally consigned. Bastards have long been disparaged, and even Edmund's proud cry in *King Lear* – "Now, Gods, stand up for bastards!" – did not dispel a stigma that persisted until recently. Over the centuries, bastards have been called *spurious* and *base-born*, and phrases such as *child of shame, merry-begotten child, bachelor's child, illegitimate* and *born out of wedlock* were used to mark their inferior status. Much more desirable than bastards were legitimate children, born in wedlock, formerly known as *muliers*; this latter word appeared in the fourteenth century, and derives from the Old

Orgy: originally the name of the secret nocturnal rites held in ancient Greece in honour of the god Dionysius. The word derives from an Indo-European source meaning to do, and is thus related to both organ and ergonomic.

French *moiller*, meaning *wife*, which in turn evolved from the Latin *mulier*, meaning *woman*. Legitimate children were also called, from the fifteenth to the eighteenth century, *natural children*, thanks to the notion that having children in wedlock is the natural thing to do. Confusingly, however, the term *natural children* was also used, from the sixteenth to the nineteenth century, to denote bastards, thanks to the rival notion that it's actually more natural to have offspring out of wedlock, as do all other creatures on the planet, and that marriage is, for better or worse, an artificial institution.

As for the word *bastard* itself, its origin reflects its stigma: it probably derives from the Medieval Latin *bastum*, meaning *packsaddle*, implying that such children were furtively conceived on the road, perhaps even on horseback. This origin is even more apparent in the French *fils de bast*, meaning *child of the packsaddle*. A similar notion gave rise to the term *bantling*, which emerged as a synonym for *bastard* in the late sixteenth century: the word probably derived from the synonymous *Bänkling*, a German word formed from *Bank*, meaning *bench*. A bantling, in other words, is a child conceived not in a marriage bed, but on a bench.

LOVE COMES IN SPURTS

Or, the Exciting Climax, in which Orgasm Words are Briefly Considered

"THE MOMENTARY TRICK" IS what Shakespeare calls it in *Measure for Measure*. "That sweet fury" is how John Cleland refers to it in *Memoirs of a Woman of Pleasure*. "Her crisis" writes D.H. Lawrence in *Lady Chatterly's Lover*. "The Big O" is the term celebrities have lately thrown about on talk shows. They are alluding, of course, to the orgasm: the physiological pinnacle, the crescendo of pleasure, the zenith of delight, the few seconds of bliss that mark the beginning of the end of a sexual encounter.

All of these synonyms for *orgasm* are coquettish euphemisms: while they veil the bare physiological event with one hand, they eroticize it with the other. *The Big O*, for example, modestly diminishes the ugly word *orgasm* to its first letter, and yet at the same time that one letter implies the cry of ecstasy, the fervent

"Oh!" that coincides with the moment of climax. This rhetorical technique of simultaneously camouflaging and intensifying the moment of orgasm can also be seen in more extended descriptions, such as the following passage from James Joyce's *Ulysses*, where a display of fireworks becomes an allegory of Gerty's sexual rapture:

> She would fain have cried to him chokingly, held out
> her snowy slender arms to him to come, to feel his lips
> laid on her white brow, the cry of a young girl's love,
> a little strangled cry, wrung from her, that cry that has
> rung through the ages. And then a rocket sprang and
> bang shot blind blank and O! then the Roman candle
> burst and it was like a sigh of O! and everyone cried O!
> O! in raptures and it gushed out of it a stream of rain
> gold hair threads and they shed and ah! they were all
> greeny dewy stars falling with golden, O so lovely! O
> so soft, sweet, soft! Then all melted away dewily in the
> grey air: all was silent.

The double move of simultaneously camouflaging and intensifying the orgasm is also evident in one of the earliest words used to denote it – namely, *die*. *Die* is a euphemism to the extent that it appropriates a pre-existing word as a kind of code, and yet eroticizes the notion of the orgasm by associating it with the most intense, mysterious and ultimate human experience: death. This sexual sense of *die* was especially popular in the sixteenth and seventeenth centuries, where it was often employed in erotic songs such as "My Lovely Wanton Jewel," where a nymph proclaims, "I could never wish a sweeter dying." John Donne also plays on this sense of *die* in his poem "The Canonization," where the speaker tells his beloved, "We die and rise the same, and prove mysterious by this love," thus fusing imagery of sex with that of resurrection. A more extreme and perhaps unsettling instance of this sense of *die* appears in the late-seventeenth-century poem "Xamolxis and Perindo," where a young woman, at the moment when she joyfully succumbs to the advances of her seducer, "cries 'Oh, oh! Unkind: you kill me,' and so dies." The French, too, have long employed a similar figure of speech with "la petite mort," which was borrowed by English in the early twentieth century as "the little death." This construing of orgasm as a kind of death heightens, as mentioned before, the eroticism of the sexual climax, but it may also reflect the fact that orgasm, or at least male ejaculation, was once thought to diminish the vital essence of a man. That archaic belief is also suggested by the verb *spend*, which has been used to denote an orgasm since the seventeenth century. For example, in "The Cabinet of Love," an erotic work from the early eighteenth century, the term is used to describe the simultaneous orgasm of two lovers: "at one instant both together spent." That word, with its mercantile overtones, implies that one has a finite reserve of orgasmic energy or sexual potency that is incrementally expended with every climax. An orgasm, in other words, comes at a cost.

Carpopedal spasm: a contraction of the hands or feet that occurs during orgasm.

Like *die*, the word *come* has been used to signify an orgasm for many centuries. In Thomas Nashe's erotic poem "The

Choice of Valentines," written in the late sixteenth century, a woman warns her lover that he may not "come too soon," and that he isn't allowed to fall asleep until she too has climaxed. Shakespeare, too, seems to imply the *orgasm* sense of *come* in *Troilus and Cressida*, where Cressida says, after spending the night with Troilus, "My lord, come you again into my chamber." She then adds, "You smile and mock me, as if I meant naughtily," to which the ever-eloquent Troilus replies, "Ha, ha!" Later on, in the early eighteenth century, Thomas D'Urfey also plays on the double sense of *come* in his bawdy ballad, "As Oyster Nan Stood by her Tub," where the bartender, just as he is finishing a quickie with Nan, replies to a gentleman who has called out to him from another room:

> But being call'd by Company,
> As he was taking pains to please her;
> I'm coming, coming, Sir, says he,
> My Dear, and so am I, says she, Sir.

More recent than the erotic euphemisms "die" and "come" are the more learned clinical equivalents, *orgasm* and *climax*. The word climax, as mentioned earlier in connection with the related word *clitoris*, was originally a term found in classical rhetoric, denoting a series of ever-more-forceful steps in a formal argument. It wasn't until the early twentieth century that *climax* developed its *orgasm* sense. An even more recent word, in one sense, is *orgasm*,: it wasn't used as a verb until the 1970s – in other words, up until thirty years ago, no one had ever said, "I orgasmed." As a noun, *orgasm* is somewhat older. It developed its *sexual climax* sense at the beginning of the eighteenth century, though earlier on, dating back to the seventeenth century, it had been used to signify an emotional outburst of any sort. Even further back, *orgasm* developed from the Greek *organ*, meaning to *swell*.

〜〜

If we assume that the typical human experiences an orgasm three times a week; and if we assume that each orgasm lasts about five seconds; and if we assume that a human might conceivably be orgasmic for sixty years; then the total time that the average human spends orgasming in his or her life is a mere thirteen hours. In contrast, in a single month many people spend more than thirteen hours commuting to and from work, and most people devote more than a thousand hours of their life to brushing their teeth. The "momentary trick" is indeed fleeting, and yet its pursuit has always been a personal and cultural obsession, one that has motivated so much of human history. Linguistically, too, the quest for "the sweet fury," for "the Big O," is ultimately behind all of the love words and sex words explored in this book. Fitting, therefore, that this conclusion, like a fugacious orgasm, is over almost before it began.

Acknowledgements

The following individuals, over dinner or via email, helped me refine the title, form and content of this book: Elizabeth Dawes, Zbigniew Izdorczyk, Dorothy Tennov, Clive Holden, Alissa York, Al Marshall, John Brubacher, Michael Kurtz, Sue Sorensen, Peter Sorensen, Richard Almonte and Adrienne Weiss. Any errors, infelicities or bad puns in the book are my own doing.

Works Consulted and Recommended for Further Reading

Adams, J. N. *The Latin Sexual Vocabulary*. Johns Hopkins University Press. 1982.

Almond, Jordan. *Dictionary of Word Origins*. Citadel Press. 1995.

Apperson, G. L. *Dictionary of Proverbs*. Ware, Wordsworth Editions. 1997.

Arango, Ariel C. *Dirty Words: The Expressive Power of Taboo*. Jason Aronson. 1996.

Ashley, Leonard. *The Dictionary of Sexual Slang*. Barricade Books. 2002.

Ayto, John and John Simpson. *The Oxford Dictionary of Modern Slang*. Oxford University Press. 1996.

Ayto, John. *Dictionary of Word Origins*. Arcade. 1993.

Ayto, John. *The Oxford Dictionary of Slang*. Oxford University Press. 2000.

Barfield, Owen. *History in English Words*. Lindisfarne Books. 2002.

Barnhart, Robert K. *Chambers Dictionary of Etymology*. Larousse Kingfisher Chambers. 1999.

Brohaugh, William. *English Through the Ages*. Writer's Digest Books. 1998.

Carrera, Michael A. *The Language of Sex: an A to Z Guide*. Facts on File. 1992.

Carrera, Michael. *The Wordsworth Dictionary of Sexual Terms*. Wordsworth Editions. 1998.

Chantrell, Glynnis. *Oxford Dictionary of Word Histories*. Oxford University Press. 2002.

Chapman, Robert L., Barbara Ann Kipfer and Harold Wentworth. *The Dictionary of American Slang*. HarperCollins. 1998.

Dalzell, Tom. *The Slang of Sin*. Merriam-Webster. 1998.

Evans, Rod L. *Sexicon: The Ultimate X-Rated Dictionary*. Citadel Press. 2002.

Francoeur, Robert T. , Timothy Perper and Norman A. Scherzer. *A Descriptive Dictionary and Atlas of Sexology*. Greenwood Press. 1991.

Freeman, Morton S. *Hue and Cry and Humble Pie*. Plume. 1993.

Goldenson, Robert M. and Kenneth N. Anderson. *The Language of Sex from A to Z*. World Almanac. 1986.

Green, Jonathon. *Cassell's Dictionary of Slang*. Cassell. 1998.

Grey, Antony. *Speaking of Sex: The Limits of Language*. Cassell. 1996.

Harvey, Keith and Celia Shalom. *Language and Desire: Encoding Sex, Romance and Intimacy*. Routledge. 1997.

Herbst, Philip. *Wimmin, Wimps & Wallflowers*. Intercultural Press. 2001.

Kacirk, Jeffrey. *Forgotten English*. Quill. 1999.

Kramerae, Cheris and Paula Treichler. *A Feminist Dictionary*. Pandora Press. 1985.

Lighter, Jonathan E. *Random House Historical Dictionary of American Slang*. Vol. 1. Random House. 1994.

Lighter, Jonathan E. *Random House Historical Dictionary of American Slang*. Vol. 2. Random House. 1997.

Love, Brenda and Paul Mavrides. *Encyclopedia of Unusual Sex Practices*. Barricade Books. 1994.

McConville, Brigid and John Shearlaw. *The Slanguage of Sex: A Dictionary of Modern Sexual Terms*. MacDonald. 1984.

Metcalf, Allan. *The World in So Many Words*. Houghton Mifflin. 1999.

Mills, Jane. *Womanwords: A Dictionary of Words about Women*. Longman. 1989.

Moore, Bob. *NTC's Dictionary of Latin and Greek Origins: A Comprehensive Guide to the Classical Origins of English Words*. McGraw-Hill. 1997.

Morris, William. *Dictionary of Word and Phrase Origins*. HarperCollins. 1988.

Onions, C. T. and Robert D. Eagleson. *A Shakespeare Glossary*. Clarendon Press. 1986.

Partridge, Eric. *A Dictionary of Slang and Unconventional English*. Macmillan. 1967.

Partridge, Eric. *Shakespeare's Bawdy*. Routledge. 1968.

Pei, Mario. *Dictionary of Foreign Terms*. Delacorte Press. 1991.

Pinkerton, Edward C. *Word for Word*. Verbatim Books. 1982.

Rawson, Hugh. *Devious Derivations*. Castle. 2003.

Rees, Nigel. *Dictionary of Word and Phrase Origins*. Cassell. 1999.

Richler, Howard. *Take My Words*. Ronsdale. 1997.

Richter, Alan. *Dictionary of Sexual Slang*. John Wiley & Sons. 1993

Richter, Alan. *The Language of Sexuality*. McFarland. 1987.

Room, Adrian. *Brewer's Concise Dictionary of Phrase and Fable*. Harper Collins. 2000.

Room, Adrian. *Brewer's Dictionary of Names*. Helicon. 1999.

Room, Adrian. *Cassell's Dictionary of Word Histories*. Sterling Publications. 2002.

Room, Adrian. *Dunces, Gourmands, Petticoats: 1,300 words Whose Meanings Have Changes Through the Ages*. McGraw-Hill. 1997.

Rubinstein, Frankie. *A Dictionary of Shakespeare's Sexual Puns and Their Significance*. Macmillan. 1989.

Safire, William. *Language Maven Strikes Again*. Henry Holt & Co. 1991.

Shipley, Joseph T. *The Origins of English Words: A Discursive Dictionary of Indo-European Roots*. Johns Hopkins University Press. 1984.

Spears, Richard A. *Forbidden American English*. NTC Publishing Group. 1998.

Spears, Richard A. *NTC's Thematic Dictionary of American Slang*. NTC Publishing Group. 1999.

Spears, Richard A. *Slang and Euphemism*. Signet. 1982.

Spender, Dale. *Man Made Language*. Routledge & Kegan Paul. 1990.

Thorne, Tony. *Dictionary of Contemporary Slang*. Bloomsbury. 1997.

Vogels, Josey. *My Messy Bedroom: Love and Sex in the 90s*. Vehicule Press. 1998.

Watkins, Calvert. *American Heritage Dictionary of Indo-European Roots*. Houghton Mifflin Co. 1985.

Watts, Karen. *21st Century Dictionary of Slang*. The Princeton Language Institute, Random House. 1994.

Weekley, Ernest. *An Etymological Dictionary of Modern English*. Dover. 1967.

Westheimer, Ruth K. *Encyclopedia of Sex*. Continuum. 2000.

Williams, Gordon. *A Dictionary of Sexual Language and Imagery in Shakespearean and Stuart Literature*. Three volumes. Athlone Press. 1994.

Williams, Gordon. *A Glossary of Shakespeare's Sexual Language*. Humanities Press International. 1997.

Wilson, Robert. *Playboy's Book of Forbidden Words*. Playboy Press Book. 1972.

Electronic Resources

Bullough, Vern L. and Bonnie Bullough. *Human sexuality: An Encyclopedia*. (Garland reference library of social science; vol. 685) www2.rz.hu-berlin.de/sexology/GESUND/ARCHIV/SEN/INDEX.HTM

Middle English Dictionary. ets.umdl.umich.edu/m/med/

New York Times Historical Newspaper Online via Proquest. www.proquest.com

Patterweb: Early Modern English Dictionaries Database Search Utility. www.chass.utoronto.ca/english/emed/patterweb.html

The Oxford English Dictionary. 2nd ed. Oxford: Clarendon Press, 1989. OED Online. Oxford University Press. www.oed.com